What happens if you track down the earliest known reference to every holy well in England? The vivid traditions of these sites, many of them hitherto unknown, cast a new light on whether holy wells were taken over from pagan precursors, and what the Reformation meant for sacred landscapes. Colourful tales of saints, sprites and charlatans reveal the lively side of medieval popular religion.

With this book the study of English holy wells moves out of the realms of romanticism and myth-making into the light of history. Jeremy Harte draws on maps, miracles, legends and landscapes to present his detailed discussions in a readable and often witty manner.

English Holy Wells comprises three volumes. Volume One is supplied with a CD-ROM of Volumes Two and Three to make the complete work available at an affordable price.

Jeremy Harte is a folklorist with a particular interest in sacred places and supernatural encounters. His other books include *Explore Fairy Traditions, Cuckoo Pounds and Singing Barrows, The Green Man* and *Alternative Approaches to Folklore.* He is curator of Bourne Hall Museum in Surrey.

English Holy Wells:

A sourcebook

Volume 1
The making of the
English holy well

Jeremy Harte

Heart of Albion

English Holy Wells: A sourcebook

Jeremy Harte

Cover illustration:
Lady Well at Lewisham.
From an 1827 lithograph by H. Warren;
courtesy of Jeremy Carden.

ISBN 978-1-905646-10-4 (Vol 1 plus CD)
ISBN 978-1-905646-13-5 (Vol 2 only)
ISBN 978-1-905646-14-2 (Vol 3 only)

Published by

Heart of Albion Press
2 Cross Hill Close, Wymeswold
Loughborough, LE12 6UJ

albion@indigogroup.co.uk

Visit our Web site: www.hoap.co.uk

Printed in England by Booksprint

Acknowledgements

My thanks are due to all the staff at the London Library whose support, as they laboured upstairs and down with stacks of Camden and Dugdale, has been well beyond the call of duty. This book, like much independent scholarship, would not have been possible without the existence of that wonderful institution and I urge all serious readers to join it. Thanks are due also to the staff of the British Library, and to the local studies librarians of England, who responded to my queries with unfailing enthusiasm. The online resources created by enthusiasts at the Megalithic Portal and Modern Antiquarian were invaluable, as was the early mapping made available at www.old-maps.co.uk.

The contributions of virtual colleagues on the wells-and-spas mailing list have been a constant support and a welcome reminder that other people were interested in this stuff too: thanks to Andy Anderson, Carl-Henrik Berg, Christine Buckley, Gill Burns, Graeme Chappell, Gill Edwards, Terry Faull, Sarah Head, Bea Hopkinson, Chris Kimberley, Jennifer Scherr and many others, including those unflappable conference organisers Maddy Gray and Graham Jones, now virtual no more. John Billingsley, Keith Briggs, Katy Jordan, Rik Lee, Richard Pederick, Freda Raphael, Jonathan Roper, Jacqueline Simpson, and Alex Walsham provided inspiring conversation. Tony Hilton of the North West Catholic History Society was generous with his researches into Lancashire.

Thanks are due to those who have been kind enough to act as hosts on site visits: Adam Stout (who contributed much information on Glastonbury), Neil Mortimer, George Nash, and the late (alas) Jennifer Westwood. Bob Trubshaw, the best of publishers, navigated the byways of rural Leicestershire in search of sites and never asked when the book would arrive, or how long it would be when it came. Bruce Osborne provided vital books at short notice, along with assorted spa waters and recommendations to put the computer on standby while I joined him at the Salsa class. Now this task is over, I may be able to take up his advice. Janet Bord and Tristan Gray Hulse have played many parts as correspondents, friends, and hosts.

Special thanks must go to James Rattue, who has contributed more to this book than anyone. His generosity, at an early stage in the project, in making over his files of otherwise unrecorded wells has given it whatever completeness it may have. The errors, of course, remain my own. And thanks to my extended and long-suffering family, who have lived with the wells for over three years: to my mother, to Jess and Gabe, and to Judith, Adrian, Bex and Alex – they are the true saints.

That's about it, really. At this stage in the acknowledgements, it is conventional to put in some fulsome praise for the shadowy figure who made the coffee, sympathised with writer's block, and proofread the index. Put-upon helpmates may be glad to know that in this case the author made his own coffee; so you see, it can be done. But I still remember a summer day long ago, when the children who are now grown up were not even born, and we went down the Dorset lanes to St. Wite's Well; never knowing how things would turn out, and maybe they haven't turned out so badly after all. Thanks, Gill.

Contents

This book consists of two parts – first a history of English holy wells, and then a survey of the evidence from which the history was taken. In order to make the whole work available at a manageable price, the second and third volumes of the book have been supplied as a CD.

Volume One: The making of the English holy well

Volume Two

Volume Three

CD-ROM

Volume Two (as PDF)

Volume Three (as PDF)

Analysis of sites (as Excel spreadsheet)

Illustrations

Volume One

Abbreviations and conventions

Abbreviations have been kept to a minimum, but note CH for County History, OE for Old English, ON for Old Norse, OS for Ordnance Survey, RO for Record Office, and TM for Tithe Map (although strictly speaking, field-names are taken from the apportionment not the map). In looking up record offices, remember that many of these no longer advertise under that name, and will be found as regional libraries or history centres.

References to the Ordnance Survey are set out for users of both grid square and digital systems. TL (5,2) 017 171 can be read as the grid square reference TL 017 171 or the digital reference 501700 217100, whichever is convenient. These will direct you to the part of the map where a place-name can be found, but they may not be exact references for the well.

All place-names have been capitalised in modern style, except for the references in Anglo-Saxon charters. Place-name references from Latin sources are given in the nominative.

The conventions for dates are:

1500x50 for documents dated to some time between 1500 and 1550.

1500/1 for mayoral, regnal and accounting years partly in 1550 and partly in 1551.

Head entries, such as 'Lady Well at Turvey', are given in standardised form. Spellings of words such as 'holy', 'lady', or the names of saints have been regularised in the head entries, so variant forms like Ann and Anne will both appear under 'St Anne'. Saints' names are given in a modern vernacular form – Osyth and Giles rather than Osgyth and Aegidius.

A well is located at the nearest settlement, which may not necessarily be the parish in which it is found. Settlements which do not appear on a standard road atlas are given some further identification; thus Fernyhalgh is identified as 'near Preston'.

All translations can be found in the work cited unless the reference states 'tr. from text', in which case they are my own.

The spreadsheet (included on the CD) has fields as follows:

Region, following the boundaries identified in note 10 of Volume One.

County, using the abbreviations in Gelling & Cole (2000).

Settlement name.

Date, by century, when the well is first mentioned.

Date, up to the eighteenth century, when the well is last mentioned.

Type of well: H for Holywell, S for saint's well and M for well of the Virgin Mary

Types of place-name in which the name of the well survives: W for spring-name, R for stream-name, F for field-name, T for street-name, P for personal name, and S for settlement or house name.

Dedication of the well.

Type of dedication: U for saints of the universal church, R for regional saints, L for local saints.

Buildings which share a dedication with the well.

Location of the well.

Surroundings of the well: N for natural setting, V for rock face or niche in a wall, B for basin, D for draw-wells, and W for well-houses.

Reported quality and contents of the water: U for unfailing, P for powerful, M for mineral, C for chalybeate and S for sulphurous.

Diseases which the well was said to cure: E for eyes, S for skin, R for rheumatism and O for other.

The Holy Well at Alderley Edge. An engraving of 1828 by T. Picken.
(From Bakewell 1843:11.)

Introduction

The Devil is in the detail. That's not strictly true, of course – the Devil is in the Monk's Well at Wavertree near Liverpool, where he laughs at stingy pilgrims – but it's a good working principle.[1] Only through close attention to detail, wherever it comes from, can we hope to discover something new about holy wells. That is what this book sets out to do. Every well (and there are over a thousand of them) has its own story, by turns beautiful, heart-breaking, grim and passionate – not to mention plain bizarre, as we will find in due course when we meet with the invisible dragon of Longwitton, the dancing stars of Biddestone and the woman in St Ives who took a talking hare for her lover.[2] But all these stories come together to answer a single, simple question. Why did people in England decide that certain springs and wells were sacred? When did this happen and what use did they make of them afterwards?

But surely we know this already? Many books have already been written on holy wells and with a little judicious cutting and pasting their conclusions can be turned out again to make many more. Holy wells, we will be told, are links with a distant past when the blessings of nature were better understood and belonged to those ancient cults against which the Church preached in vain. They were an important part of the religion of the ancient Celts and will be found in the Celtic fringes of the British Isles. Missionaries travelled through the landscape converting these shrines to the new faith and everywhere that we find a well with a saint's name, we know that he stayed to consecrate a spring. The natural beauty of the surroundings at holy wells, and the constant life-giving flow of their waters throughout the driest of summers, evoked a religious gratitude. Their waters had natural healing powers and this led the wise missionaries to change their old pagan dedications to Christian ones so that the medicinal effects would be attributed to God and his saints. Pilgrimages sprang up and people travelled many miles so that they could be cured by the sacred waters. After the Reformation, the saints were forgotten, but the medicinal reputation of the waters lived on and they achieved new celebrity as spas.

This is a compelling, evocative story, which sounds entirely convincing, but it is a myth. Like other myths, it presents its subject as an eternal archetype, free from the grubby dealings of history. People find it hard to believe that holy wells were actually things invented by other people and not healing revelations from the timeless world of nature. Some aspects of this story may be true, in whole or part,

St Mary's Well at Newcastle.
(From Welford 1885–7: 1.308.)

while others are demonstrably false, but taken as a whole the myth has stifled historical research into an important subject.

Why is there a myth of the holy well? It cannot be for want of enthusiasm on the part of researchers. Throughout the country, enthusiasts have put on their wellies and tramped through mud and midges to find the legendary waters, coming back to record and share their experiences. There have been three sequences of journals devoted to holy wells and there are now two lively online discussion groups.[3] Does that leave anything to be said?

People love to track down and visit holy wells. There is something healing about these old places, for the spirit as much as the body. But the discipline of the pilgrim does not necessarily produce good historians. The water of these ancient shrines, however laborious the fieldwork that identifies it, will be just that – water. It is people, and the spiritual world to which people alone have access, which make its sacred reputation. The holy well is not some ideal from outside of time and change. It is a loose but convenient label which brings together all kinds of stories which people have told in successive generations about the landscape in which they live.

So until we realise that there are many kinds of holy well, each produced in response to different circumstances at different times, our study of the subject will suffer from a radical foreshortening of the historical perspective. It is as if there was a literature on 'the sacred stone' which indiscriminately jumbled up war memorials, megaliths, tombstones, crosses, obelisks and altars. It is a challenge to unscramble the complex of sites which meet us when we go looking for wells, since unlike the churches or chapels with which they are often associated, holy wells do not offer architectural clues to their status. They look just like any other water supply. It is the documentary record which marks them out.

Working without documents, and quite often disregarding the documents that they already have, researchers tend to place great stress on the early origin of wells. The casual reader of landscape archaeology is likely to be confronted with something like: 'Churches were built to "Christianise" the site of a pagan well or spring. Wells dedicated to the grotesque Celtic child-eating goddess Annis emerged in a much-sanitised guise as dedicated to St Anne, while St Helen was conveniently on hand to commandeer all of pagan Elen's springs' (Muir 2007: 154). This is rubbish from beginning to end. There was no Celtic goddess Annis. There was no pagan deity Elen. The well-cults of St Helen and St Anne developed in historic times for clearly identifiable historical reasons and Christianisation had nothing to do with it.[4]

Over a decade ago, James Rattue's *Living Stream* revolutionised this field of study by showing that holy wells did indeed have a history: they were not just survivals from some mysterious antiquity, but were created, adapted and discontinued over time. If researchers have failed to build on Rattue's foundation, it is for lack of the basic machinery of documentation – the deeds, rentals and surveys as well as the cults and legends and miracles – that would make further research possible. That is what this book is for.

But have we gone too far in taking the romance out of holy wells? Is there not something a little arid about all these charters and customals, when we could be walking upstream through the woods to a source in the living rock, where the water gushes out beneath the hart's-tongue fern and the primroses? How dry, by comparison, were those long afternoons spent over battered county histories while the dusty sunlight passed through high library windows. But there is life here, too. The documentary record does something that pilgrim fieldwork will not: it liberates us from our own responses to the holy wells – whether pious or profound or just plain clichéd. Everyone who was ever associated with a holy well had their own life, in their own unique human moment, which is gone forever. They can only be found in written history; they will not appear on site visits, however long we gaze at the still waters. That is why history matters.

In the pages that follow, we will meet with a great deal of more or less humdrum evidence, but we will also encounter a parade of vivid characters. Here is a woman who takes a gulp of well water, lurches forward and throws up a three-foot-long snake on the church pavement; there are shivering monks gathering up the bloody dust of their martyred master in a dark cathedral and steeping it in the deep well waters. We see bemused and guilty guildsmen watching as the water from a holy well steadfastly refuses to boil and the sacred eel squirms in the cauldron. Now comes a knight riding across a bone-strewn old battlefield where he calls on God to witness the powers of a new saint, leaps off his horse and hacks a spring out of the ground by sheer faith. Now a vexed farmer paces past the dying bodies of his cattle to uncover once again the holy waters of a well which he should never have obstructed. At one site a boy sits by the fire as an apparition moves slowly along the gallery above a desecrated well; at another, secret pilgrims stand, head bowed, by the cottage that was once a well chapel. To the sound of confused shouting, a Rogationtide procession passes by and the boys who beat the bounds are soused in the once-sacred waters. Mr Miller plays his flute to the unresponsive cows that graze around one holy well; Mr Blubber and his friend the Devil scheme to take the water of another away from the public. We hear from an elderly lady who would not go near her local holy well at the fated hour of twelve lest she be crushed by a standing stone as it returned from its midnight drink, and from an old gentleman who 'was liggin' a dying and he axed for a cup o' watter from the Holy Well, and they sent and fetched it, and he took it and went off upon his feet'. There is no shortage of life at England's holy wells.[5]

The making of the English holy well

What is a holy well?

A great deal is known about holy wells, but sometimes it is hard to marshal our knowledge. That may be because, as Father Horne put it many years ago, 'it is not easy to define a holy well' (1923: 7). Robert Hope, who stands at the head of holy well research, listed some 400 in his *Legendary Lore of the Holy Wells of England* (1893). This is only a very provisional figure, though, for all sorts of springs came into the bounds of Hope's insatiable curiosity. In his pages we meet with wells that were dressed with flowers or hung with rags, wells near crosses or trees or churches, wells haunted by ghosts or fiends or fairies, wells whose waters cured barrenness or scurvy or eye disease, wells which featured in legends of giants and dragons and fierce wild boars, wells named after forgotten worthies or local landmarks, cold wells, salt wells, iron wells and wells whose water was accounted remarkably pure. And as if that was not enough, he also includes the lore of rivers, lakes, pits and the occasional bath.

In this, the most inclusive sense, a holy well is almost any source of water which plays a significant cultural role in its community. Tristan Gray Hulse, who knows more about the subject than most, has suggested a definition as follows: 'A natural (or, rarely, an artificial) source of water, either with or without some form of associated material structure, for which, either in the past or in the present, some evidence (either actual or presumed) of some form of cult can be demonstrated: evidence of cult to include onomastics; topography (i.e. associations in space – the 'sacred' landscape); history; archaeology; hagiography; legend; pilgrimage; bathing or drinking for sanative, penitential or other ends; presence of votive deposits; architecture; folklore and local oral/written tradition; &c.' (1995).

That '&c.' gives the game away. Wells with cultural significance are so numerous, and so indeterminate as a category, that it would be impossible to list them exhaustively for a single county, let alone for the whole country. So the aspirations of this survey are much more modest. In what follows, a holy well will be taken as one that has a sacred name – one that is dedicated to a saint, or called 'holy'. A glance at some of the county surveys prepared by James Rattue suggests that holy wells in this purely onomastic sense constitute a small proportion, perhaps a fifth, of all the wells that a cultural historian might consider interesting. But what we lose in numbers we will gain in clarity.

St Anne's Well at Audenshaw as drawn in 1890. (From Speake & Witty 1953: frontispiece.)

Francis Jones, perhaps the most clear-minded of holy well researchers, conceived of wells under four classes. A was wells bearing the names of saints, B those associated with churches, C healing wells, D those with secular people's names, and E the wells which featured in local legend. It will be seen that our onomastic category of holy wells corresponds with Jones' Class A. Between England and Wales, however, there is one significant difference. In Wales, the holy wells always bear the name of a saint, although this is not marked out as a special name in any way. 'It is Ffynnon Seiriol but never Ffynnon Sant Seiriol, Ffynnon Ddewi but never Ffynnon Ddewi Sant' (Jones 1954: 7).

The rules of naming in England are quite different. Except for a handful of early examples, the form is always 'St X's Well' and this makes it much easier to identify holy wells about which nothing else is known. The only figure not to be commemorated in names of the St X's Well type is the Virgin Mary. Whereas her wells are consistently Ffynnon Fair in Wales and Tobar Moire in the Highlands, the corresponding dedications in England are divided in the names they use. A quarter of them are St Mary's Well, as one might expect, but the remaining three-quarters are called Lady Well, a name which has no parallel in Welsh or Gaelic, or indeed Latin.

It's true that local names and local pronunciation often conspire to make identifications difficult. Under the influence of Protestantism, the prefix 'saint' lost much of its meaning for people and from the eighteenth century onwards we meet with some bizarrely irregular developments. St Augustine becomes Tosting at Leicester and Paston at Cerne Abbas. At Fersfield in Norfolk, Tann is St Anne; Cuthbert transforms to Cuddy at Bellingham in Northumberland; and at Frosterley in neighbouring County Durham, St Botolph is reduced to the undignified Bot. St Helen appears under the guise of Sayntelling, Stelling and Sellan in Yorkshire, while at Santon Downham outside Thetford she has been secularised to Tenant.

Much easier, however, is the simple loss of the prefix 'saint' from before the name. In the case of locally venerated figures like Aldhelm or Alkmund, this is not a problem because we know who they are talking about. But there are also the saints of the universal church, who were often pressed into use when giving Christian names to children. Millions of people since the Norman Conquest have been called Anne or Andrew, and naturally some of them have owned and given their names to wells. In the survey which follows, I have been fairly rigorous in requiring evidence that a name is in fact that of a saint. 'Anne's Well' is not to be taken as 'St Anne's Well' unless there is some solid evidence in favour of it.

Relax your grip on that point and almost any speculation is possible. At one end of the spectrum we have quite reasonable suggestions, such as that of White Kennett (1818: 192) when he proposes that the Anglo-Saxon *Eadburgewelle* in Canterbury is named after St Eadburh, who was indeed a Kentish saint, though not originally associated with Canterbury. But as the antiquarian literature accumulates, speculation becomes more and more preposterous. Another Kentish site, Goose Well, is transformed into Holy Ghost Well (Igglesden 1900–46: 26.27–8). Sinner's Well near Leek in Staffordshire stands revealed as St Cena's Well, the Well of the Holy Supper (Cope 1945). And so on.[6]

England is also unique in a third form of name: the sites which are called Holy Well and nothing else. Names of this kind go back to 800 at least and are clearly much earlier than the phrase 'holy well' employed denotatively to describe a particular kind of well, a use which is not found before the seventeenth century. To avoid confusion, sites with this kind of name will be described as Holywells, with a capital H to distinguish them from holy wells in the more general sense. The corpus of sites which we are dealing with, then, consists in outline of three types: the Holywells, the wells of the Virgin – which are mostly Ladywells – and the saints' wells.

Inventing holy wells

Robert Hope, as we have seen, described 400 wells in England, of which only about half were holy wells in the onomastic sense. His magpie mind fastened on every detail which had been sent to him by fellow-readers of the *Antiquary* and for the purposes of his curiosity, one well was as good as another. To a large extent, Hope's compendium pre-empted the need for any other study of holy wells and remained the standard work until the twentieth century was nearly done. It is an open question what would have happened if the work had been done instead by one of the more historically competent figures working in the field at this time – by Charlotte Burne, or Edward Peacock, or indeed by John Charles Cox, who could tell sense from

Holy Well at Longthorpe as engraved in 1855. (From Thompson 1913–14a facing 113.)

nonsense but was kept too busy by his work on Derbyshire churches and by editing the *Antiquary* itself.

But the spirit of the age was, in any case, against a systematic history of holy wells. The 1890s were the heyday of the early folklorists and they had placed their trust in Tylor's theory that survivals from the prehistoric world could be found embedded, like flints in puddingstone, within the matrix of later culture. Historical background was unnecessary to these identifications, and would only have confused the issue, for whatever looked old *was* old, and probably pagan to boot. Between the original publication of Hope's material in the *Antiquary* and the issue of his book, George Lawrence Gomme had laid down the law: the cult of wells 'could not, under any circumstances, have been brought over by, and become prevalent through, the medium of, the Christian Church' (1892: 80).

This must have tended to discourage study into their historical origin. Still, it is a surprise to find Hope (1893: 90) tranquilly listing St Govor's Well, in the ancient surroundings of Kensington Gardens, as one more holy well among the rest. The dedication had been transferred from Llanover in Monmouthshire as recently as 1856 by Sir Benjamin Hall, Lord Llanover, when he was made First Commissioner of Public Works. Hope knew this – he had read the correspondence in *Notes & Queries* about this well (Williams 1860; Buckley 1875) – but it simply did not register with him as relevant.

Nineteenth-century holy wells are not uncommon. In Devon alone, we have Holy Well at Killerton, with its imposing Romanesque surround, built by members of the Acland family after the spring was opened by navvies in the 1850s. Arthur Troyte Acland improved the ambience by writing a 'Legend of the Holy Well' (Amery 1894: 80–1). St Mary's Well at Holsworthy was dedicated in 1882 by the Rev George Wright Thornton (Day 1934: 66). And Sabine Baring-Gould, the doyen of High Church antiquarianism, had his own personal holy well, built in the grounds of the family home at Lewtrenchard and dedicated to St Petroc (Faull 2004: 54–5).

Piety, of a romantic kind, was the inspiration for these modern dedications. A hundred years earlier, there had been another motive: when spas were all the range, any local manager with a flair for marketing would have noticed how saints' names gave a certain cachet to their product. In 1740 a visitor to the spring at Humphrey Head found the English seaside in all its damp winter charm. 'It's a Melancholy Scene for Water drinkers, on Cold wet Sands, and they seldom appear till after 9 o'Clock… Common People swallow from 3 to 8 Quarts for a thorow Brush upwards and downwards' (Short 1740: 54–5). Not surprising then, that by 1800 it had become Holywell Spaw, with the Fairy Chapel to be seen in a nearby cave, and a walk-on part in a romantic ballad (Stockdale 1872: 159). All this was aimed at a better-paying class than the 'Common People'.

Skipperham Well at Ashill in Somerset became dedicated to St Skipperham, or St Kipperham, or St Nippenham – any saint would do – until they finally hit on St Cyprian (Horne 1923: 38). Also in Somerset, a mineral spring seen at Edington in 1791 – it 'contains sulphur and steel, and stains silver yellow in two hours… against the change of weather it smells like the foul barrel of a gun' (Collinson 1791: 3.433) – had become much more genteel by the 1830s and was now called Holywell. Another spring at nearby Shapwick, where 'dogs afflicted with mange, would recover their healthy appearance by being thrown into the spring', got its name of Holywell at the mid-eighteenth century, shortly before the dogs were banished and a pump room and enclosed bath built for the accommodation of patients. The spa failed, as so many spas did, but the name stuck (Aston & Costen 1990: 39–40).

Today, nothing distinguishes these sites from hundreds more. It is only close attention to the documentary record that enables us to catch them in the act of creation: today they look just like any other holy well, and they have soon picked up the same magical reputations and traditions. Spring Well at Denton in Lincolnshire became St Christopher's Well at some point between 1784 and 1803, for no better reason than that the local landowner liked the name and wanted to build a tea-house there. A hundred years later, its waters were much in demand for their curative waters. Fairies haunted it and children knew that a sip from the well would make their wishes come true (Healey 1995a).

At Denton the dedication seems to have been spun out of thin air, but often, as at Skipperham's Well, it was arrived at by creative manipulation of existing place-names. The spring-name Chadwell (*ceald wella*, the 'cold spring') is routinely transformed into St Chad's Well. This kind of development, turning a word with another meaning into the name of a saint, is called hagiologising. The villages of Aspatria, Marwell, Everingham and Botolph Claydon, none of them originally connected with a saint, have all been laid under contribution for hagiologising forms and now boast wells dedicated Sts. Patrick, Mary, Everildis and Botolph. John Hardestie of Harrogate, who lived to be 96 in the arduous trade of water-carrying from John's Well, has became St John after his demise and the well is renamed accordingly (Grainge 1871: 131). Elsewhere Cat's Well has turned into St Catherine's, Senton's into St Anne's and Gulwell into St Gudula's. This is exactly the same toponymic speculation which generated the imaginary dedications of the antiquarians, but at these sites it has spilled out from the pages of books and taken up a real life in the landscape. St Gudula's Well lies banked in by mossy stone slabs, with a plaque to give its name and an old wayside cross nearby (Faull 2004: 84–5).

Samuel Loxton's 1918 drawing of St Anne's Well at Brislington.
(From Lovegrove 1986.)

The spring is a source of real pride to the locals and its origin in a local historian's *jeu d'esprit* of 1882 in no way invalidates the importance that it has now. After all, every holy well was created at some date or another.

Nevertheless, in a book which is focussed on holy wells of the Middle Ages, these post-Reformation dedications are a potential distraction. I have therefore separated them out and given them a section of their own after the main survey. Of course there are borderline cases, just as there are with the doubtful and spurious dedications of wells and the discovery of a single early reference could put any of these sites among the known medieval sites. These modern wells include shrines which are as important as any from the earlier centuries. It is a surprise to find Lady Well at Fernyhalgh and St Anne's Well at Brislington among them, but that is what the evidence says. Lady Well was a focus of post-Reformation Lancashire Catholicism around the walls of an old chapel and did not acquire its origin legend (modelled on that of Durham) until 1730. A revived devotion turned from the roofless medieval building to the ever-flowing spring beside it. Brislington was an important centre of pilgrimage until 1536, but there is no mention in the abundant early records of a well there. Not until 1885 do we hear of St Anne's Well and then like Lady Well it seems to have been adopted as a centre of Catholic veneration when the original chapel was in ruins.[7]

If modern dedications are so common, can any reference to a holy well be trusted? Gomme thought that every well was ancient; we are beginning to suspect that all except the handful recorded in the Middle Ages are modern. This is an extreme position and it underestimates the continuity that exists in English cultural life, especially in place-names. Throughout the seventeenth and eighteenth centuries, we meet with fields, woods, lanes, streams, farmhouses and hamlets named after holy wells. The names had usually ceased to carry a sacred meaning for the people who used them and were just convenient labels. They must go back at least to the 1550s, when Catholicism lost the countryside; it remains to be seen how much earlier they are. Into the early nineteenth century, people could still point out the holy wells that had been handed down by tradition, and much of this knowledge is embodied in the first large-scale edition of the Ordnance Survey.

Holy wells in England and beyond

So far, our enquiries into holy wells have consisted largely of winnowing out the evidence. We have moved from an overview of all culturally significant wells to the wells with holy names, and from that smaller body of sites we have progressively excluded the speculations and imaginations of local antiquarians, the wells that were created after 1600, and the ones which appear in sources so recent that it is hard to believe they go back to the Middle Ages. That leaves us a body of sites with which are recorded in medieval documents, or which appear from later place-names and traditions to have maintained their identity as holy wells since the Middle Ages.[8]

From a total of some 1500 English wells considered in this survey, about 900 are likely to be medieval in origin. 'English', in this context, needs some qualification. Hope's original survey included Cornwall, the land of holy wells, but I have not been able to follow him. It is easy enough to copy uncritically from the dozen books published on the subject, but to provide a serious evaluation of the 150 or more wells reported from the region, which has its own historiographical tradition on the subject going back to the 1820s, would require a detailed knowledge of Cornish topography and language. Perhaps someone will take up the challenge later.

One thinks of Cornwall as an area uniquely blessed with holy wells, in a Celtic heritage shared by Wales, Ireland, Brittany and the more remote parts of Scotland. How true is this? Simply comparing the number of wells is misleading, since it does not take into account the great disparities of size between the countries. If we take the density of sites as a more realistic guide, then England with its 900 sites turns out to have 5 wells for each 250 square miles. The one national survey for Scotland (Morris & Morris 1982) lists about 350 wells with holy names; that would be only 3 per 250 square miles, with the highest densities in the south, and the Western Highlands almost barren of sites, though clearly more research is needed. For Wales, Jones (1954: 31–3) enumerates some 500 wells in his Class A, the saints' wells: that is 17 wells per 250 square miles. In Cornwall it is likely that local patriotism and High Churchmanship have made excessive claims for the number of holy wells, but at least 100 in Meyrick's directory (1982) seem to be early, and that yields 18 per 250 square miles. There are no national surveys for Ireland or Brittany, and in any case the meaninglessness of 'pre-Reformation' as a category in these countries makes direct comparison difficult. But it is clear that in southern Britain at least, England has a much lower density of wells than the Celtic West.[9]

But what of the distribution of wells within England? Are they evenly spread, or is there a similar disparity between the numbers of wells in different areas? Analysis of the data is difficult, not least because English local history is traditionally organised by county, and counties vary in size: one site more or less would hardly be noticed in Devon, but would have a disproportionate effect in Rutland. With this in mind, I have divided up the country into fifteen regional blocks of about 3000 square miles each.[10] The figures – like all the statistics which will follow in this introduction – are based on the corpus of medieval wells in the survey.[11] According to these, the distribution of wells in the different regions of England is as follows.

Distribution of wells by region

Region	Wells per 250 sq. miles
North-East	6.6
Cumbria	5.0
West Riding	7.5
East and North Ridings	4.1
North-West	4.8
North of Midlands	5.5
Lincolnshire	3.1
Welsh Border	6.6
Midlands	5.9
East of Midlands	2.6
East Anglia	1.5
Home Counties	4.7
West Country	5.7
Mid-West	2.9
South-East	2.7

Clearly there is an unequal distribution here. East Anglia, the region with the fewest wells, varies by a factor of 5 from the West Riding, which has the most. The traditional view, first articulated by Isaac Taylor, is that 'the numerous Holywells, rare in the east of England, but more frequent as we approach the Welsh border, are survivals of a Celtic cult' (Taylor 1898: 390). Well, perhaps. The Celts are certainly absent in Norfolk and Suffolk, but then Yorkshire and Derbyshire with their numerous wells are hardly a Celtic stronghold either. In early history, of course, these regions were Celtic – so was the whole country – but that does not explain why Cumbria and the West Country, where the cults of Welsh and Irish saints continue to this day, should come out at a lower rating. What is happening here and is it significant in any historical sense?

The uneven distribution of English holy wells has been remarked on before.[12] Rattue was the first to attempt a statistical analysis, although his map (1995a: 17) is derived from a list of all wells with names, not just holy wells in the narrower sense. He considers three factors – population density, social and economic backwardness, and the level of investigation by researchers. One would have though that regions with many people would have many holy wells to serve them, but the exact opposite is true; wells vary inversely with population density. East Anglia, with the least number of wells, is recorded in Domesday Book as having the most people, while the West Riding with the most wells appears in the same source with the fewest people. Admittedly that was because William I had just killed many of them off, but Yorkshire had been thinly peopled even before the Harrying of the North.

The search for holy wells

Rattue's third factor, the level of investigation by researchers, cannot have had much influence on the distribution of sites. It's true that the study of holy wells has been traditionally conducted county by county, leading to piecemeal coverage and not all researchers work to the same standards. No county survey has ever quite lived up to the standard set by Taylor (1906) for Lancashire, with his painstaking consultation of OS maps, systematic fieldwork and exact citation of authorities. Nevertheless, every county in England has received some kind of holy well survey apart from Bedfordshire, Berkshire, Huntingdonshire and the Isle of Wight: small counties from which few wells are recorded and which have therefore failed to tempt anyone to write about them. If the recorded distribution of wells in England is uneven, it's not for want of people trying to find them.[13]

But what about the primary sources? A really successful county well survey cannot start from scratch: there has to be some material made available by previous research. Ideally this should include a classic county history from a writer with an interest in wells, a learned society with a record of studying folklore, early coverage by the Ordnance Survey, fieldwork by at least one obsessive well enthusiast early in the century when local tradition was more reliable, and most of all, good coverage by the English Place-Name Society.[14]

Would this explain the unequal distribution of holy wells in England? Hardly. If we take the three cases of Norfolk where wells are rare, Cumberland where they are at middling density, and Northumberland where they are common, there is no sign of dependence on the availability of primary sources. Norfolk has two volumes of the Engish Place-Names Survey (EPNS) covering rural areas, with a third for Norwich; the county historian, Francis Blomefield, had a holy well in his own parish and was interested in others; and three researchers – Burgess, Manning and Pennick – have all set out to find the lost wells of Norfolk, without noticeable success. Cumberland and Westmorland, too, seem to have everything going for them, including a very active county society, full coverage by the EPNS, and two exhaustive modern surveys of the literature; but they still only reach the median level for density of wells. On the other hand Northumberland, which has the most holy wells per square mile next to the West Riding, has no EPNS volume at all. The unequal distribution of wells must be a historical fact, not a side-effect of the process by which information was gathered.

It may be that the variation has nothing to do with the number of holy wells that there originally were, but reflects instead a difference in their survival. Many researchers have speculated wistfully on a time, in the Middle Ages or even earlier, when every parish had its own holy well. This happy state of things would have been brought to an end by the Reformation – and that was certainly something that fell with differing impact on different parts of the country. Seen in this light, the shortage of holy wells in East Anglia would be a natural consequence of the Puritan movement there, while their modern prevalence in the north and west would be a consequence on the irregenerate residual Catholicism of these areas – a consequence of the 'social and economic backwardness' noted by Rattue.

It's a nice try, but it does not work out in practice. Norfolk may have been a Puritan county, but it is also the scene of two Catholic well shrines, at Bawburgh and Walsingham, with unbroken continuity of use up to the present day. On the other side of the country, Lancashire retained so many recusants that it may be said, from the landscape point of view at least, to have escaped the Reformation; but the North-West is not remarkable for the density of wells known there, standing just below the median point. Besides, the theory that medieval England was full of holy wells can be tested directly against the evidence. We know of some 120 wells which appear in early records, but which had vanished completely from the map by 1600. Whatever made them disappear, it was not the Reformation. And when this density is plotted out – small sample size though it is – much the same pattern emerges as before. The West Riding has lost 13 medieval wells, because it had many wells to lose; in East Anglia only 2 are known to have disappeared. There is a more than fivefold difference between the two regions, as there is with the much larger figures for all holy wells. The uneven distribution already existed in the Middle Ages.

A less sophisticated theory for the distribution of wells was offered by Richard Morris, who announced (1989: 86–7) that it was all a matter of geology. Springs are naturally commoner in some areas than others, holy wells are a particular kind of spring and therefore they will be more or less common in different parts of the country according to the water supply. We may wonder by what geological fluke Cornwall, which occupies much the same geological formations as Devon, should have more than three times as many wells, or why wet Wales should be so much more prolific in them than even wetter Cumbria. The absurdity of this theory lies in its assumption that holy wells constitute a predictable percentage of springs in general. In fact they have come into being wherever there was a need for them and do not have to be natural springs. Over a dozen are draw-wells, dug down to the water table. St Cuthbert's Well on Farne was a sump, draining water from the surrounding rock.

The distribution of holy wells

But if the distribution of wells is not due to the presence of researchers, or to the availability of source material, or to survival after the Reformation, or to the availability of water, or to that final standby, the influence of the Celtic fringe, then what *is* it due to? It all depends on what kind of wells we are looking at. The problems of interpretation have been magnified because we insisted on treating the holy well as a single cultural category, forgetting that holy wells have originated at

Saints' wells and wells of the Virgin	
Region	**Wells per 250 sq. miles**
West Riding	4.7
North-East	4.4
Cumbria	4.1
Welsh Border	3.7
North-West	3.3
Midlands	3.3
East and North Ridings	3.2
North of Midlands	3.2
West Country	3.2
Home Counties	2.5
South-East	2.2
East of Midlands	1.9
Mid-West	1.6
Lincolnshire	1.5
East Anglia	1.2

different times, under very different circumstances. In fact, if we tease out the Holywells from the saints' wells, then two very different patterns of density will emerge. To begin with the saints' wells and wells of the Virgin, their regional distribution is shown on page 14.

Set this on the map and at once it makes sense. It is the saints' wells, not wells in general, which are distributed in inverse correlation with population. They are most common in rocky, upland counties with few villages and many shepherds – Fox's Highland Zone (1959: 29). They fall in numbers as we move eastward to the gentler corn-growing landscapes, where most people lived. The wildest region has four times as many wells as the tamest one.

And what of the Holywells? The table below shows their pattern of distribution.

Holywells	
Region	**Wells per 250 sq. miles**
Midlands	3.2
Welsh Border	2.9
West Riding	2.8
West Country	2.5
North-East	2.2
North of Midlands	2.2
Home Counties	2.2
North-West	1.9
Lincolnshire	1.6
Mid-West	1.2
Cumbria	0.9
East and North Ridings	0.9
East of Midlands	0.7
South-East	0.5
East Anglia	0.3

This is quite different. The Midlands, which were just above median in the distribution of saints' wells, have the highest density of Holywells – more than ten times that of East Anglia. Whatever reasons people might have had for giving this type of name, they were evidently most persuasive in central England. The numbers are still high in adjoining regions, but tail off as we move from the centre, whether it is to upland Cumbria or the thickly populated South-East.

The springs called Holywell

The name Holywell is a compound of Old English *halig* and *wella*. It is an ancient name; *halig* and its ancestral forms in Germanic had begun, even before Christianisation, to have much the same sense as Latin *sacer* and *sanctus*.[15] In place-names, the qualifier is often used for natural features – trees, stones, fords and streams. There are also particular kinds of places, *stoc* and *stow*, which are said to be *halig*. These were not necessarily areas set aside for cult or worship. Holywick in Buckinghamshire and Hallington in Northumberland were the *wic* and *denu* belonging to religious houses. At Reading, the *Haliwater* ran the monastic mill. 'Holy' in these names is evidently to be understood, not as being 'numinous, awe-inspiring' but in the more pedestrian sense of 'dedicated to the Church'.

But Holywells remain by far the most numerous names with *halig*. There are some 340 of them in England, constituting 38 percent of holy wells in the more general sense. Generally speaking they are easy to recognise in the toponymic record, since *halig* has developed smoothly into the modern 'holy'.[16] There are only a few other place-names which have developed in such a way that they can be confused with Holywells, although as a qualifier, *halig* can be confused with *hol*, the word which yields modern 'hole'.[17] Field-names often have spellings such as Hollywell; this is nothing to do with holly trees, but is simply a way of showing, by modern spelling conventions, that the first vowel ought to be pronounced short. Until the twentieth century, Holy- in place-names retained its short *o*, as it still does in Holyhead. But familiarity with the phrase 'holy well' has now induced most people to pronounce Holywell place-names with the long *o*.

Confusion with another element has occurred at Holywell near Castle Bytham at Lincolnshire. Nowadays they will show you the holy well, a decorative feature in the grounds of Holywell Hall, but this is a response to false etymology, as the settlement name is derived from *hæl*, meaning 'omen'. From the sixteenth century this was confused with *halig* and the question arises whether this has happened anywhere else. Certainly Morris (1989: 85) thought that other Holywells might derive from *hæl* and therefore presumably lay claim to some pre-Christian origin. But there is no philological evidence for this. Old English *æ* has its own distinct sound-development, becoming Middle English *e*, and in any case *hæl* is a very rare element in names.[18]

The situation is a little more complex in the North of England, where Old Northumbrian had a regional variant of *halig* which was pronounced *hælig*. This yields Middle English forms like *Heliwell* and modern Hellywells. The southernmost example of these appears at Tibshelf in Derbyshire, where there was a *Heliwelle* in

St Helen's Well at Stainland.
(From Crabtree 1836: 499.)

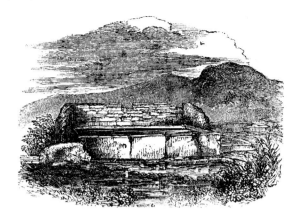

1321: there is also a *Helliwell* at Rubery in Worcestershire, but this is so far outside the Old Northumbrian area that it must be an aberrant form. Otherwise we have four modern forms in Cumberland (Blencogo, Catlowdy, Dalston and Haresceugh) and fourteen in the West Riding. These begin with a twelfth-century *Heliwelle* at Glasshoughton, followed by medieval forms at Baildon, Bradfield near Ecclesfield, Cudworth, Hipperholme, Priestley Green and Stainland, with modern fieldnames at Attercliffe in Sheffield, Atwick, Huddersfield, Manningham near Bradford, Thrybergh, Tinsley and Worsbrough.

The medieval names always have the central vowel as -*i*-, so clearly they derive from *hælig* 'holy' and not *hæl* 'omen'. At Glasshoughton the Old Northumbrian form alternated with the usual *halig* up until 1496, while at Stainland someone living near the spring is recorded in the late thirteenth century as *de Sacro Fonte*, showing that the meaning of the place-name was still transparent. But by the end of the Middle Ages, the well at Stainland had a chapel of St Helen beside it, suggesting that the place-name had become opaque and people were now guessing that Helliwell meant 'St Helen's Well'.

If the word *hælig* had become meaningless by the end of the Middle Ages, then any place-names containing it must have been coined at an earlier date, certainly before 1400. But the form has a wide currency; in Cumbria and West Yorkshire, these names account for 50 percent of all the Holywells. Two-thirds of the Helli- forms, moreover, are found only in modern fieldnames, or in landmarks on the Ordnance Survey map. If it were not for this accidental variation in Old English dialects – something which, as it happens, only applies in two out of the fifteen English regions – we might never have suspected that modern names had such an early history. It goes to show that, despite the incontestable evidence for modern origin of some holy wells, the place-name record can generally be trusted to take us back to the late Middle Ages.

How old are the Holywells?

But how much further back than that can we go? There is evidence for Holywells from six Anglo-Saxon charters. These describe the boundaries of Withington in Gloucestershire, 800s; Ruishton in Somerset, 854; Fontmell Magna in Dorset, 932;

Stoke near Ipswich, 960s; Olney in Buckinghamshire, 979; and Portesham, again in Dorset, 1024.[19] The distribution of these references is not very meaningful and shows only that charters have been better preserved in the south and west. But the fact that it is always Holywells that are found on these estate boundaries must be significant. Detailed description of landmarks in boundary clauses continued throughout the Middle Ages, and post-Conquest charters regularly feature saints' wells – St Hilda at Aislaby in the 1110s, Andrew at Sawley in 1147, the Virgin at Scotforth and Helen at Gosforth around the beginning of the thirteenth century, with Andrew at Sturton and Werburgh at Brill a little later. If names of this kind are not featuring in Anglo-Saxon charters, it must be because they did not exist then.[20]

To the list of pre-Conquest Holywells we can add the well at Halwell near Dartmouth, recorded in the tenth-century Burghal Hideage, and the settlement of Holywell in Huntingdonshire, first named in a will of 986. Domesday Book contributes the hamlets of Halwill near Holsworthy, Holwell near Radipole and Holywell near Oxford to this list. Again, it is noticeable that there are no corresponding manors named after saints' wells.

Generally it will be found that Holywells are much more embedded in the landscape than saints' wells or wells of the Virgin. Most of them – 65 percent of the total – have given their name to a field, a stream, a road, a farm or a hamlet, as well as to the original well.[21] Indeed, many of these adopted names – 41 percent, or 140 sites – have outlived the spring-name with which they originated. At these places, we can still see the river or the lane called Holywell, but we have lost any record of the well after which it was named. More than 80 wells survive only in the names of fields and 25 are known because they have given rise to settlements called Holywell. The contrast with saints' wells is as striking as it was with the boundary clauses. Only 8 percent of saints' wells have given their names to another landscape feature nearby. Though there are 400 of these sites – considerably outnumbering the Holywells – there are only 18 fields and 10 settlements that take a name from them. Clearly Holywells and saints' wells function in different ways within the landscape.

It is not surprising, then, that the most famous well-shrine of the Middle Ages in Britain should be at a town called Holywell, but it is unexpected that this should be in Welsh-speaking Flintshire. In 1247, when the name was first recorded, the ethnic status of the county was less decided – it had nearly become part of Cheshire – which is why St Gwenfrewi is better known in Anglicised form as Winifred. Holywell Wood in Monmouth (*Halliwell* 1343) is in another area which was long undecided between Wales and England (Charles 1938: 224, 262). Jones lists twelve English-language Holywells in Wales, most of them as one might expect in Monmouthshire and Montgomeryshire, but with one on the Lleyn Peninsula and another in the Vale of Neath.[22] The names do not appear to be modern; Hally Well at Meifod near Welshpool still retains the *a* of *halig*. But they cannot be nearly as old as the names east of Offa's Dyke. Generally, English field-names and local names are not found in Wales before the thirteenth century.

There are also Holywells in Cornwall (Meyrick 1982: 36, 84). Halwell at Linkinhorne is so far east that it could have been coined at the same time as the Devon examples, but Holy Well at Cubert is much further into Cornwall, in a region west of Newquay which was not Anglicised until the thirteenth or fourteenth centuries. These Welsh and Cornish examples give important insights into the chronology of Holywell names. Evidently it was still possible for a spring to be named in this way after about 1200, when some English began to be spoken in the Celtic West and before 1550, when the Reformation put an end to the tradition. But the naming of Holywells must have been a dying tradition by then, since otherwise the name would be just as common in east Cornwall or Pembrokeshire as it is in Devon or Gloucestershire, and this is clearly not the case.

What we need, as a test case, is a region where a language other than English was spoken for a limited period in the Middle Ages and where there was a special name for holy wells. And such a region does exist, away from the Celtic zone. It is easy to forget that for hundreds of years the Viking kingdom of York was as foreign and unEnglish as Galloway or Dublin. By the late ninth century, this region had been extensively colonised by speakers of Old Norse, which was just about mutually intelligible with its sister-language of Old English, but had a quite distinct vocabulary for many features of the landscape. A spring, which was OE *wella*, would be called ON *kelda* by the invaders. The last Viking King of York died in 954 and over the next hundred years the county was gradually brought back under English rule. Old Norse speakers were gradually assimilated into the English-language community, although they continued to use many distinct dialect terms that they had carried over from their previous language.

This is why a spring at Melmerby in the North Riding is called Hallikeld instead of Halliwell. This was a place of some importance – it was the meeting-ground for a wapentake, or divisional administration, and appears in Domesday as *Halichelde* – and it must have been named by one of the first generations of Scandinavians to take up English, though they still retained the word *kelda* for spring from their parent language.[23] It cannot be a native Old Norse coinage, because the qualifier is OE *halig* not ON *helgi*. We have another *Halykeld* from the 1150s at Wharram-le-Street in the East Riding, examples from Knaresborough (1257) and Ripon (1367) in the West Riding, and in the North Riding from Liverton (1210s) and Kirby Sigston (1226), as well as the only post-medieval instance, Halleykeld Rigg on the Ordnance Survey in Sawdon. All these examples come from a compact area, centred between York and Middlesbrough.

The use of *kelda* for well in English dialect cannot have begun much earlier than the eleventh century. Before that date, there was no incentive for Norse-speaking families, coming as they did from the dominant ethnic group, to adopt the language of their social inferiors. At the other end of the period, *kelda* seems to have died out as a vocabulary word sometime in the thirteenth century[24] This means that our seven Halikelds must have acquired their reputation as holy wells sometime between 1050 and 1250.

So what does this all tell us about the history of springs called Holywell? The distribution shows that these names are a native English coinage and not adopted from Celtic precedents; this is something which one would have suspected anyway from the lack of a Welsh or Cornish lexical equivalent. If the relative frequency of the names is any guide to their chronology, then the custom of calling springs Holywells will have begun in the Midlands and then spread out into the adjoining districts. It was almost as popular in the Welsh Borders, the West Riding and the West Country – regions which were not settled intensively by the English until the eighth century. Mercia itself was converted in 655, although the early episcopate probably had more urgent problems than the blessing of springs. It seems reasonable to think that the earliest recorded sites, Withington in the 800s and Ruishton in 854, represent a tradition which had grown up over the previous hundred years.

Six Holywells are recorded in boundary charters and since these represent a more or less random sweep of the countryside, they must have been frequent elsewhere. By the tenth century, they were common enough to give rise to settlement names. The village of Holywell in Huntingdonshire was an important place when Athelstan Mannessune bequeathed it in his will of 986; many years must have elapsed since the first straggling houses were built around the church, or the church appended to the well. The frequency with which Holywells gave their names to fields, farms or hamlets suggests that they were there early enough to influence later toponymy, and also that they might be found in lonely spots where they formed the only identifiable landmark. Large numbers of Holywells must have been dedicated in the West Riding and Cumbria at a time when Old Northumbrian *hælig* was still the usual word for 'holy' and this tradition goes back to the twelfth century if not before.

But the creation of Holywells cannot be attributed to a single historical period. At Wanswell in Gloucestershire and Leigh in Worcestershire, wells which were originally identified by other names seem to have been redefined as holy.[25] In the North Riding and its outskirts, the Christianised descendants of Scandinavian settlers were dedicating Halikelds at dates between the eleventh and thirteenth centuries. At least one Welsh example, at St Winifred's Well, was coined by English landowners in the thirteenth century and a few others in Wales and Cornwall must be later than that. The tradition may have carried on in a small way until the Reformation, but by then it seems to have been eclipsed by other forms of devotion.

Holywells and the early Church

This is what the place-names say. But does it fit in with the wider historical record? In about 1020 Cnut, who was himself a Christianised Scandinavian of the kind that we have held responsible for the Yorkshire Halikelds, passed a law stating that 'it is heathen practice if one worships idols, namely if one worships the heathen gods and the sun or the moon, fire or flood, wells or stones or any kind of forest trees' (*Councils & Synods* 1964–81: 1i.489). That sounds very much as if the names which compound *halig* with words for 'well' – or, indeed, for 'tree' or 'stone' – defined pagan sites, not Christian ones. It suggests a long survival of heathenism, against which the Church could only make slow headway. The early folklorists certainly interpreted the evidence in that way and so indeed did the legislators and clerics who passed the original laws. But the perspective of ordinary folk, the people who were being legislated about, was more complex than that.

Prohibitions of worship at wells, trees and stones were issued throughout Catholic Christendom over a period of a thousand years. Throughout that time, the formula remained remarkably constant, as one might expect from a culture with such respect for the written word, but the world moved on nevertheless. When Caesarius of Arles and Martin of Braga denounced the worship of wells in the sixth century, they were battling against paganism in its literal, historical sense. The peasants of rural Gaul were still attending well-shrines like that of Coventina or Sequana and it was the duty of a good missionary bishop to stop them. But already in the sixth century, the cult of saints' wells was attracting devotion of a different kind. Gregory of Tours recovered from splitting headaches at the well where Julian of Brioude had carried his own head after it was severed by the executioner's sword; water was the medium which cured him, but it was St Julian who earned his gratitude. The *numina* which had been immanent in the old religious landscape were yielding, site by site, before the more personal mediation of holy men, living or dead. 'Wherever we look, in the early centuries of the cult of saints', says Peter Brown (1981: 126), 'we see the victory of a language drawn from observed human relations over the less articulate and less articulable certainties of an earlier age'.

The well-cults of early Christian England came from the same clerical culture which had inspired Gregory of Tours. It is true that the pagan Anglo-Saxons, like almost every other culture, had their own traditions of sacred waters. They may even have used the name Holywell to describe them. But the veneration of wells was already an established Catholic practice when St Augustine came to land and they would have spread through the land whether Æthelbert and his people had been pagans, Arians, or secular humanists. New wells could be established and venerated with any need to convert existing ones and there is little reason to think that they did; Holywells are rarest in the southern and eastern parts of England, the areas where pagan place-names are thickest on the ground.[26]

People preferred the new saints to the old gods – so much so, in fact, that they soon took control of their new-found faith and began venerating saints of their own making. Charismatics and village messiahs appealed to an audience which had absorbed Christian ideals of the supernatural but did not want to see access to it locked up in the hands of bishops. Boniface of Devon, in his reforms of the Frankish church on the borders of Germany, had trouble in 744 with a wonder-worker called Aldebert, an intimate of God and his angels who worked miracles at his own network of crosses placed in the open fields and meadows – and at springs (Gurevich 1988: 65-8). Significantly, Boniface complained about these cult places, not because they were pagan, but because they took the rituals of prayer and confession away from established minsters. But the future of the religious landscape lay with minor shrines of this sort, some of which would eventually become parish churches and chapels, while others survive as our isolated rural Holywells.[27]

Aldebert worked wonders and foretold the future, as charismatics usually do. He had his special ways of doing so and these were castigated by his enemies as magic. And it is in connection with magic – and especially the divination of the future – that the denunciation of wells returns to the attention of legislators, after a long period in the eighth and ninth centuries in which it does not seem to have caused any concern

(Blair 2005: 168, 481). The Viking occupation of the North had brought about a crisis in the church, partly through the arrival for the first time in centuries of real-life pagans on English soil and partly through the loss of confidence that this disruption brought. In response to this, Wulfstan the Archbishop of York began to issue legislation against the cults of tree, well and stone in the early years of the eleventh century. These appear in the text known as the *Canons of Edgar*, issued after 1005, in the *Northumbrian Priests' Law* of about 1010, and in the laws of Cnut noted above (*Councils & Synods* 1964–81: 1i.320, 463, 489).

Wulfstan drew on the authority of tradition in his denunciations, using words which would already have been familiar from the penitentials associated with Egbert and Theodore (Thorpe 1840: 293, 371, 380). A penitential is a guide for the priest at confession, enumerating those sins which the faithful might commit either knowingly or in ignorance and giving a set tariff of penance for them. The tradition went back to the lists of forbidden practices in Caesarius and his contemporaries, but had been formalised. Making vows at a well earned you three years on bread and water, reduced to a year if you had only taken part in feasting there.[28]

In the penitentials these faults rank fairly low in a long catalogue of sins, but they had much greater importance for Wulfstan. His lawcodes make the extirpation of heathenism a primary duty, introduced at the beginning as part of the lawful establishment of church and state. And this is not just aimed at those Vikings who still hanker after the cults of the Æsir, for all sorts of magic and divination come under the same ban. In his *Homilies* (1957: 148, 184) Wulfstan condemns the cult of wells and trees as a breach of the faith received at baptism. Ælfric had said the same in the 990s in his homily *On Auguries* (1881–1900: 1.373). 'Some men are so blinded, that they bring their offerings to an earth-fast stone, and to trees, and to well-springs, even as witches teach'. The earlier penitentials had expressed concern about vows being made 'at trees, wells, or stones, or at chapels (*cancelli*), or anywhere except at God's church'; they wanted to curtail the extension of Christian rituals to illicit sites. But for Ælfric and Wulfstan, these excesses have become demonic. The Devil, with his agents the witches, is acting from within to subvert Christian society. Of all his arts, the divination of the future is most subversive, since it subverts the trust in God's Providence which should typify the well-ordered Christian society. Magical wells, with their long tradition of foretelling things to come, were especially suspect.[29]

But the popular mind did not necessarily make such hard and fast distinctions. The countryside contained a variety of religious practice – learned magical practices like necromancy, popular superstitions involving sun and moon and natural features, cults of supposed saints remembered in name only and enthusiasm for new miracle-workers, visionaries and faith-healers, both living and dead. The same forms of worship were to be found across this whole spectrum of belief. Everywhere people made vows, lit candles, repeated prayers and collected chips of holy wood or phials of holy water. It was the business of bishops and kings to draw a line through this ragged medley of popular faith and to say what legitimately belonged within the Church and what was to be condemned as lying outside it. According to how that line ran, a holy well might be authorised or it might be excluded. The cult itself

Holy Well at Stevington. (From Fisher 1812.)

would still have originated in a broadly Christian world, even though it might condemned in formulae dating back to the days of the conversion

Holywells and the later Church

Before a century had passed, Wulfstan's campaign for a single-minded Christian society had been reduced to more manageable proportions. The provisions made by the Council of Westminster in 1102 are realistic. 'We hear that there are those who, with rash enthusiasm for novelty, have treated the bodies of the dead, springs and such like with the reverence that is due to a holy shrine. This is not to be done without the authority of the bishop' (*Councils & Synods* 1964–81: 1ii.678). This ruling is summarised as 'supposed saints and shrines at wells', which puts it in a firmly Christian context. Furthermore, the Council of Westminster is not calling for an outright ban on these cults, but for episcopal control of them. If the dead man turned out, on due intervention, to qualify as a saint, then his relics and his well could be culted without further concern. No longer a rash novelty, it would become part of the wider religious landscape.

This is what St Hugh of Lincoln was doing at the close of the twelfth century when thanks to his 'stern admonitions' at Berkhamsted, Wycombe and elsewhere, 'people were known to have rejected the worship of springs' (*Magna Vita* 1864: 348). St Hugh is presented in his *Life* as an ideal pastoral bishop and the fact that this portrait – wells and all – is modelled on Sulpicius Severus' *Life* of Martin does not argue against the truth of its details. St Martin, as Hugh knew well enough, had fought to convert the pagans; now Hugh was bringing the superstitious back into the fold, by telling them that their beliefs were no better than paganism. The boundary between lawful and illicit faith was open to negotiation, though; the survival of the field-name *Halliwell Mead* at Wycombe suggests that its cult was accepted later on.

Not far away is another Holywell at Bisham which seems to have been the scene of a religious scandal in 1385 when Bishop Erghum of Salisbury suppressed its cult. Crowds were coming in from Wycombe and Great Marlow, speaking excitedly of the miracle of a bird which nested in a bush over the well and, made tame by the holiness of the place, did not fly away even when they handled it and placed offerings in its nest. They also told how a man had recovered his sight by bathing his eyes there; but the Bishop brusquely attributed the cure to cold water and ordered the Rural Dean to fill in the well, tear up the tree and pronounce greater excommunication against those who visited there. (*Victoria CH Berks.* 1906–27: 2.14)

The example of Bisham shows that a Holywell could be created as late as the fourteenth century. If the site had it not come to the attention of the bishop, it would feature in the records as just another field-name. That's the problem with these records of suppression; they tell us about the cults that failed, but we know very little by contrast about those which succeeded. It is not easy to be a saint. The reputation which strikes awe into one community may leave another unimpressed and both landowners and clergy looked askance at any charismatic who challenged their authority.

The early career of St Robert of Knaresborough was a series of forced moves and evictions from one hermitage to another around the royal forests of Yorkshire. Eventually he found a settled position in a cave not far from the town, where his reputation for sanctity was accepted by all; he even bested King John in a pious battle of wills and received a small estate of land alongside the Nidd. Some forty years after Robert's death in 1218, one of the streams draining this land was called the *Halikeldsike*, although it became better known to later tradition as St Robert's Well (*Metrical Life* 1953; Purvis 1927–9: 391–2). From Knaresborough's point of view, St Robert had timed his death badly; just three years earlier, the Fourth Lateran Council had begun the process by which decisions on canonisation were reserved for the hands of the Pope.[30] A dossier was put together for Robert's cult, but it was never formally endorsed and to this day his sainthood remains a matter of local opinion. This is the context in which we should understand *Halikeld*, one of the last -*kelda* names, and one of the most clearly dated, for it must have originated after St Robert received the field from the king in 1216 and was certainly current by 1257. The place-name enshrines an element of Yorkshire caution among his contemporaries. Maybe he was a saint in heaven and maybe he wasn't, but he had certainly been a holy man and there was no harm in saying as much. This is the role of reserved judgement which Holywell spring-names seem intended to fulfil.

Where are the Holywells found?

The pilgrim to holy wells will find them in a variety of settings. Some live up to romantic expectations, trickling among ferns from out of the living rock, or secluded under the shade of some old tree beside the village churchyard. But they will be found in many other places – beside the road, on windswept hills, in marshy spots on the banks of rivers and at undistinguished corners of fields.[31] There is just as much variety in the structure and appearance of wells. We have natural springs,

Locations of Holywells	
location	**percent**
Isolated	32
Outskirts	48
Central	20

running through the grass or filling pools; banks of rough rock or arches cut in field walls with the water running out through a spout; wells which fill a sunken or raised basin; and well-houses, some built in local vernacular style and some with architectural pretensions. As one might expect from their more rustic origin, Holywells are more likely than saints' wells to be housed in the simpler kinds of structure. They comprise 57 percent of the natural settings and 47 percent of the spouts. Saints' wells and wells of the Virgin, by contrast, make up 86 percent of the basins and 89 percent of the well-houses.

The variety of locations for wells almost defies topographical analysis, but it is possible to consider them under three broad headings. First there are the central sites, where wells are found in towns and villages, churchyards and chapelgarths, or the closes of cathedrals, monasteries and hospitals. Then there are locations on the outskirts of settlement, with wells situated in the open fields or hunting parks, or next to a single house or farmstead. And finally come the completely isolated sites out in the countryside, sometimes on a boundary.[32] If we distinguish these three levels for the Holywells, the distribution of their locations turns out to be as the table above.

This suggests a delicate balance between centrifugal and centripetal impulses. The ideal site for Holywells, it seems, must lie away from settlement, but not so far removed from ordinary life as to be out of reach. This resembles the typical situation for a hermitage and in fact St Anthony, the father of hermits, is depicted as choosing just such a site. In his *Life* we read that 'he came to a very lofty mountain, and at the foot of the mountain ran a clear spring, whose waters were sweet and very cold… Anthony then, as it were, moved by God, loved the place… So… he abode in the mountain alone, no-one else being with him.' [33]

The isolation of the hermit's cell was tempered by his dependence on the outside world for food and other gifts. St Jerome, the most distinguished of St Anthony's successors, appears sometimes in art as a gaunt figure by a desert well, at others as the master of a well-stocked library. Both images contained an aspect of the truth, as they did for Robert living in his cave on the outskirts of Knaresborough, where he could retreat for contemplation, but from which his servants could easily solicit the alms of travellers passing over Grindal Bridge on the way into town.[34]

At Holywell Haw near Loughborough there was a *heremitorium de Halliwellhaga*; it was already a hermitage when the property was given to Garendon Abbey in 1180, and afterwards the monks ran a small dairy there (Potter 1842: 189–91). The name of Halywell, surviving at a grange held in the village of Sulgrave by St Andrew's monastery in Northampton, may have originated in the same way (Bridges 1791: 1.127). The Priory of Holywell at Churchover was founded in the 1250s. Its situation by Watling Street looks very much as if a hermit had settled down by the Roman road at a small cell, remembered afterwards by the name of his holy well. Subsequently the situation was regularised by a grant from Robert de Cotes, who wanted a chantry and thought the place should be under proper supervision, so he made the hermit's successors into canons of Rocester Abbey. Unfortunately they were 'in a lonely and dangerous situation on the highway where robbers often conceal themselves to make raids', something which cannot have much troubled the original poor hermit but was a great vexation to his more prosperous successors. In 1325 the chapel of Holywell was transferred to a new site (Hamper 1821: 76–8).

At Croxton Kerrial, William Parcarius de Lions had a park full of heathland and 'all that scrub land around the spring called Haliwelle'. This was included in lands bestowed on Croxton Abbey in 1162, but the well in the park may represent an earlier and less costly attempt to maintain a holy man at the lord's expense (Dugdale 1817–30: 6ii.877). If he succeeded in bringing some of the waste under cultivation, well and good; if not, at least his prayers were a blessing. The 'ancient and ornamental hermits', paid to strike contemplative poses in eighteenth-century landscape gardens, have a longer pedigree than one had supposed. Many famous monasteries were to stem from such unpromising beginnings.

A park is private ground, however overgrown, and nobody would have been allowed to maintain a holy well there without the lord's consent. Robert of Knaresborough had found himself evicted from hunting-grounds on more than one occasion. This suggests that a place like Holywell at Blaisdon, first mentioned in a grant of those parts of the king's waste 'which are within the bounds of the Forest of Dean', must have had some official encouragement (*Rotulorum Originalium Abbrevatio* 1805–10: 2.122). When Henry son of Conayn refers to 'my park of Halikeldale' at Liverton, it implies that he or his predecessor had sponsored the holy well there and presumably some kind of hermit beside it (*Cartularium de Whiteby* 1879–81: 2.377). If they had hoped to combine land clearance with spiritual advancement, this was a success; fields that had been enclosed here were given to Whitby Abbey in the1210s and the village of Liverton was established at about the same time, stretching in an orderly row south of the church, which is itself as near the holy well as is possible without infringing the park bounds.

The equivalent setting for urban wells lay on the outskirts of town. Here the hermit could find some spare land to till, cultivating the generosity of passers-by at the same time; when the roads were so uncertain, a place of prayer for travellers was much appreciated. The crofts of Halliwell at Chesterfield lay 'on the high road leading from Chesterfield to Whytington on the east, and the road leading from Chesterfield to Neubold on the west'. A small chantry chapel of St Helen was built here in the fourteenth century, over a hundred years after the well is first mentioned (Bestall 1974–80: 5.181–2). At Colchester, on the south side of Harwich Road about half a mile beyond East Bridge, we arc told of a Holywell in 1339; next, a chaplain is

Holy Well at Kings Newton.
(From Hope 1893: 59.)

recorded there in 1344 and then a chaplain-cum-hermit in 1387 (*Victoria CH Essex* 1903–2001: 9.336). This suggests a development of religious institutions at this site, beginning with the well and gradually becoming more formal.[35]

There is a similar development at Coleham, a suburb of Shrewsbury, where in 1356 we hear how Roger the hermit attends the chapel of St Mary Magdalene. He tills an acre taken from the waste nearby at Spellcross ('the cross where speech was held') and more hermits follow, the last one in 1526. It is not until 1571 we hear for the first time of a Magdalen Well, but this must have existed in some form for the needs of the hermits (*Victoria CH Shropshire* 1908–1985: 2.23). At Stanley in the West Riding, the chapel of St Swithin is first recorded in 1284: according to tradition it was founded so that Mass could be said for the sick at a time of plague in a spot outside the town itself. There was a hermit living here in 1355 and his water would have come from the St Swithin's Well near the chapel (Walker 1934: 193–4, 446).

Wells dedicated to saints

As these examples show, the demarcation line between Holywells and saints' wells was occasionally breached. At Buxton, *Bukston juxta Halywell* as it was called in 1461, the well had been dedicated to St Anne by the early sixteenth century. A reference to *Chaddewalle* in 1301 at Tushingham in Cheshire was clearly understood as St Chad's Well, even if that wasn't originally what it meant, but in 1620 the spring was called the Holy Well. The eponymous spring at Holywell near North Shields was known as St Mary's by 1769; the area around St Edward's Well at Maugersbury was called Holy Well Head in 1766; at Spaunton Bank near Lastingham, St Mary Magdalen's Well is found in Holy Well Close, and at Repton St Anne's Well is among the Holy Well Hills.

That's about all the overlap that can be found between wells called holy and those dedicated to saints. Holy Well at Folkestone was 'called also St Thomas's Well', but this is on the Pilgrims' Way where everything is linked with St Thomas sooner or later. Seven or eight examples out of a corpus of 900 is not many and generally speaking the two categories are distinct. When William Fitzstephen in his 1174 *Description of London* said that 'Holywell, Clerkenwell, and St Clement's Well are of most note' (Stow 1912: 502–3), he evidently thought of St Clement's as a different sort of name from Holywell, not as a particular example of something called 'a holy well'.

As we have seen, saints' wells do not feature in Anglo-Saxon charters or early settlement names; the first one on record is St Cuthbert's on Farne in about 700, although this was not actually named after the saint and seems to have been atypical in other ways. After that there is a long pause and then in the 1080s and 1090s comes the work of Goscelin of Saint-Bertin. Goscelin was a hagiographer brought over in the wake of the Conquest, at a time when many English monasteries needed to draw on the spiritual capital which was locked up in the relics of their local saints. What could better impress the Normans than a new *Life* and one written by a Continental to boot?

Writing in Latin, Goscelin normally uses the 'St X's Well' form of phrase The first native-language form is from Guisborough, where *Hildekelde* is recorded in the 1150s, followed by Brill in Buckinghamshire, where we have *Seyntburwell* in 1273, although this is almost immediately followed by the form *Warboroughwell* in 1298. It looks as if in Old English the well had been named directly after the saint, as in Welsh. Referring to the saints as such began in the tenth century and became habitual after the Conquest; Middle English *saint* is taken from Old French and not directly from Latin *sanctus* .[36]

There are some 120 saints with wells dedicated to them. Already in the Middle Ages national cults were recognised as being distinctive; John of Tynemouth in his *Nova Legenda Anglie* had assembled a collection of their lives, including those of Wales, Scotland and Cornwall in his *Anglia*. Then there were New Testament saints and the martyrs of the early church, as well as saints like Catherine who were known to everyone, despite being more or less imaginary, and cults like Lambert and Leonard which came to England later from the Continent. It seems best to follow John of Tynemouth in marking out British saints from non-British and to leave that second category without any further subdivision.[37]

On this basis, there are about 80 wells in England dedicated to local saints, 100 to regional ones and 220 to foreign saints, Biblical saints and other dedications such as the Trinity. The contrast with Wales is instructive; here the proportions are exactly reversed, wells with foreign dedications being the fewest and those of local saints the most numerous. If you consider the number of saints, rather than just the number of saints' wells, Wales has half the number of non-British names in its dedications (16 as against England's 38). Both countries have roughly 25 saints with regional reputations, but it is in the number of local saints that Wales excels, with some 140 where England has about 60. The much smaller size of Wales makes this all the more remarkable. Although the wells dedicated to foreign saints form about the same percentage of all holy wells in both counties, they are still nearly three times more common to the square mile in Wales than they are in England. But, whilst always remembering this disparity, the fact that Wales is especially rich in the wells of obscure local saints, while England is distinguished by Holywells, suggests that the two kinds of dedication may have a similar origin.[38]

The wells of local saints

Not that England is without its local saints. At Meare in the Somerset Levels, people would proudly show visitors how St Benignus had came to this place in bygone days and planted his staff, which grew into a tree. His servant Pincius had many comic misadventures with a devil, after which his master saved him the three-mile trip to gather water by telling to strike the ground with his staff. 'At once a fountain burst forth, the source even today of a wide river, good for fishing and safe to use for various purposes' (William 2002b: 348–51). Actually the Brue doesn't rise anywhere near Mere, but why spoil a good story? Traditions of Benignus, or Beonna as his name seems to have been in Old English, were recorded in the saint's *Life* by William of Malmesbury, but William, though a conscientious historian, clearly did not have much to work on and simply gave a decent Latin guise to the local legends.

The same process can be seen in the accounts of Nectan, written by a devotee of the saint at Hartland in north-west Devon. The earliest text, of the twelfth century, is a list of miracle stories told by local people and from these we learn that Nectan had a well with a stone nearby that had been coloured by his blood. There was a sacred eel that swam around in this well and in a grove nearby grew an ash-tree, called the Magpies' Tree, which should not be cut or damaged on fear of incurring the saint's displeasure (Grosjean 1953; Doble 1970). A few years later, in 1168, Arroasian canons were installed at Hartland and one of them was detailed to write up a proper *Life* of Nectan. Out went the eel, the tree and the never-explained magpies. Instead we are told how Nectan came to Stoke, lived a hermit's life and was eventually beheaded by robbers while searching for his cows on the waste ground a mile away. He picked up his head, walked back to the spring and put it down on the blood-marked stone and only then did he die, to be buried in the church nearby. Though the story of the martyrdom must come from tradition, a certain amount of tidying up has taken place. But it is clear that nothing much was really known about St Nectan. The name appears to be Irish; his relics are said to have been found in the tenth or eleventh century.

At Braunton, the cult of St Brannoc is recorded in the ninth century. You could see 'his cow, his staff, his oak, his well and his servant Abel' in stained glass in the church and, although this does not survive, it was probably one of the miracle windows which became popular in the fourteenth century (Risdon 1811: 337; Roscarrock 1992). At Ilam, St Bertram (originally Beorhthelm) had another ash tree and a well, but his story is not recorded until the seventeenth century (Plot 1686: 207). St Edwold was identified as the brother of a king of East Anglia, although the location of his cult in an obscure corner of Dorset suggests otherwise. Guided by a vision, he came to the Silver Well at Stockwood and thrust his staff into the ground 'It can be seen there to this very day, a majestic ash tree' (*Nova Legenda Anglie* 1901: 1.362–4). St Decuman sailed with his cow on a cloak that crossed the Bristol Channel to Watchet and was killed by robbers, after which he carried his head to a spring and near the later site of his church (*Nova Legenda Anglie* 1901: 1.265, Doble 1962: 28). He has a well at Rhoscrowther, too; the Welsh explain that the Somerset well is a fraud and that St Decuman really stepped back on his cloak and returned home to Pembrokeshire to wash away the blood before dying properly (Jones 1954: 37).

All these stories were worked up from the common repertoire of hagiographical motifs.[39] If they repeat each other, so much the better; the *Lives* of saints are not histories, but acts of sacred testimony. That would explain the otherwise surprising frequency with which beautiful but pious princesses are killed after conflict with male relatives or admirers. The story of St Arild at Kington is basically that of St Winifred at Holywell, even down to the red bloodstains that mark out her well, though admittedly these are only recorded in recent tradition (Quinn 1999: 223). A well broke out when St Sidwell of Exeter was beheaded with scythes by haymakers on the instigation of her stepmother (Swanton 1986). Another arose after St Urith of Chittlehampton had her head cut off. This was also done by workers in the meadow, with their scythes, persuaded to the deed by her stepmother (Andrews 1962: 233–41). At Halstock the well of St Juthware flowed after she was beheaded, in this case by her brother and he had been prompted by the malice of – yes – her stepmother (*Nova Legenda Anglie* 1901: 2.98–9).

The same motifs are repeated again and again, but why? Not much was actually known about St Urith, so the parishioners of Chittlehampton could have commissioned virtually any story about her, but clearly they were happy with one that showed a high degree of repetition. As long as the narrative was cast in suitably devotional form, they were not going to bother about matters of detail. Facts were free, but opinion was sacred.

As a matter of fact, we don't even know what their saint was originally called. Mostly she appears as Urith, but in an early relic list she is Hyaritha. After some thought, John Rhys suggested a Celtic etymology from Iwerydd, but an equally good case could be made for a mistaken reading of the Welsh *gwyryf*, 'virgin' (Blair 2002b: 557). Juthware is recognisably OE Guthwaru, while Sidwell appears as Sidewelle from the tenth century, whatever the ultimate etymology of her name. Arild looks as if the second theme was OE -hild, but it is not easy to see what the first one could be – and the name could have been altered, or even invented, to resemble other Old English examples. After all, Gwenfrewi of Wales – 'white Brewi' – has been Anglicised to Winifred, as if she had really been an Old English *Winethryth.

One of the most contested saints' names is that of Alkelda, whose holy well can be found at Middleham in the North Riding. For many years it was received wisdom that she was a holy well personified – one of the *halig keldas* which we have seen to be common in that region. Certainly there is an St Alkelda's Well, although it is not recorded before the nineteenth century (Barker 1856: 18). But the early forms of her name all show medial -*i*-, not -*e*-, and furthermore it is almost unknown for the qualifier *halig* to lose its original *h*. Accepting these problems with the *kelda* derivation, and allowing that Alchhild is a quite legitimate name, we can restore Alkelda to her position as a real historical figure.[40] She must have been active before the ninth-century Scandinavian conquest of the North, although the legend that she was strangled by Viking women is unlikely to have any truth to it. Generally speaking, the hagiographers were obsessed with the violent death of their female saints. It is as if, having imagined a paragon of all the virtues, they could not think of any way in which she could show them except through being martyred. As far as women were concerned, the only good saint was a dead saint.[41]

That is not quite fair; we have a few legends in which the maiden's flight from the lustful suitor is followed, not by martyrdom, but by the successful achievement of a hermit's life. St Pandonia (presumably OE Pendwynn) fled for refuge to her kinswoman, the Prioress of Eltisley in Cambridgeshire, and it is at Eltisley that her well is found (Leland 1906–10 1.1). She is said to have been a Scots king's daughter, which would have made it a long flight, but the hagiographers always liked to create a royal genealogy for their heroines, especially when there was little more than a name to go on. With St Bee, as with St Alkelda, it is suspected that the name has created the saint. Her hagiographer tells us how she received a ring as a miraculous token of her espousal of Christ, but that is because his main concern is to weave together every tradition, related or unrelated, that could be linked to the name of his patron. In this case the church of St Bees had a sacred bracelet on which oaths were sworn in what seems to be a Christian imitation of ancient Viking practice, and *beag* is Old English for 'ring'. The ring itself seems to have been late ninth century, so the cult (and by implication, her holy well) cannot be older than that (Todd 1980). St Wite's Well lies near Whitchurch Canonicorum and St Wite appears in one source as a virgin martyr, but nobody knows by whom she was martyred, or when, so this may simply be an attempt to create a story on the usual lines for an otherwise unknown woman saint (Gerard 1980: 16).

The cults of obscure saints

If saints were to survive as something more than a name and a well, they needed the continuity and support of a religious house.[42] It is because the minster communities at Eltisley and Whitchurch did not last that we have no *Lives* of Pandonia and Wite to go with their wells. Binsey has been more fortunate, since its local saint became the patroness of a rich and well-situated foundation at Oxford. Soon after its foundation in the 1120s, St Frideswide's Priory commissioned a *Life* of their patron. There was the usual jumble of local tradition to be harmonised into a satisfactory whole and it is not until the first reworking of the material in the mid-century that we hear about the well she created by her prayers at Binsey.[42]

But curiously, the *Life* does not call it St Frideswide's Well, as the story seems to demand, but St Margaret's. The church has the same dedication and this suggests that there was some pre-existing tradition which could not be overridden just for the convenience of the hagiographer. The situation of the well, too, shows deliberate planning; it lies just west of the building, on the central alignment of the building. The church and well, along with an adjoining farmhouse, form a compact block within an old earthwork, which is called Thornbury in Frideswide's *Life*. It was here that Edith Lancelin retired to live in holy solitude at some time in the 1120s. She may have been was following the example of the saint, or the saint's actions may have been unconsciously modelled on her own; it is not clear which, but the dedication of church and well to St Margaret is likely to be Edith's work.

When the old English minster churches fell into decline after the Viking invasions, many local saints were relegated to obscurity and it is clear from the fantastic nature of most twelfth-century *Lives* that their authors knew no more of the facts than we do. For a glimpse of the pre-mythological stage we have to rely on passing mentions, such as that from Daylesford in Worcestershire. Here 'a servant of God named Bægia' received a grant of land in 718. The charter boundaries run past the stream *Baeganwellan* which evidently took its name from the man of God – because he had fetched the daily water of his hermitage here, perhaps, or more prosaically because he had landowner's rights in the well along with the rest of the property that was now being granted for a minster (Mawer & Stenton 1927: 121). The spring-name survived until the eighteenth century and there is still a Baywell Wood, but that is all. No St Bay, no relics, no fantastic life; a holy tradition, which might have flourished in the more accomodating climate of Wales or Cornwall, survives for us as a bare place-name.

No doubt similar stories lie behind the obscure saints who appear in relic lists and other sources, although St Makedran's Well at Farlam is the only well to appear in a medieval text, in 1195. The name sounds Gaelic or Irish, which would make sense in at a site not far from Carlisle and the border. At Loweswater, also in Cumberland, we have a St Ringan's Well. Ringan is attested as a Gaelic form of Ninian, but it is not obvious why this would be used locally and the only reference is a late one. Another Gaelic form of Ninian is Trinian and curiously there is a St Trunnian's Well at Barton-upon-Humber, though it is hard to see what Ninian could be doing in Lincolnshire. St Trunnion may have got muddled up with St Aniel of Burton upon Stather and either of them may be the St Anyon who was claimed by one local to be the real patron of St Helen's Well at Brigg. At Warrington we hear of Elphin, who could be OE Ælfwine or Welsh Elffin, and there is the mysterious doublet of Farmin at Bowes and Firmin at North Crawley. St Hawthorn, who had a well on the Wrekin, may be an unrecognisably corrupt form of some Old English or Welsh name, or he may just be a hagiologised tree.

There are no early records for St Tinniver's Well at Beckley or St Urian's Well on the Isle of Wight, though the cults of these saints certainly existed before the wells are mentioned. Another Devon saint, Wardred of Lee, seems to have been provided with a well as late as 1971. The 'famous Well dedicated to St Begga' seen in 1726 at Begbroke (Hearne 1885–1918: 9.238) sounds suspiciously like a hagiologising form but this is not formally proven, while we have already noted the spurious wells of Gudula at Ashburton, Cyprian at Ashill, Everildis at Everingham and Govor at Kensington.

But some traditions, like those of St Sidwell at Exeter clearly go back to an early period. The story of her death in the hayfields was already current in the 930s and, like many episodes in hagiography, it seems to have been composed around existing landmarks, in this case the saint's well outside the city walls. Then there is the mystery of her name, which appears from the earliest sources in two divergent forms,

St Oswald's Well at Oswestry, as depicted about 1825 in an engraving by George Yates. (From Roberts 1879: 97.)

Sidewelle and Sativola; neither form can be easily derived from the other and it would make much more sense if both were developments of a lost Celtic original.[44] Here, if anywhere, we may suspect that the cult of a well venerated by the seventh-century British had survived the English conquest of Devon.

On the other hand, St Urith has a name of doubtful etymology, a derivative legend, no connection with a minster or other early site and an unexpectedly late cult. She was the focus of generous pilgrimages in the fifteenth and sixteenth centuries and, since pilgrim cults were normally short-lived, it seems quite possible that St Urith was only discovered in about 1400 and that her story, including the well, was modelled on those of other saints.

Saints in the landscape

The cults of obscure saints generally go back to the minster period – say the eighth or ninth centuries – but, as with Holywells, the kind of expectations which created these early sites remained in force for many years, up until the end of the Middle Ages. The village saint was a living figure, one whose patronage and reputation rose and fell over the years. New intercessions needed new stories, so that fresh links were made each generation between the saint's life and the local landscape.[45]

This is clear from the zest shown in the *Lives* for associating natural landmarks with the saints. These cannot all go back to the supposed era of the story. Wells, of course, are everlasting and stones are almost as indestructible, so it is possible that these could have kept a sacred reputation from the time of conversion onwards.[46] But the *Lives* are just as interested in holy trees – and trees do not last for ever. They grow old and die. In fact the ash, a favourite tree in these stories, is particularly short-lived, reaching its full height after about 100 years and then succumbing to disease and age when it is 200, or exceptionally 300 years old. Stories will only attach themselves to mature trees, not to saplings; so if we find local people pointing out a particularly fine and sacred ash, it follows inevitably from the facts of tree life that it cannot have had that status for more than 200 years. Before then, the tree would only just have begun to grow and would not have been worth noticing.[47]

St Kenelm the boy martyr planted a twig in the ground just before he was buried; it sprouted miraculously into an ash tree and when his body was exhumed a spring burst out nearby. So says Goscelin in the 1070s and, following the 200-year rule, it is quite feasible that the ash tree could have been woven into the legend within a generation after the death of the historical Kenelm in the 820s. The *Life of St Edwold* also includes 'a majestic ash tree', though this text only survives in the *Nova Legenda*. Supposing the original version to be as early as Goscelin's time, and supposing that Edwold really was, as his legend states, a brother of St Edmund of East Anglia – both of them very questionable assumptions – then this tree, too, could go back to the time of the saint venerated near it. On the other hand, the ash tree which Reginald of Durham associated with St Oswald in 1165 cannot possibly have existed when the saint died in 642. Two centuries would have passed before it even sprouted, even supposing (which is unlikely) that Oswald ever came anywhere near the site at Oswestry which now claims to be his death-place. Similarly, the Magpies' Tree venerated at Hartland in the twelfth century cannot have anything to do with St Nectan, who flourished before the English conquest of Devon.

The most extreme disjuncture of tradition and history comes at Ilam, where the locals continued to point out St Bertram's ash in the seventeenth century. 'The common people superstitiously believe, that tis very dangerous to break a bough from it: so great a care has St Bertram of his Ash to this very day' (Plot 1686: 207). But if it was flourishing in 1686, the tree must have begun to grow only a century or so before the Reformation. It is tempting to suppose that it was only the last in a long line of sacred trees, but there is no evidence for this; it would be a purely imaginary projection of the actual records and one which gives no credit to the inventiveness of folk tradition. Confidence in the immemorial lineage of these traditions is shaken when one thinks of the oak tree which featured in the tales of St Brannock at Braunton and was portrayed in an window (apparently of the fourteenth century) at the parish church. This oak, like the sow which identified the site of Brannoc's church and the marvellous wolf-guarded cow which he bought back to life when it was dismembered by wicked men, was taken wholesale from the Pembrokeshire *Life of St Brynach*. At some point between the twelfth and fourteenth centuries, the legend must have been transferred to the north Devon coast and the storytellers had no problems in finding a suitably impressive old oak to embody it.

The respect paid to tall ash trees and weather-beaten thorns at modern wells, often cited as evidence of a pagan origin, is really proof of the opposite; the trees have grown long after the Reformation and so did their cults. We don't know much about the tree which was venerated at Bisham in 1385, but it was described as only a bush and the fact that it was grubbed out rather than felled suggests that it cannot have been of any great antiquity. The miraculous bird of Bisham, like Oswald's raven and Nectan's magpies, clearly derives from a stratum of folk belief which was more at home with the natural world than official Christianity could be, but that is in itself no proof of an early date.[48] Research into sacred trees at wells, and into the holy wells themselves, is bedevilled by this confusion between the archaic and the genuinely ancient. Archaic imagery can arise at any time. It does not provide evidence for survival from an early period.

Local lore saw no difficulties in linking saints with trees that had grown three or four hundred years after their death. At Pucklechurch, recent folk tradition has transplanted a story of St Aldhelm from Bishopstrow, where it is first recorded, to a tree (yet another ash) twenty miles away (Walters 1928: 97). And if trees, why not wells? St Brannoc's Well, like his tree, was evidently rediscovered at a new site. The storytellers' work of fastening holy men and women into the landscape did not happen once and for all at the beginning of their cult. It must have been a continual process, moved and modified as old landmarks disappeared and new ones acquired the patina of age. It is only the written texts of hagiographies which fix this process. Until then, we can never be certain that the well which claims such venerable antecedents is not simply a new focus for an old cult.

Saints brought into history

In any case, we cannot always be confident of dating saints through the *Lives* which bear their names. Obscure but well-loved local saints could be stitched into the framework of Anglo-Saxon history, just as they were tied down to the landscape. At Maugersbury near Stow-on-the-Wold there is a St Edward's Well, but local opinion is divided on who this St Edward was. Some think that he was a local hermit, but the parish church is dedicated to Edward the Confessor, while according to an early charter there were lands here given by Æthelred, presumably in expiation of his murdered brother Edward the Martyr. It seems that an otherwise unknown Edward has been associated with his more famous namesakes in order to boost the prestige of the town.[49]

According to his *Life*, St Walstan of Bawburgh was also a scion of a royal house – apparently that of East Anglia, since he was born at Bawburgh near Norwich. His father was called Benedict, his mother Blida, and he died in 1016. Obviously nothing like this is known from the pages of history and the choice of 1016 as a death-date may reflect the convention by which it marked the end of the Saxon and the beginning of the Danish monarchy. Walstan is being placed in a historical never-never land of the late Anglo-Saxon period.

When it comes to dating Walstan's cult, the style of his *Life* is more helpful than its content. It first appears in the Wynkyn de Worde edition of the *Nova Legenda*, but is evidently earlier; however, the text contains words which are not current before the thirteenth century (Twinch 1995: 36). Pilgrims to Walstan are recorded in 1255 and the chancel of the church was rebuilt fifty years later, no doubt funded by their offerings. The name Walstan is a good Old English one, but everything else about him has the flavour of the early thirteenth century. He left his royal home to become a farm labourer at Taverham, where he endured many slights until at last his death, attended by sights and wonders, revealed what a saint he had been. A fashion for worker-saints had grown up in response to the cult of St Francis, who died in 1226 and who, like Walstan, had left a wealthy family to live a humble life among the poor. The astonishing episodes surrounding Walstan's last journey, in which the oxen drawing his death-cart create holy wells every time they stop to piss and leave wheel-ruts in the pliant water of the local stream, sound more like the imagination of the local peasantry than the contribution of a pious litterateur.[50]

Farm-worker though he was, Walstan also had to be a king, in accordance with the fairytale convention by which all saints were of royal blood. We have already met with vague claims of royal origin in the stories of Edwold, Pandonia, Bega and Frideswide. At Gloucester they venerated St Cynburgh, another of these runaway princesses; she fled from the unholy prospect of marriage and took on a new job as a baker's assistant outside the south gate of the city. Her employer's wife disliked her, just as the farmer's wife at Taverham despised Walstan, and she killed the girl, throwing her body in a well which became the focus of her later cult. Thus the fifteenth-century story (*Historia Monasterii Sancti Petri* 1863–7: 1.lxv–lxviii). A dedication to St Cynburgh is recorded here in 1141 but it is much more likely to refer to the historical abbess of that name than to the servant-princess, who has been created as the focus of a later cult. Miracles are first recorded at her shrine in 1267, which would fit with the thirteenth-century predilection for saintly labourers.

Other women were remembered as mother-abbesses, leading and guarding a holy community. This was much more like reality; perhaps the obscure saints who are commemorated in this way had indeed lived such lives, but it is equally possible that in the absence of real evidence the hagiographers used this trope to graft them somehow onto the pages of the history books. Geoffrey of Burton upon Trent, the author of the *Life of St Modwen*, has written of his delight in finding a copious historical account of this otherwise unknown saint and it seems almost churlish to point out that he achieved his end by fusing her with two completely different women, St Monnina or Darerca of Armagh and St Monnena of Perthshire.[51] St Edith of Polesworth, whose well near a hermitage remained a focus of cult in the sixteenth century, has been identified with two known Ediths – sisters of Edgar and Athelstan respectively – but is unlikely to have been either. She has a second well dedicated to her, at Church Eaton, but this was a later development; the advowson of the church was presented to Polesworth Abbey in about 1170 and the dedication must date from after this event. St Osyth of Essex has a detailed *Life* written in the twelfth century, but since this represents her as being killed by Vikings in 653 its historical accuracy can be taken as nil. She was popular enough to merit the dedication of another well at Bishops Stortford, in addition to the one at St Osyths which appears in her *Life* (Bethell 1970). St Osyth of Aylesbury, with a well on the outskirts of that town, seems to have borrowed the *Life* of her namesake in Essex, for want of a better. It is hard to see why either of these two saints should have inspired the dedication of St Osyth's Well at Richmond in the North Riding. Can there have been a third, equally unknown Osyth? Or is this another dedication to a servant-saint – in this case, St Zita of Lucca?

The element of fantasy, always strong in the *Lives* that depend on local tradition, is found throughout that of St Fremund (OE Freomund) of Cropredy. The story makes him a son of Offa, summoned by the needs of his country from a hermit's life. He triumphs against the Vikings, but is beheaded by a treacherous Englishman; undismayed, the saint picks up his head and walks to a spot near Harbury, where he thrusts his sword in the ground, praying for water, and after a well has streamed from the spot he dies (*Nova Legenda Anglie* 1901: 2.694). This is only the beginning of a series of wonderful post-mortem adventures, but it incorporates the theme of the sacred journey which is so common in these lives (Blair 2002a: 484). Among these saints who carry their heads after death – the cephalophores – we find Nectan, Decuman, Sidwell, Urith, Juthware and Osyth of Essex. Sometimes the well springs up at the place of their death and they walk from it to the site where they know their tomb must be; sometimes the well is found, or created, at the end of the miraculous journey and they use its water to cleanse away the blood from their matted hair. Either way, the journey moves from the dishonour of martyrdom to the to the saint's new and higher power as an intercessor in heaven. It is also a move from one cult site to another, from the well to the shrine. If the length of the journey varies – about a hundred yards for Sidwell, a mile and a half for Osyth – it is not to increase the sense of miracle, but because that was the distance between two places which the storyteller wanted to bring together into a single narrative.

The miraculous creation of wells was part of the death-journey of Walstan, linking cult sites at Taverham, Costessy and Bawburgh. The journey of Kenelm to his final resting-place at Winchcombe Abbey involved the miraculous rising of wells at Clent and on the outskirts of Winchcombe itself. The *Life of St Ethelbert* traces the route from his place of martyrdom at Marden to his shrine at Hereford, with miracles taking place along the way; there are wells of the saint at both places, though they do not feature in the *Life*. At Derby, the presence of St Alkmund's Well just outside the city, at the place where his relics would have entered when they were translated in the ninth century, suggests a similar concern with the saint's passage through the landscape. The same need to validate a sacred geography appears in the *Life* of Rumbold, in which the saint prophecies his coming death and announces that he must be buried successively at Kings Sutton, Brackley and Buckingham, a cult sequence which is corroborated by wells at the latter two places (Hagerty 1988). There is a St Rumbold's Well at Astrop near Kings Sutton, too, but that is just a modern renaming of a medicinal spa. This *Life* is perhaps the most unhistoric of all hagiographies. Any sense of the real Rumbold or Rumwold has been jettisoned for a tale of marvel in which the heroic infant, grandson of the heathen Penda, calls for baptism immediately after birth and after three days of edifying preaching dies and is enshrined.

Celtic saints

The traditions of obscure saints, whether they survive only as place-names or have been worked up into fictitious *Lives*, do not constitute evidence for the era at which they lived. It is true that the well-cults which are recorded in the eleventh and twelfth centuries could in theory have been remembered at the same spot for four or five hundred years. There is nothing impossible about this, for similar cults are recorded at an early date in the handful of Insular *Lives* that go back to this period. But such an unvarying chain of transmission is not likely; tradition is too mutable and inventive for later legends ever to serve as proof for early conditions.

If this is true for the conversion period in England, the same doubts must apply on an even greater scale to the English wells named after Celtic saints of the fifth and sixth centuries.[52] St Nectan may belong to that era, although we do not hear of his cult until the tenth century, and it is posssible that it was his relics, and not the saint himself, that crossed the sea and found a new home in Devon. The same is true of

St Decuman, since the rival claims for his cult by Pembrokeshire and Somerset suggests that he was imported from one to the other. Until the eleventh century his relics seem to have been based at a minster church near Watchet, now lost to the sea. Although it is possible that St Decuman's Well had previously existed as a secondary focus of the cult, it seems more likely that when his shrine was transferred inland, his legend and its landmarks were relocated too. Further along the Somerset coast, we have St Erne's Well at Weare, surviving only in place-names, but suggesting a cult of the sixth-century Ernin. On the island of Steep Holm (notionally in Somerset, though in fact in mid-channel between England and Wales) Caradoc of Llancarfan located a well of St Gildas (Williams 1901: 2.409). Since Caradoc knew no more about the author of the *De Excidio* than we do, his story of the saint's hermitage and well must be a twelfth-century fiction, perhaps one of his own drafting. This suggests that the other traditions may also derive from clerical contacts across the Bristol Channel and not from memories of the lost Celtic past of Somerset and Devon.

In any case, contemporaries like John of Tynemouth had a much weaker idea of the 'Celtic saint' than we do today. A saint was a saint and if their patronage had been found particularly effective in any area it would spill over into the neighbouring regions. The Cornish St Petroc had a considerable following in Devon.[53] The number of his holy wells has been much exaggerated; at Dunkeswell, Harpford and Newton St Petrock the traditions are only recorded recently and at Lewtrenchard and Westleigh they are definitely spurious. But there is at least one medieval well of St Petroc, recorded in the precincts of Torre Abbey in about 1230 (Watkin 1923–4: 137). It is stretching a coincidence to suppose that this abbey should have found a pre-existing holy well in the grounds chosen for it in 1196 and it is much more likely that the dedication was made by the monks. The well rose next to the kitchen and supplied water for the divine office, washing and other uses; it was a more practical source than we might expect from a holy well. The same seems to be true of the well dedicated to St Egwin, which rose next to the fishponds in his abbey at Evesham (*Chronicon de Evesham* 1863: 216).

Another cross-border dedication appears at Dewsall in Herefordshire, which not only takes its name from a well dedicated to the patron saint of Wales, but uses the Welsh form of the name, Dewi. Significantly, this is the only medieval settlement in England to be named after a saint's well, as opposed to 20 or more villages or clusters of farms called Holywell; in this, too, it follows Welsh practice. West Herefordshire was effectively outside England and saints such as Clodock (Clydawg) are recorded in the book of Llandaf, not in English sources. Unfortunately the only mention of his well is in a modern source, while the Shrewsbury reference to a spring of St Brochfael Ysgythrog, King of Powys, seems to be the work of Iolo Morgannwg. The Welsh St Asaph makes an unexpected appearance at a Northamptonshire well in 1915, but this seems to be an antiquarian conceit. Many wells were visited on May Day and that happens to be the feast day of St Asaph.

St Winifred makes several appearances in England, which is unexpected from a saint whose cult was so strongly localised at her Flintshire Holywell. In fact these other St Winifred's Wells derive, not from any spread of her cult, but from an imitative tendency to name local wells after the famous site. The well at Lansdown seems to owe its name to Mary of Modena, who visited Bath in 1687 after a pilgrimage to the Flintshire shrine. At both sites her her prayers and wishes had been for the conception of a child to carry on the Catholic line of James II and the dedication of the well at Lansdown seems to be a tribute to this (Peach 1883: 1.5, 158). There are other duplicates of St Winifred's Wells in Shropshire, just over the border from Wales. One at Lilleshall goes back to 1804; at Shrewsbury, the name is found as a variant on what is normally Holy Well; and at Woolston there is an enigmatic building, serving as a courthouse and bath-house, which was identified as a well of the saint in 1837.[54] The St Winifred's Well at Holywell near Castle Bytham seems to have been introduced just because the name reminded people of the Welsh shrine, while that at at Brough is an error for St Mary's Well, made by someone to whom all holy wells suggested Winifred. At Crediton, Ripon and East Dereham she has got mixed up with Winfred, Wilfrid and Withburgh, while the Winifred's Well at Sherborne is a hagiologising form of an unrelated place-name.[55]

The cult of St Patrick gave rise to several wells in north-west England, though none of them are medieval. The earliest, that of Bampton in Westmorland, takes its dedication from the nearby church and the well at Lancaster may be associated with a chapel in the parish church there. Patterdale in the same county is a hagiologising form, since the settlement was originally named after a secular landowner called Patrick. St Patrick's Well above Bromborough Bridge, overlooking the Mersey, is supposed to have been the saint's point of departure for Ireland; at Slyne he is supposed to have made a spring arise on his travels when he begged for water and was refused (Cox 1895: 244; Billington & Brownbill 1910: 2). These stories are all modern, popular amongst the local Irish communities and probably coined by them, but they show the kind of cultural influences through which a cult can spread.

Influence from across the Scottish border is not so evident, perhaps reflecting the lesser number of wells in that country. Hope lists a St Boswell's Well in Northumberland, but that is a mistake; his source is referring to the Roxburghshire St Boswell's. Columba (Columcille) had a well at Casterton in Westmorland, with a chapel alongside it. Here the origin is not in much doubt, since both well and chapel reflect the piety of the lords of nearby Warcop, where the church is dedicated to the saint. The cult of St Kentigern, more popularly known as Mungo, is a rare example of a Celtic saint who is venerated almost exclusively in an English county. Apart from his role as patron of Glasgow Cathedral, St Mungo is confined to Cumberland, where he has wells at Bromfield and Caldbeck. The spa well of St Mungo's at Copgrove in the West Riding lies at some distance from the others, while early references have aberrant forms such as Mungnaye and Mugnus, suggesting that the well was not really dedicated to St Mungo at all. St Magnus of Orkney is not inconceivable in an area of Viking settlement, or we may be dealing with another obscure local saint whose name has become unrecognisable.

In the late nineteenth century, Cumbrian archaeologists were seized by a passion for retracing the footsteps of St Kentigern and would join up his surviving dedications into long itineraries, supposed to reflect the saint's missionary journeys through the district. Holy wells formed part of this pattern, although the evidence was often suspect; at least four bogus 'St Mungo's Wells' were created in this way. Since Cumbrian churches were founded later than most – probably after the tenth century – there is no reason why they should record the actual life of St Kentigern, who died in 603. They simply reflect the spread of his cult in a later age. The same goes for St Ninian, whose wells at Brisco, Whittingham and Loweswater are recorded in the nineteenth century. They may represent earlier traditions, but are hardly likely to go back to the fifth-century heyday of the saint himself.

The earliest English saints

As we cross the boundary from legend into history, the possibilities of identifying an actual date of origin for a well become greater, but the value of the wells as independent historical testimony grows less. With the obscure local saints, the existence of dedicated wells did at least prove that they were figures of importance at an early period, even if the cult itself might postdate the era of the saint by some centuries. But the veneration of historical saints tells us nothing that we do not already know about their earlier careers. The medieval authors could consult their Bede, just as we can; and it is in the pages of Bede that almost all of these figures are to be found.

The father of English history has preserved two accounts of the creation of holy wells. The earlier, and most mystifying, appears in the *Passio* of St Alban. There are pre-Bedan versions of this text, which appears to go back to a fifth-century original.[56] There is nothing else like this in the canon of Insular hagiography; it belongs instead to the world of Late Antiquity, with a trial and execution under Roman law in a Roman city. As Alban is borne to his death, he prays for water and a spring rises from the ground. Then, bizarrely, as soon as his thirst is satisfied, it disappears again. Usually, saints' *Lives* introduce the motif of the spring, stone or tree to link past and present by referring to some landmark which can still be seen in the reader's own day. From this perspective, a spring which flows and vanishes again is a completely pointless addition to the story. Evidently the author is playing by some quite different set of rules, but it is not easy to see what they are. There is nothing in later history about this spring; the Holywell recorded at St Alban's from 1250 onwards is not the same site.

With St Cuthbert's Well at Farne, we are on more familiar ground. After so many nebulous and spurious characters, it is refreshing to arrive at a saint with an actual biography. Shortly before 680, Cuthbert transferred from the monastery of Melrose to that of Lindisfarne and obtained permission to establish a hermitage on Farne, where he had a well dug for water supply. After a short period as Bishop of Lindisfarne, he returned to his hermitage in 687 to die and by at least 705 the well was being honoured in his memory. As in other episodes of Cuthbert's *Life*, the element of miracle is kept deliberately low. We are told only that, following the example of Moses, he predicted that water would be found in stony ground and that its waters were reliable and pleasant to the taste (Colgrave 1940: 98–9). Nevertheless, this is enough to establish it as the first securely dated holy well in English history.

St Cuthbert's Well at Bellingham. (From the Northumbrian County History Co, 1893–1935: 15.226.)

The cult of St Cuthbert soon acquired a regional character. By 995, when his relics were securely enshrined at Durham, he had become the special saint of the North and kings from southern England sought his favour as they would that of any other territorial magnate (Bonser, Rollason & Stancliffe: 1989). Durham Priory was a great landlord and employer; the special veneration given to St Cuthbert's church and well at Bellingham by one Sproich in the 1160s is not unconnected with his day job mending bridges on the Tyne, for which he was paid by the Priory almoner (Reginald 1835: 242–5). There are six other Cuthbert wells in the North. That at Wetheral lay near a 'monks' ford' in the 1200s and was evidently established by the monks of Wetheral Priory, founded in 1106. Scorton in the North Riding is supposed to have been near a religious foundation; at Offerton in Durham and Edenhall in Cumberland the dedication is shared by the church, as at Bellingham. There are more recent references at Tweedmouth and South Shields, with two from further south – Doveridge in Derbyshire and Donnington in Shropshire.

The other northern saints have a more circumscribed cult. St Aidan's Well at Bamburgh, like his church there, represents his cult at the royal centre nearest to Lindisfarne. The St Wilfrid's Well in Ripon supplied water to the cathedral dedicated in his honour and that at North Stainley lies within the Liberty of Ripon. This was identified by tradition as the original estate held by the saint when he died in 709. And so it may have been, but the wells are more likely to represent a later sense of regional identity; the one at North Stainley was on the boundary of land confirmed to Ripon Cathedral in about 1255. The only outlier to this group, at Halton in Lincolnshire, shares its dedication with St Wilfrid's church there.

Another saint familiar from the pages of Bede, St John of Beverley, has a very local reputation. A supposed well in Beverley Minster is spurious and another at Holme Church nearby seems to have been given the saint's name late in the nineteenth century, while the first mention of that at Driffield also comes from the 1890s. St John's most celebrated well is at Harpham, where he was born, according to a tradition that goes back to the time of Leland – and no further. Given the abundant twelfth-century material on his life and miracles, the absence of any earlier references to Harpham is fairly damning and the tradition is likely to date from the end of the Middle Ages. The fact that nineteenth-century guides were able to point out the very cottage in which St John was born (Smith 1923: 123) does not inspire confidence in the accuracy of their story.

Landmarks in the lives of saints

The dedication of wells to mark the birthplaces of saints is not uncommon. St Osyth of Aylesbury had one at Quarrendon, or Bierton if Leland's attribution of the site is mistaken, while St Edith's Well at Kemsing marks the supposed birthplace of St Edith of Wilton. St Wendred's Well at Exning and St Werburgh's at Brill served the same function. The historical standing of these saints varies greatly, but the common pattern is of a princess born at some small royal centre, a *villa regalis*, who afterwards goes on to achieve holiness and distinction at a religious house elsewhere and is then enshrined, often at a third or fourth location. Meanwhile the original place of her birth is sinking into a common village, with only a few memories of past grandeur to call on. By dedicating a well, local people were remembering the saint and hoping that she and her pilgrim devotees might remember them.

St Boniface had a well at his birthplace in Crediton, although his Saxon name of Winfred evidently confused local people, as it appears as Winifred's well from 1879 onwards. Bede himself has a well at Jarrow, doubtless inspired by the belief that he was born there. If, as seems likely, Bede was born at Monkwearmouth instead, then the tradition would have been inspired by false antiquarianism. In the same way, Colchester acquired a well of St Helen only after the story of her birth there became current in the twelfth century. There is no mention of the well at Quarrendon/ Bierton in Osyth's *Life*, even though this has several miracle stories centred on her birth, which would offer a natural opportunity to mention it, so the cult probably originated at some time after the *Life* was written. It was certainly flourishing by the late Middle Ages, when townsfolk pointed out not only St Osyth's Well but her comb, her girdle and the ball she used to play with as a child (Campana 1996: 102). This is typical of the sentimental domestic piety which loved Infancy Gospels and stories of the Virgin's girlhood. Wells found their place in the biographies of many later figures. St Richard of Chichester had a well at Droitwich, where he was born in 1197, while a fifteenth-century chapel at Charlcombe was dedicated to St Alphege, the martyred Archbishop of Canterbury. He was born at nearby Weston in 954, but the dedication at Charlcombe seems more likely to have been taken from books than local memory.

In the more fabulous *Lives*, a well is always the scene of miracle and marks some crisis in the life of the saint – their birth or death, or the establishment of their future shrine. Only in the more historic accounts do we find wells performing the more mundane duty of water supply, just as they do in the Irish lyrics that celebrate the hermit's simple life in the forest. The *Passio* of Sts. Wulfade and Rufinus is an unusual text in several respects – it is very late (thirteenth or fourteenth century), it uses many of the conventions of romance rather than hagiography and it describes the well of a saint other than its heroes. The author had evidently been to Stowe near Lichfield and seen the well of St Chad there, which he introduces into his story as a feature in the woodland glade where the saint rests in his cell, awaiting the destined arrival of the young prince whom he will baptise (Dugdale 1817–30: 6i.227–8). There are many other wells of St Chad, but analysis of the cult is bedevilled by the presence of hagiologising forms from OE *ceald*, 'cold'. Indeed, the only other site to have a historic connection with Chad is that in Lastingham, where he succeeded his brother Cedd at the monastery founded in the 650s. Both saints have wells in the town, where St Cedd's was dignified in the nineteenth century by a stone wellhead, made of material plundered from the nearby Rosedale Abbey. It is unusual to have wells commemorating two local saints, or in this case three, since a third site (recorded only in the twentieth century) is dedicated to St Ovin, who was also connected with the abbey. There are no early records of cult at these sites, which may be some antiquarian's attempt to turn Lastingham into a kind of Bedan theme-park.

There are three wells of St Swithin, but like Chad he may owe some of his cult to mistaken etymology. The well at Walcot is the only one within the region of Wessex where the historical Swithin was active and where people would have been familiar with his shrine at Winchester. The other two are in Yorkshire – one at Copt Hewick, the other at Stanley. Rattue (1995b) has pointed out that there is another Swithins Well in the West Riding, without the prefix 'saint', and this has been derived from ME *swithin*, 'moor cleared by fire'. This makes it probable that the other two names are both hagiologising forms, although that at Stanley must be an early one, since St Swithin's chapel was already established by 1284.

These dedications to St Swithin are exceptional in the North Country, where cults more usually reflect the northerners' determination to resist incorporation into a uniform kind of Englishness. But other parts of the country have their regional cults too. St Botolph (OE Botwulf), the apostle of East Anglia, had a well at Hadstock which was still attracting pilgrims just before the Reformation, and one recorded in the thirteenth century at Weybourne. This is in north Norfolk and looks as if it is the last point on the coast from which the Boston Stump would be visible, so there may perhaps be a link with St Botolph's cult there. At two outliers (Farnborough in Warwickshire and Frosterley in Durham) the dedication seems to have been taken from a neighbouring church or chapel.

St Aldhelm, bishop of Sherborne in 709, played a similar role in the cultural memory of the West. Although he lived long after the conversion, his rule over the diocese coincided with its expansion westwards into formerly British territory, so he was remembered as the first English bishop there. His well at Pucklechurch is associated with legends of the archaic type: St Aldhelm used its waters to cure the sick and thrust his staff into the ground where it turned into a mighty ash tree to shelter the congregation. Unfortunately the well is not recorded until 1712 and the tree even later. The cult may be an early one – Pucklechurch was another *villa regalis* – but its legend probably came from Bishopstrow in Somerset, where William of Malmesbury recorded stories of a sprouting staff in the 1120s. William had a particular respect for Aldhelm, the patron of his own monastery, and collected stories about him from Doulting, where the saint had died before being carried back and enshrined at

St Aldhelm's Well at Doulting. (From Fairbrother 1859 facing 131.)

Malmesbury. Nothing is said in William's account about a holy well, which suggests that the well of St Aldhelm at Doulting was created between his time and its first mention in the 1540s. It is the one example, outside legend, of a well at the place of a saint's death, matching with and motivated by the same concerns as the birthplace wells which we noted earlier.

There were stories of St Aldhelm at Malmesbury, too. In a dell down by the river, below the monastery, William was told how the saint 'got his rebellious body under control by immersing himself up to the shoulders in a spring which was near the monastery. Impervious to the winter's icy cold or the summer's mists arising from the marshes, he would pass the nights there uninterruptedly. Only when he had sung through and got to the end of the whole Psalter did he bring his labours to an end' (William 2002a: 243–4). His successor at Sherborne, Bishop Daniel, had another well nearby, used in the same way. It is curious to think of the erudite and accomplished Aldhelm spending his nights in such obsessive austerity, but he may have learnt to do so from Maeldubh, the Irish founder of Malmesbury. If he really did so, then this well would have been associated with his cult from the time of his death in 709, making it one of the earliest attested holy wells.

Certainly the practice of standing in cold water to pray is attested in the Irish tradition and appears in the lives of several Insular saints. Gildas, Illtud, Gwynllyw, Congar and Kentigern are all said to have spent their nights in this way; Bede describes the water vigils of Cuthbert and Dryhthelm, while St Chad's Well at Stowe was later pointed out as the spring where he subdued his rebellious body. In later times we find the hermits Wulfric and Godric deliberately digging pits so that they could immerse themselves for prayer; in Godric's case, the pit afterwards became his holy well. Like Cuthbert, Ethelfled of Romsey would slip out of bed so that she could practice this austerity unknown by others, a piece of spiritual modesty which left her open to charges of having taken a lover.[57]

As this might suggest, the lives of women saints were more circumscribed than those of their male counterparts. Unlike their fictional counterparts, they were not at much risk of being martyred and their exercise of power was circumscribed. Their rule was confined instead to their own religious houses. Thus the Life of St Enswith tells how prudent she was in providing a water supply to her monastery at Swetton from springs a mile away. These survived in tradition as her holy well and, to make the miracle greater, the water was said to run obediently uphill on its journey to the conduits – something it was apparently still doing in the later eighteenth century (*Nova Legenda Anglie* 1901: 1.298; Hasted 1778–99: 3.379). The Kentish royal nunnery of Lyminge produced two saints – Edburgh, whose well in the village is recorded in 1484, and Ethelburgh, who is commemorated in a well near the archbishop's palace at Ford. There seems to have been something of a vogue for holy wells in the precincts of bishops' palaces. The primates had one of St Blaise at their residence in Bromley, one of St Dunstan at Mayfield and another at Otford dedicated to, and possibly created by, Thomas Becket. There is a Ladywell near the precincts of Bewley Castle in Bolton, the residence of the bishops of Carlisle. In the southwest, there is a St Mary's Well in the grounds of the Bishop of Exeter at Chudleigh, and the Bishop of Bath and Wells had his own spring of St Andrew which watered the palace moat along with the city of Wells.

Another St Edburgh is venerated at Bicester. She was a daughter of Penda, part of the kinship of saints from the first Christian generations of his royal house whose memory reconciled the Mercians to their unequal partnership with Wessex in a united England. At Brill, the cult of St Werburgh – another of Penda's daughters – may have had some such motive, or it may reflect influence from her later shrine at Chester. There was a late Anglo-Saxon settlement at Bicester, focussed on the minster which contained St Edburgh's relics, although the cult also owes much to the monastery founded under her patronage in 1182.

Holy wells compensate for lost saints

The changing fortunes of geography left many saints from the seventh and eighth centuries in villages which had become obscure. New towns and cities, unknown in the age of conversion, grew in power and were hungry for sacred relics of their own; since the canon of indigenous saints was more or less fixed by 850, they could not call on new patrons, but had to obtain old ones from their unwilling neighbours. The classic account of *furtun sacrum* occurs at East Dereham, the resting-place of St Withburgh (OE Wihtburh). The resourceful abbot of Ely came to this village, a dependency of his abbey, and laid on a great feast for the inhabitants. While they were occupied, a party armed with saws and crowbars broke into the church, removed the relics of the saint from her shrine and conveyed them quickly down the Norfolk lanes to a waiting boat. By this time the furious inhabitants of Dereham were in pursuit but the abductors had made too much headway to be caught and St Withburgh was soon enshrined beside her sister St Audrey in Ely Cathedral.[58]

This explains the devotion paid to St Withburgh's Well in East Dereham churchyard. The spring is first recorded in about 1110, forty years after the theft; it rose, or was supposed to have risen, at the place where her body was exhumed from its first grave and translated to a shrine in the church. Now the body was gone and nothing was left but a well, so they culted that instead.[59] It was the only link with their patron that was left, for the cult of saints in England – like that in Wales, but unlike practice in the Continent – resisted the partition of bodies. The literature on resting-places takes it for granted that a saint will lie at one particular minster, not here and there in scattered reliquaries. Because sacred bodies were indivisible, other sites saw a virtual enshrinement of their saintly paraphernalia – staffs, books and bells – and the veneration of holy wells followed naturally from this. Trees and wells had the special attraction of belonging to a particular place and its community. They could not be appropriated or taken away by tidy-minded authorities and this was what made them appeal to people who wanted spiritual comfort in their own familiar setting.

Compensation wells of this kind are found wherever the relics of some saint had been translated to some larger and more important establishment.[60] There is a well at Ryhall, the original site from which St Tibba, another of these royal abbesses, was taken to Peterborough, and another at North Crawley, from which the obscure St Firmin was taken to Thorney. We have already met with St Edwold, who was translated from Stockwood to Cerne Abbas, and St Juthware from Halstock to Sherborne, with wells being pointed out in both cases to keep up their memory in the original village. Cuthbert's well at Farne acted as a compensation well after his relics had found their final home in Durham. The most famous example is St Winifred, whose relics were translated in 1138 to Shrewsbury. It is unlikely that the spring at Holywell would ever have achieved such celebrity if it had not been standing in for an absent saint.

Some of these cases involve the transport of relics to new foundations across the country, but other translations are on a very local scale. St Walstan was moved only a mile or so through the Norfolk countryside from Taverham to Bawburgh, assuming that his *Life* is based on details of an actual cult. St Chad moved to Lichfield from its suburb at Stowe, and St Sidwell to Exeter from its extramural suburb, still called St Sidwells after her. At Slepe in Huntingdonshire, the body of St Ive was discovered, and as soon as it became clear how important he was, taken off to Ramsey Abbey. But his well and reputation remained behind, of such importance that the original name of Slepe is now forgotten and the place is called St Ives (*Chronicon Abbatiae Rameseiensis* 1886: lxxi).

It is unusual for a saint's cult to give rise to a place-name; the English are quite different from the Welsh or Cornish in this. But the generic *stow*, with a general meaning 'place of assembly, special place' is found at Clent, formerly known as Kenelmstow, and at Stowe near Lichfield with its cult of St Chad. At Stow-on-the-Wold (*Edwardestowe* 1107) and Plemstall (*Plegmundestowe* 1291) the wells of local saints seem to have been reidentified with more famous figures of the same name

St Kenelm's church at Clent. (From Parkes 1797.)

from history. Padstow, which once had a well of St Petroc, acquired its name during the tenth-century English incursions into Cornwall, and at Morwenstow near the border St Morwenna's Well still survives. But names in -stow continued to be coined after the Anglo-Saxon period. The other Stowe in Gloucestershire, with its St Margaret's Well, must be post-Conquest, and so must the *stow* at Hallaton near St Morel's Well.[61]

The legendary cults of sacred kings

The relics of a saint were worth competing for. They held a secret power, especially when the saint had been a person of power in their life. The cult of saint-kings is one of the curiosities of early medieval piety. To be royal was to be the focus of an imaginative popular empathy which was not altogether separate from religious feeling. And this was much more the case when the royal person had suffered a brutal death. Almost any royal figure who was young, good-looking and cut off in their prime by an untimely death could count on the adulation of the crowd. Normally the Church put a stop to this sort of thing, but for a short period in the late eighth and early ninth centuries, the cults of martyred kings received official authority.[62] It was hoped that the internecine conflicts of rulers could be controlled, if not entirely suppressed, by dramatic honours paid to their victims.

47

Like other hagiographies, the stories of royal martyrdom follow a standard pattern. The prince is lured to some remote outpost, often a hunting lodge in the forest; the murder is carried out by a wicked servant of the ruler and strenuous attempts are then made to hide the bloody deed. But then miraculous signs proclaim the sanctity of the dead man – sometimes a light from heaven, but often the breaking out of a well.

The legend appears in its fullest version in the *Life* of St Kenelm (OE Cynehelm), in which it has been considerably worked up from the facts. The historical Kenelm, who died at the age of about 25, has been reinvented as a boy-saint and his innocent sweetness contrasts poignantly with the perfidy of his sister Quendred and her lover Ascapart. Young Kenelm is taken to the lonely Clent hills, where he plants the twig that will grow into a majestic ash tree, announces foreknowledge of his death and is finally beheaded and secretly buried. But through a series of marvellous incidents his fate becomes known and, when his body is exhumed, a well rises up in token of his sanctity (Love 1996: 50–89).

Miraculous episodes aside, it is hard to escape the conclusion that the historic Kenelm really was killed at Clent in the early ninth century and that the well, and probably the ash tree, were pointed out as tokens of his martyred state not long afterwards. What other reason did Clent have to lay claim to his cult? Its spring is another of those compensation wells that keep up a link with a saint whose relics lie elsewhere – not, in this case, because they had been moved from an old shrine to a new one, but because they were taken almost immediately to royal burial in the mausoleum of the Hwiccian and Mercian kings at Winchcombe.

Another attempt to forestall royal murders by venerating their previous victims seem to have been made in the case of Ethelbert. He was invited from his kingdom of East Anglia to become son-in-law to the great Offa in 794 and found himself butchered for his pains. Offa repentantly had him enshrined at Hereford Cathedral and St Ethelbert's Well, just to the east of the building on the site of an old cemetery, was already old in 1250 (Whitehead 1978). Another well in the nave of Marden church is supposed to have risen from the spot in which the body was first buried; but this story, despite its archaic look, is not recorded before 1804 (Duncumb 1804–1915: 2.137) and no mention of this miracle appears in the *Life* by Osbert of Clare, though this gives a wealth of topographical detail for Ethelbert's last journey.

In Kenelm's *Life* there is an episode which tells how the men of Gloucestershire, hotly pursued by their Worcestershire rivals, have almost reached their goal at Winchcombe when they collapse from weariness and thirst. As they lay the coffin down, a well miraculously rises to quench their parched throats and so they struggle on for the last mile. The conflict between two communities for the dead saint is paralleled by, and probably taken from, Sulpicius Severus's *Life of St Martin*, but it has been superimposed onto the familiar landmark of a well on the hill's edge just out of town. In the same way, St Alkmund's Well lies just outside Derby. The minster which enshrined the saint's relics lies outside the town walls on the ridgeway road leading to the north and the well is just off this road. The circumstances of St Alkmund's death – whether by murder or in battle – are uncertain, but die he did, in about 800 and he was culted at Derby in the days when it was called Northworthig, before the Vikings came. The reputation of the well may go back to that date, although as it is so near to the minster it may have been added to the story later; certainly it existed by the 1190s (*Cartulary of Darley* 1945: 173–5; Radford 1976: 55–8). At Tamworth there is a well of St Rufinus, but it is not clear how this links with the *Passio* of Sts. Wulfade and Rufinus, who are supposed to have been baptised by St Chad at his holy well in Stowe, and were venerated at the village of Stone in Staffordshire. Since the two convert princes were supposed to have been killed by their pagan father, the King of Mercia, it is possible that the murder was thought to have taken place at Tamworth and that the well is linked to the event. But this is speculation and the whole story seems to have been made up at a late date, sometime between the Conquest and the thirteenth century.[63]

Sacred kings in history

There is no doubt about the historicity of the last of these figures, St Edward King and Martyr. He was killed in 979 in the forest of Purbeck, at a lonely spot called Corfe and his body was then concealed. So far the story is a reprise of Kenelm's, although it is not clear if it was adapted to conform to a mythic archetype, or simply reflects the realities of assassination. The only places where an Anglo-Saxon king could be safely killed were obscure hunting lodges, where he would be away from his retinue and the news could be kept quiet long enough for the necessary political machinations to take place. St Edward is the only saint of the West Saxon house to be venerated after his death and his cult may have been promoted by Ælfhere, ealdorman of Mercia, who knew the legends which were familiar in his homeland. St Edward's Well is first recorded by Goscelin in the 1080s (Fell 1971: 8) and served as a local reminder of lost sanctity after the king's body was carried first to Wareham and then to Shaftesbury. Corfe was an obscure place – its castle was not built until after the Conquest – which meant that here, as at Clent, there would have been little motive to create a well here at any time after the initial period of the murder. The *Life* tells us that Edward's body was exhumed from a marshy place, the sort of place where water would begin to flow after a little digging.

Not all royal martyrdoms were the work of domestic intrigue. St Edmund was captured and killed by the heathen Danes in 869 and not long after was taken as the patron saint, first of his native East Anglia and then of England as a whole. Hunstanton, a *villa regalis* of the king, had a source of five or twelve springs celebrated under his name by the 1150s (Arnold 1890–6: 1.99–100). Hunstanton remained a centre of Edmund's cult in later years and the wells may have been added to its other holy places at any time after his death. There was another St Edmund's Well recorded at Finchingfield in about 1180.

The most disputed of these royal shrines is at Oswestry, where tradition located St Oswald's ash tree and well. The facts about St Oswald are well known from the pages of Bede – although even Bede seems to have had some reservations about him. An early programme for the *Ecclesiastical History* does not make any mention of the Northumbrian king who plays such a large part in the final version (Stancliffe & Cambridge 1995: 35, 112). Maserfelth, where Oswald died in battle in 642, seems to have been an obscure place; not only has its name not survived, but in his accounts of the miracles worked there, Bede relied on the report of ordinary people and not the clergy or aristocrats that he usually preferred as witnesses. Maserfelth appears to have been in Northumbrian territory, since Oswald would not have been remembered as a saint by his traditional enemies. Oswald was venerated at a second location, the place where his arm and head were exhibited after death. This was presumably near one of Penda's royal vills, from which the trophies were retrieved by Oswy in 643.[64]

Reginald of Durham in his *Life* of 1165 doubles up these two locations and identifies them both as Oswestry. He explains that after Oswald's right arm and head were cut off, a great bird like a raven flew away with the arm to its nest in a withered ash tree. The tree grew green again and when the arm dropped out from this tree, a clear unfailing spring broke out from the hard rock (Simeon 1882: 1.355–8). Oswestry does indeed mean 'Oswald's tree', but there was more than one Oswald in Anglo-Saxon England and there is no reason to think that this instance belongs to the saint of that name. Place-names in the form So-and-so's Tree are not uncommon and always refer to landownership (Gelling 1990–2006: 1.229–31).

It seems more likely that people in this part of Shropshire, long after the original giver of the name had been forgotten, wanted to link it with the growing cult of St Oswald, probably after his relics had been translated to Gloucester in 909.[65] The hero-king now shared in the general prestige of martyred royalty – something which would have troubled Bede, who wrote at a time when the distinction between men of prayer and men of war was much more clearcut. This veneration of martyred princes was typically Mercian; the wells of St Oswald at Astbury in Cheshire and Winwick in Lancashire are nearer to Mercia than to the Northumbrian heartland of the saint's cult. There was a minster at Winwick, but it was a late foundation, probably of the tenth century (Blair 2005: 342). St Oswald's Well at Elvet must postdate the arrival at nearby Durham in 995 of St Cuthbert's monks, who carried the king's head among their other relics.

A well at Lee St John is linked with the battle of Heavenfield fought by Oswald in 634; the site was remembered in processions and a church dedication from Bede's time onwards, but the well, venerated by 'the devotees of the Romish communion' in 1715, might be one of the sites created by Catholic piety after the original shrine became roofless (Hodgson 1916: 13). The Cumbrian and Yorkshire dedications at Burneside, Grasmere and Hotham are witness of a northern cult, though clearly devotion to Oswald in Cumbria cannot date from his own time, but from a later period when the region had become part of Northumbria. It is tempting to regard Kirkoswald, where the spring rises underneath the church, as part of the same pattern, but the well was not called St Oswald's until 1893 and in eighteenth-century sources it is anonymous. St Oswald's Well at Newton under Roseberry, in Cleveland, is a hagiologising form based on the name of the nearby hill. Roseberry Topping was *Ousebergh* in 1404; earlier forms do not sound so much like Oswald, so the dedication of the well and its adjoining chapel are unlikely to be earlier than the fifteenth century.

The saint-abbesses

Roseberry Topping was originally dedicated to Odin, although all memory of the Norse god had faded by the time his name was mistaken for that of the Christian saint. But, as this example shows, place-names associated with the early saints do not necessarily go back to the era in which they lived. The great patrons of monastic foundations had an afterlife which extended for many centuries. St Milburgh, abbess of Much Wenlock, died in 717 but continued as the undisputed mistress of lands in Shropshire until the Reformation. Wells dedicated to her are recorded at Much Wenlock in the thirteenth century and Brockton in 1573 but they could be reflecting contemporary piety and not going back to the Anglo-Saxon age.

The well at Stoke St Milborough is recorded in 1321 and appears later in a legend of the fleeing princess type, in which St Milburgh escapes from a lustful prince mounted on her white ass, which falls in exhaustion and creates a well. But this story is a exemplary warning not to confuse the archaic with the truly old, since it was created at some time in the nineteenth century by the conflation of two genuine medieval stories (Eyton 1854–60: 4.6; Brown 1990: 80–1, 86–7). Nevertheless there been early tales of this kind at Stoke, though without the well. Storytellers liked to use the *topos* of the beautiful, vulnerable virgin to add a little romance to the life of someone who in real life had been a successful and well-connected administrator, and the place-name itself suggests that the place had long been associated with her ownership or her cult. Other wells at places called *stoc* can be found at Hartland (St Nectan), Stockwood (St Edwold) and Halstock (St Juthware). The practice of naming settlements after saints was more Welsh than English and both *stoc* and *stow* show a westerly distribution.[66]

Medieval monks were men of their time. Like their secular contemporaries, they loved the idea of a graceful, high-born lady ruling over wide lands; figures such as St Milburgh are not far removed from the world of Eleanor of Aquitaine. Thus the author of the *Liber Eliensis* is half in love with his patron and inspirer, St Audrey (OE Æthelthryth, Lat Etheldreda). Like the lady of the troubadours, she is beloved but unattainable – largely, of course, because she had been dead for five hundred years. This raises the question of whether St Audrey's Well at Ely really went back to her own time, or had been created by later admirers. The well is certainly said to have sprung, like St Edward's or St Withburgh's, from the delved ground after the saint's body was translated to a new shrine in 679. Given the low-lying environment at Ely, this is not an implausible story. On the other hand, the region was exposed to the full shock of the Danish invasions and religious life of any kind, let alone the cult of the patron saint, was not restored until the 970s. The author of the *Liber Eliensis* seems surprisingly well informed about the circumstances of its creation - 'the monks made a pit like a cistern' – while an earlier source of the 1120s mentions the well, but not as a holy site (*Liber Eliensis* 2005: 63, 454). It may be significant that Ely had been taken over in 1070 as a centre of armed resistance for Hereward the Wake, a time when the island would have needed all the water supply it could get. The traditions of St Audrey's Well in the 1180s could be a retrospective consecration of a shaft well dug for more urgent reasons a hundred years earlier.[67]

St Hilda's Well at Hinderwell.
(From Atkinson 1874: 1.223.)

Another well of the saint, at the nearby farm of Barton, may reflect the abbey's ownership of the estate. There is also a St Audrey's Well at Grantchester, a village and ruined city which appears in Bede as the place where the abbess Sexburgh found a Roman stone coffin and took it for the enshrining of her sister and predecessor. This is not something that would have made much stir at the time, but in later years anyone reading their Bede would have associated St Audrey with Grantchester and it is this which accounts for the well.

The influence of Bede is shown most strongly at Whitby, the later name for *Streoneshalh* where the abbess Hilda established a minster in the 650s. Hilda is Bede's ideal type of the mother abbess, just as Oswald is his exemplar of the Christian king, and in neither case is it certain that their contemporaries would have given them the pre-eminence which they have gained through the pages of the *Ecclesiastical History*. In any case, the culture which she represented was annihilated by the Viking invasions. The conventual life did not return to Whitby until 1078, when three monks from Winchcombe and Evesham travelled north in a deliberate attempt to restore the lost glories of Northumbrian Christianity. With well-thumbed copies of Bede in hand, they were able to identify the almost-lost site of *Streoneshalh* and to found what would soon become one of the wealthiest Benedictine houses in Yorkshire.

There is strong evidence, then, for a late dedication of the three wells of St Hilda in the region – one recorded at Aislaby in about 1110, another at Guisborough in about 1150 and the third at Aldfield in the 1310s. The Aislaby well is on the boundaries of Whitby Liberty, as St Wilfrid's Well at North Stainley was in the liberty of Ripon, and both are likely to have been named by the landowners of the monastic estate which owed so much to the saint. The vernacular forms, *Hildekelde* at Guisborough and *Sayntehildekelde* at Aldfield, are compounded with *kelda* not *wella*, a use of language which (as we saw above) was limited to the period between 1050 to 1250 and found in the area stretching from York to Middlesbrough.

Also in Cleveland is the St Hilda's Well found in Hinderwell churchyard. The first reference comes from 1779, but the dedication must be earlier since there is clearly a connection with the settlement name. The older forms of this begin with Hilder-, but they start to be replaced by the modern version in the fifteenth century, so the association with St Hilda must go back before then.[68] But does Hilderwell mean 'St Hilda's well'? The Domesday form *Hildrewelle* cannot come from OE Hild; it could only derive from a putative ON variant of the name, in the genitive form *Hildar*. There is no evidence for this, nor is it likely that such a form would have been compounded with *wella* rather than *kelda*. On the whole, an origin in OE **hyldre*, 'elder tree', seems much more likely. The well would therefore be a hagiologising form, created after the revival of Hilda's cult in the North.

These dedications to St Hilda exemplify the piety of post-Conquest religious houses which rediscovered or invented the wells associated with St Frideswide at Binsey, St Edburgh at Bicester, St Audrey at Ely and St Oswald at Oswestry. A kind of vicarious cult for St Heiu, abbess of Hartlepool and Hilda's predecessor, may explain the name of St Ive's Well at Pontefract; it is not easy to see how the name could derive either from the Cornish St Ive, or the eponymous saint of the Huntingdonshire town.

The later English saints

It is clear that saints associated with the heroic age of the English church were being remembered in the dediation of wells at subsequent periods, up to and after the Conquest. There are also a significant number of sites associated with saints of a later date, from the tenth century onwards. St Edith of Wilton, who died in 984, had a well in 1409 somewhere near Wilton itself and another had been dedicated to her at Bristol by 1391. Her well and church at Stoke Edith are clearly a hagiologising form from the place-name, which in fact commemorates Edith the wife of Edward the Confessor. The cult and well of St Edith in Kemsing has been assigned to Edith of Wilton, on the understanding that she was born at this Kentish village, but there is no independent evidence for this and it may be that Edith of Kemsing was another saint of the same name.

At Plemstall, *Seint Pleymondes Well* (1302) was associated, at least in later tradition, with the Plegmund who became Archbishop of Canterbury in Alfred's reign and died in 914. He is supposed to have been elevated to the primacy from a secluded life as a hermit in this Cheshire hamlet. There is no independent evidence for this, which suggests that the dedication is a hagiologising form associating this place-name with the only famous Plegmund known to history.[69] Another Archbishop of Canterbury, St Alphege, gained a more secure position in cult after his martyrdom at the hands of the Danes in 1012. The dedication of his well at Charlcombe outside Bath is probably of the fifteenth century, if it is contemporary with the chapel nearby. A chantry of the saint, founded at Solihull in 1277, was associated with a spring known variously as St Alphege's Well or the *Holywalle*.

Foremost among these early archbishops is St Dunstan, who appears in Osbern's *Life* working a miracle at an unidentified thegn's estate, presumably somewhere near Canterbury. He has been invited to dedicate a church, the supply of water runs out and he makes a perennial spring flow from the rock (Stubbs 1874: 109). Osbern wrote a century after Dunstan's death in 988, so the reputation of the well must have grown up quite rapidly. It is the first story to link a miraculous well with a historical character and the first to link a well with a parish church rather than a regional minster. There are other wells of St Dunstan; the one at Mayfield Palace has an obvious link with him as archbishop, and that at Witham Friary must have something to do with Dunstan's cult at Glastonbury, but it is not see easy to see the connection at Tottenham, where his well is recorded in 1619.

The cult of St Dunstan was based on biography, but that of St Augustine of Canterbury was worked up long after the death of the historical character. In earlier years, the role of Augustine had deliberately downplayed in favour of his master Gregory, the prestigious saint of Rome. Not until the eleventh century did St Augustine's Abbey at Canterbury begin to promote the cult of their patron as Apostle of the English and, as part of their campaign, they commissioned Goscelin to write two *Lives*. The hagiographer had to stick to the record as it appeared in Bede, but he supplements the facts of Augustine's brief seven-year episcopate with some more marvellous tales of his travels through Britain and Ireland, including a visit to Cerne Abbas. Goscelin already knew Dorset, having worked for Hereman when he was bishop of Sherborne in the 1070s and he would have picked up the story then.

We are told that a priest attached to the minster at Cerne, bed-ridden with some infirmity, had a vision of St Augustine arrayed in his archbishop's robes. The priest was told to make for the saint's well and wash himself while repeating the fiftieth psalm – a more moderate version of the duty to recite a whole psalter while standing in a well, as the hermit saints had done. The priest follows instructions and is rescued from the jaws of death (Migne 1844–80: 150.760–1). Clearly this story must postdate the foundation of Cerne Abbey in 987. Goscelin reports the miracle after giving the usual story of the well's creation, telling how Augustine struck the earth with his staff while travelling through Dorset and so made water flow from dry ground. But it is tempting to invert the stories and to suppose that the cure happened first, at a time when the cult of St Augustine was being promoted after many years of neglect and that only when the spring had received its name was it fitted out with a chapel and a legend.

Another of Goscelin's *Lives* enables us to pinpoint the origin of a holy well with more precision. In 1002 a farm worker, ploughing a field near Slepe, uncovered a stone coffin. It is not described in any detail, but one suspects it was a Roman sarcophagus, like the one which was appropriated for the burial of St Audrey at Grantchester. The ploughman's discovery caused a stir, everyone wondering who the occupant of this tomb might be, until through means of a dreams the dead man identified himself as St Ive or Ivo.[70] How this Persian saint found himself in rural Huntingdonshire was never quite made clear, but his cult suggests the widening horizons of the late Anglo-Saxon world. The body was translated to Ramsey Abbey, but a spring had arisen at the place of his burial, another example of a grave-cut being enlarged until it struck water, as at Corfe, East Dereham and Ely.

After the Norman Conquest

The creation of wells continued after the Conquest. In 1200 abbot Eustace of Flai arrived in England on a preaching tour, with a more vigorous observance of the Sabbath as one of his main concerns. A detailed account of his message and the miracles which supported it, appears in the histories by Roger of Howden and Roger of Wendover; the texts are different, but they may both be drawing on a *libellus* or leaflet circulated by supporters of the mission. One gets the impression that it was regarded in the higher quarters of the church as a rather hot-gospelling affair, so the miracles were being quoted as proof of Eustace's divine authority. One of them happened at Withersdane: 'there was a spring there, which he blessed, and God gave such grace to its waters that the blind saw, the lame walked, the dumb spoke' (Hoveden 1868–71: 4.123). Another Kentish well was associated with the mission at Romney, where Eustace struck the ground and water flowed out. This was an old-fashioned miracle, but then he was putting over an old-fashioned message.

The spring at Withersdane was known to later tradition as St Eustace's, although the abbot was never officially given that honour. As the Middle Ages progressed, lines were drawn more sharply between the merely holy and the formally canonised. There were new saints, but they required the support of a monastic house before they could be credible. St Robert of Newminster, who died in 1159 and is apparently the patron of St Robert's Well at Levisham, had the backing of Newminster Abbey in Northumberland. Durham Priory acted as sponsor for the cult of St Godric of Finchale. The pit in which he had submerged himself as an austerity was resorted to for miracles and, though never acknowledged as a saint, he became the focus of a regional cult after his death in 1170.

To achieve immediate canonisation, a holy life was not enough. The potential saint should preferably have held high office in the church, gained the support by a powerful institution, become the subject of an unstoppable public enthusiasm and, ideally, have won the martyr's crown. All these factors came together in the person of Thomas Becket, who died in the same year as Godric. There was no delay over his canonisation – it was formally declared in 1173 – and he is the last of Insular saints to inspire devotion outside of a narrowly circumscribed homeland. When it comes to holy wells, Thomas is both a national and a regional saint. The dedications in Kent are tributes to his memory, or to the benefits which it brought in the form of pilgrim traffic. Those further afield are simply honouring him as one saint among many in the calendar of the church.

It was the need of pilgrims which led to the creation of St Thomas's Well at Canterbury. In the immediate wake of his death, there was an insatiable appetite for anything which had contacted the martyr's saving blood and the monks of Christ Church took to distributing water which was tinged, in increasingly homoeopathic proportions, with this relic. By the early fourteenth century a well in the precincts was said to have received the blood-stained dust on the day of the martyrdom and this became a sacred site in its own right.[71] Other wells in the south-east owed their dedications to some connection with the saint. St Thomas's Well at Otford first appears in the 1440s, apparently as a quite neutral description for a spring which

St Thomas's Well at Northampton as engraved in the 1830s. (From Thompson 1913–14b: facing 196.)

supplied water to the palace that Becket had once owned. By 1570, however, he was said to have created it himself in the usual miraculous way, striking the ground with his staff.

St Thomas's Well at Oxted is on the Pilgrims' Way. This is not as conclusive as it seems; the Way is a series of old tracks at some remove from the London-Canterbury road and any pilgrims who drank from the well must have been hopelessly lost. Two other wells, at Cobham and Bapchild, are just off the highway to Canterbury, where the pilgrim parties really did travel. But this simply reflects the facts of Kentish geography. The old villages all lie on the fertile coastal strip, through which the road makes its way. It suggests that the wells are older than their first appearances (eighteenth and nineteenth century) but not that they formed part of a sacred route of St Thomas.[72]

The only well to take its dedication from the known life of St Thomas, apart from the Kentish sites at Canterbury and Otford, is that at Northampton. During an earlier dispute with the king, Becket had fled secretly from the town, although unfortunately for the legend he seems to have done so from the opposite side to that on which the well stands. The connection may account, however, for the well and its associated chapel, which have borne his name since the thirteenth century. The other early record for a St Thomas's Well comes from Morpeth, where it already existed in 1239. That at Limbery, close to a chapel of the saint, is supposed to have featured in a medieval charter. At Great Ness in Shropshire and Great Malvern the wells are recorded in the early seventeenth century, but otherwise they all appear in more recent sources. There are eighteenth-century records for Box, where the church changed its dedication to St Thomas Becket at some time after 1373; Stamford, associated with another church; and Windleshaw, where a chantry chapel of St Thomas was founded in the fifteenth century. Later references are found at Plympton (another dedication shared with a church) and at Clifford, Danbury and Winton. All of these sites seem to be dedicated to St Thomas Becket, not St Thomas the Apostle, although identification is not always clear. It is curious that in three instances a well of St Thomas appears as one of a pair; it is to be found twinned with St Helen's at Great Asby, with Lady Well at Parracombe and with St Anne's at

Repton. These sites appear to have been created long after the martyrdom, when St Thomas was one among the established canon of saints.[73]

His was the last unquestioned popular canonisation. The handful of thirteenth-century canonisations were mostly of saint-bishops, the church bureaucracy being more inclined to see merit in men of their own kind. St Richard of Chichester, with his birthplace well at Droitwich, was canonised in 1262 and St Edmund Rich in 1245. Even so, St Edmund's Well at Oxford was regarded with disfavour by the Bishop of Lincoln when people began gathering there and reporting miracles in 1290. Any cult which took place outside the orderly walls of a church, even in a clerical city like Oxford – even in honour of a duly authenticated saint, was regarded with suspicion.

The conflict between rival world-views could hardly have been clearer than at the well of Simon de Montfort at Evesham. Miraculously created (or at any rate excavated with a horse's shoulder-bone) in 1274, this well was the scene of prayers and miracles for ten years until the royal ban of Edward I brought an end to its cult. The invocation of the dead earl was political as much as religious, since it implied that he had died fighting for justice and the right. Though steps were taken to prevent veneration of his body, it was impossible to prevent visits to the spring.[74]

As the Middle Ages wore on, the barriers to achieving sainthood grew higher and higher. Sir John Schorne, rector of North Marston, who died *circa* 1314, did not qualify; nor did Master Philip Ingberd, the rector of Keyingham, who died in 1325. There was nothing but a local reputation for Catherine Audley, who seems to have lived a hermit life in Herefordshire in the early fifteenth century. Yet these three quasi-saints all have their wells in the traditional style (Webb 2000: 153). It is noticeable that the later saints, canonised or not, conform to types which were established a thousand years earlier. We have the same clerical father-figures and hermits as before; in the cult of Simon de Montfort there is even the same predilection for venerating a ruler who had died by violence in a good cause. The corpus of medieval wells ends with St John's Well at Lutterworth. This took its name – or, if it had originally belonged to the hospital of St John the Baptist, changed its tradition – to commemorate John Wycliffe, for many years rector of the village, who was buried here until his body was exhumed and burnt for heresy. It is ironic that the opponent of pilgrimage and forerunner of the Reformation should have had received the honour, like so many of his predecessors, of giving name to a holy well.

How old are saints' wells?

It is a long way from Cuthbert to Wycliffe and this mass of hagiographical detail should not be allowed to obscure the starting point of our inquiry. When were holy wells consecrated and why? In the case of the Insular saints, taking both local and regional cults together, there are some 180 wells dedicated in their honour: and, following the arguments given above, 35 wells, or a fifth of the total, can be dated to within a century or two. That is still a very vague chronology. One would like more detail of the kind available at Slepe/ St Ives, with its well springing from the grave-pit of the mysterious coffin in 1002, or Evesham, where we know that Peter de

Saltmarsh created Earl Simon's well in the course of a heated political argument in 1274. But vague as it is, the historical evidence for the origin of saints' wells is better than anything previously assembled. What does it tell us?

The earliest known holy well remains that of St Cuthbert on Farne, which was dug in about 680 and was being venerated in the saint's memory by 705 at least. There is a strong likelihood that St Aldhelm's Well at Malmesbury was also culted from the time of the saint's death, since it is associated with a form of penance which he is likely to have practiced, but which does not form part of his popular image in later years. St Chad's Well at Stowe near Lichfield also has the look of an early site; the hermitage at Stowe would have existed in his time as a retreat from the cathedral. It is notable that these three early wells have no wonders or miracles attached with them: they were remembered for what they were, springs of water supplying the needs of holy men. This is the same origin as suggested above for the Holywells, except that these sites, being associated with the great saints of the church, acquired their names. Saints associated with holy wells are often said to have been hermits. In the case of Godric and Robert of Knaresborough this is true enough, but as the *Lives* of Benignus, Bertram, Edwold, Gildas, Nectan and Plegmund are all more or less fictional, their status as hermits must reflect popular expectations of sainthood.

In the ninth century we have two wells associated with royal martyrdom. St Kenelm's at Clent would have acquired its reputation not long after the death of this minor prince, otherwise its site would have been forgotten, while St Alkmund's at Derby surely goes back before the Danish occupation of the town. St Edmund's Well at Hunstanton looks as if it reflected actual knowledge of the king's residence at that place. In the tenth century we have two compensation wells – St Edward's at Corfe, which was created almost in imitation of Kenelm's following the king's death in 979, and St Withburgh's at East Dereham, likely to have been created or at least to have come to prominence after the theft of her relics in 974. The cult of St Juthware at Halstock is likely to have begun at this time; when Halstock first appears, as as a 'little minster' in a charter of 840, it is said to be dedicated to St Michael. The cult of St Juthware must therefore have grown up at some time after that date and before the time of Bishop Ælfwold (1042–58) when her relics were translated to Sherborne. The well of St Oswald at Oswestry reflects a tenth-century regional interest after his enshrinement at Gloucester and similarly provides a secondary relic for a saint whose body lay elsewhere. The well of St David at Dewsall is likely to belong to the eleventh-century, when his cult was being spread throughout Wales as an expression of national identity; before then, the founding father of St David's would have had no appeal to people in distant Herefordshire.

The great houses of the Benedictine Reform – Canterbury, Peterborough, Ely, Ramsey, Winchcombe, Malmesbury, Cerne and Sherborne – all either had holy wells, or held the relics of saints such as Dunstan, Tibba, Withburgh, Ive, Juthware or Edwold who were commemorated by holy wells elsewhere. These were the centres which, having revived the monastic life and its cults in the tenth century, were able to weather the storm of the Conquest and then to commission *Lives* which gave a permanent form to the fleeting traditions of the countryside. The saints themselves may have lived earlier on; Sidwell could well date back before the eighth century and others seem to have been the founding fathers or mothers of religious communities in the early years of English Christianity. But their memory, including the wells which fixed that memory in the landscape, would not have existed without the support of religious houses. At first these were the small minsters and later the reformed Benedictine houses which had appropriated their traditions 'The tenth-century reformers drew on this latent pool of sanctity for their own ideological aims, asserting the moral authority of their reforming programme with the church of Cuthbert and Bede' (Cubitt 2002: 450). At Lastingham, Ely, Grantchester, Oswestry, Harpham and the region around Whitby we have wells which are likely to have been identified through an enthusiastic study of Bede and not from local tradition, though this was a practice which continued long after the tenth century.

The tenth-century monastic reformers were certainly interested in holy wells. Ednoth, the first abbot of Ramsey, built a church at Slepe soon after St Ive's Well began to flow from the place of his exhumation, so that 'his tomb, the source of so many virtues, lay partly inside the wall and partly outside. This meant that whenever people came, whether the church doors were open or closed, they would never be cut off from the stream of grace' (Migne 1844–80: 155 col 89). The only other church to be extended over a holy well in this way was Clent and this was the work of Winchcombe Abbey, who were promoting the cult of Kenelm there. Now Winchcombe was a daughter house of Ramsey, re-established in 993 after an earlier suppression and it may not be coincidence that the same architectural arrangement was sponsored by two houses linked to each other.[75] Moreover, the cult of St Edward had become prominent at Ramsey soon after his death in 979, giving Winchcombe a template on which to base their affecting story of Kenelm the boy-martyr; indeed, stories about Kenelm may have been a way of expressing views about the death of kings which would have been tactless if expressed more directly when Æthelred, who was the beneficiary at least of his half-brother's murder, still sat on the throne. Corfe Castle, like Clent, had a church dedicated to its royal saint close by its holy well and Edward had received his second elevation in 1001, the year before the invention and elevation of the previously unknown well-saint Ive at Slepe (Thacker 1996: 252–3, 260, 263). The three cults certainly seem to be intertwined.

For good measure, one could add that Ramsey was active in promoting the cult of St Edmund, which would have included veneration of his well at Hunstanton; that it was among the first abbeys to promote the cult of St Augustine outside of Canterbury, not long before the presumed dedication of his well at Cerne; and that Evesham, where a holy well of St Egwin is later recorded, was a dependency of Worcester in the late tenth century, when Worcester had close links with Ramsey.

Then at some time in the early years of Cerne Abbey, a monk was cured by immersion in St Augustine's well following a vision of the saint. The cult of St Augustine was spreading in the tenth century.[76] The miracle is linked with some unlikely episodes that tell how the saint journeyed through north Dorset and created the well in the usual way with his staff. Though the anonymous monk evidently had a lively sense of the saint's spiritual care, his well would have lacked any validity in others' eyes unless it could be linked with the life of the historical Augustine during life. So the saint's biography was improved to make this sound more plausible.

The convention that a holy well must be linked with the actual presence of a saint, or of his relics after death, was slow to lose its grip. Thus the well at St Ives was validated, not just by a dream of the saint, but by the presence of his relics there. That of St Audrey was associated in retrospect with the saint's exhumation, although the tradition appears to have been created in the later eleventh century. It was the Norman Conquest which broke the convention that saints must be physically linked with their wells. The two wells of St Hilda which were created in the late eleventh or early twelfth century at Aislaby and Guisborough are a kind of retrospective homage to the saint.

A number of twelfth-century wells seem to be linked to religious houses. The presence of a hermitage gave rise to St Godric's at Finchale in the 1170s, as well as St Margaret's at Binsey in the 1120s, which although an early dedication to a foreign saint is also associated with St Frideswide. The monastic dedications to St Cuthbert at Wetheral and St Petroc at Tor are purely regional cults, with no implication that the saints in question ever came near these places. The cult of St Thomas at the end of the century gave rise to three wells – one at the site of the martyrdom in Canterbury, one with a loose historical connection at Northampton and one with a purely arbitrary dedication at Morpeth.

Two wells in Kent (Withersdane and Romney) were created by Eustace of Flai in his preaching tour of 1200. Later in the thirteenth century, we have the servant-saint cult of Walstan, with his three wells around Bawburgh, as well as that of St Cynburgh of Gloucester. There are also wells associated with the contested cults of Robert at Knaresborough, Edmund Rich at Oxford and Simon de Montfort at Evesham.

The cults of John Schorne and Philip Ingberd seem to have been established soon after their deaths in the fourteenth century and at the end of the Middle Ages comes a cluster of cults which seem to have been created by reinterpretation of earlier material. St Oswald's at Newton under Roseberry and St Hilda's at Hinderwell seem to owe their dedications to reinterpreted place-names, as does St Plegmund's at Plemstall and St Edmund's at Maugersbury; St Aldhelm's at Doulting and St John of Beverley's at Harpham are based on additional material added to the original biographies of those saints. The wells of Catherine Audley at Leigh and John Wycliffe at Lutterworth were unofficial tributes to the perceived holiness of these figures towards the end of the medieval period.

Wells were often culted in opposition to the authorities, but they were not the refuge of the ignorant or naïve. The people who venerated Simon de Montfort's memory were those who had discussed and supported him in life; belief in his miracles implies a prior belief in his political programme. This was clearly more widespread in society than one might have thought, since the waters of his well are known to have cured clergy, peasants, landowners and a citizen of London, not to mention the Countess of Gloucester's palfrey. Though we can characterise holy wells as part of popular religion, this simply means as the stories about them and the spread of their reputation relied on oral transmission rather than the written word, not that they were confined to the common people. The oral world was much larger and more consequential in the Middle Ages than it is today.

The traditions which venerated wells of indigenous saints seem to have begun with a few examples in the eighth century, just after the conversion of England was complete, and then show a gradual increase in dedications up until the twelfth, after which there is a decline, except for some antiquarian inventions later on. If this is so, then it seems that the dedication of local saints' wells became popular at least a century, and probably two, after the tradition of Holywells had begun. The absence of saints' wells from Old English charter boundaries and settlement names is striking. It is true that they might not be immediately recognisable for what they were, since the title 'saint' is not used in names before the Conquest. And in fact several early references to named wells have been claimed as dedications, among them *Eadburgewelle* in the 790s at Canterbury, *Cynburge wellan* in 926 at Chalgrave, *Ceollan wylle* in 952 at Barkham, *Eanswype wyllas* in 931 at Cold Ashton, *Chaddeswell* in 1201 at Prestbury and *Sidefollewelle* in the 1380s at an unknown site in Wiltshire. But there is no evidence that Sts. Edburgh, Cynburgh, Ceolla, Enswith, Chad or Sidwell ever had any cult at these places. As we have seen that the holy wells of the Anglo-Saxon saints were only found at places associated with their lives or relics, this must disqualify these place-names as evidence.

The wells of foreign saints

In the days when Christianity was first promulgated among the East Saxons, a fisher was at his trade on the banks of the Thames when he was called across to serve as ferryman. The passenger, as the fisher soon discovered, was his fellow-tradesman St Peter, who had come to consecrate the new abbey of Westminster, pre-empting the ceremony which was to have been performed the next day by Bishop Mellitus. As the saint stepped from the ferry, he thrust his staff into the ground first at one place and then at another, creating two springs, which 'continued to flow for many years, until at last they were washed away by the river' (Flete 1909: 41). Thus Sulcard of Westminster in about 1080; and although we may have doubts about the historicity of the original story, it does show that wells associated with St Peter existed as early as the eleventh century. But the creators of the legend, like those who wrote of St Augustine at Cerne, were clearly ill at ease with the arbitrary dedication of wells to saints. A well, to their way of thinking, was a living proof that the saint had actually been at the place where it flowed; and since this was clearly not the case with St Peter, he had to be brought to the site in a vision.

By the early twelfth century, this convention had broken down and we have the beginnings of a third phase of well tradition, supplementing the existing cults of Holywells and local saints. There are about 220 wells in England dedicated to continental or Biblical saints (excluding the Virgin Mary, to whom we shall return later). The first one known is that of St Helen at Farnhill, recorded in about 1140. The twelfth and thirteenth centuries yield a dozen more instances – St Andrew at Sawley in about 1147, St Clement at Westminster in 1174, St Helen at Derby in about 1190, St Lambert at Burneston and the Holy Trinity at Millom in about 1200. Then come four more dedications to St Helen – at Gosforth in the 1220s, at Botcherby in the 1230s, at Pudsey in 1260 and at Adel some time in the thirteenth century. A well of St Andrew is recorded at Sturton in the thirteenth century, one of St Lawrence at Nantwich later in the century and another of the same saint at Norwich in 1297.

Since St Augustine's days, churches had been dedicated to the saints of the universal church; in the early years of the conversion, of course, there was no-one else to dedicate them to. But even when the canon of English saints began to increase, it was still rare for churches to be dedicated in their honour. The cult of their relics, including secondary ones like wells, represented a separate religious tradition. By the 1140s, however, the two traditions seem to have merged and from then onwards the saints named in wells were chosen from the same stock as the patrons of churches, chapels and other institutions. There are about 40 dedications for wells, if we include the Holy Trinity, Holy Sepulchre and All Saints in the list; but the popularity of these figures varies greatly.

Saints ranked by popularity

St Helen leads the list with 50 wells. Farnhill, Derby, Gosforth, Botcherby, Pudsey and Adel we have already seen. Other wells are recorded at Cossall (1301), Gateshead (1324), Colchester (1330) Durham (1418), Newcastle-under-Lyme (1498), Farnley (1532), Dalton-in-Furness (1537), Athersley (1591), Newcastle (1593) and Almondbury (sixteenth century). Later references are found at Barmby-on-the-Marsh, Barnburgh, Bleasdale Moors, Brigg, Brindle, Burnsall, Burton-in-Kendal, Church Broughton, Eshton, Great Asby, Great Oxenden, Hartlepool, Honley, Hooton, Kirkby Overblow, Leighton Bromswold, Little Ribston, Littlethorpe, Liverpool, Louth, Lundy, Newbiggin-on-Lune, Newtown in Northumberland, Norham, North Cave, North Stainley, Old Micklefield, Reighton, Rushton Spencer, Santon Downham, Sefton, South Cave, Tarleton and Thorp Arch.

St John the Baptist has 23 wells, though only one is medieval – at Wembdon, where the cult seems to have originated with mass popular gatherings in 1464. The later references are found at Bisley, Boughton, Coley Hall, Dronfield, Evershot, Halifax, Hatherleigh, High Wycombe, Lundy, Lutterworth (unless this is John Wycliffe), Moxby, Newton Longville, Northallerton, Northampton, Ribchester, Shenstone, Skelsmergh Hall, Stanford on Teme, Stockton-on-Tees, Syston, Welham and Wem. About half of these specify that the well is dedicated to John the Baptist; the others are just to 'St John', but the Baptist rather than the Evangelist seems to be meant in all cases.[77]

St Thomas Becket, already considered above under the English saints, is next in popularity, with 19 wells (excluding the centre of his cult at Canterbury itself). The medieval ones are at Northampton (thirteenth century), Morpeth (1239), Otford (1440s) and Limbery. Later references are found at Bapchild, Box, Clifford, Cobham, Danbury, Great Asby, Great Malvern, Great Ness, Oxted, Parracombe, Plympton, Repton, Stamford, Windleshaw and Winton.

St Anne has 16 wells. The medieval ones are at Buxton (1530s), Nottingham (1557) and Rotherham (sixteenth century). Later references are found at Aconbury, Beaumont, Castle Howard, Caversham, Church Langton, Fersfield, Leadenham, Locko House, Penwortham, Rainhill, Repton, Siston and Welton.

St Peter has 15 wells, beginning as we have seen with Westminster, although that is unexpectedly the only medieval example. The later references are at Barmby-on-the-Marsh, Canterbury, Coggeshall, Coleshill, Derby, Holsworthy, Leeds, Peterchurch, Stamford, West Mersea, Whitney, Windsor, Worfield and York.

St Andrew has 13 wells. The medieval ones were at Sawley (1147), Sturton (thirteenth century) and Wells (fourteenth century). The later references are at Alnham, Ansford, Bradfield, Bradpole, Kirkandrews-upon-Eden, Lyme Regis, Moretonhampstead, Ovington, Plymouth and Stogursey.

There are no medieval records for wells of St Catherine at all, making her the only major saint for whom there is no early evidence. There are 12 later references, at

Barton-upon-Humber, Beetham, Boot, Coventry, Eckington, Exeter, Lea Town, Loversall, Stretton Grandison (unless this is Catherine Audley), Westhorpe, Winchelsea and Yealand Conyers.

St Margaret has 9 wells. The medieval ones were at Broomfield in Kent (1507) and Binsey (1519, although it already appears anonymously in the *Life* of Frideswide). Later references appear at Ashington, Burnsall, Hasbury, Leegomery, Stowe in Gloucestershire, Urishay and Wereham.

St Mary Magdalen has 8 wells. The medieval ones were at Bamburgh (1393), Coleham (1571) and Selby (1573). Later references appear at Goudhurst, Lathom, Newcastle, Spaunton Bank and Syresham.

St Cuthbert, already considered above under the English saints, is next in popularity, with 8 wells (excluding the original focus of his cult at Farne). The medieval ones are at Bellingham (1160s) and Wetheral (1200s). Later references are found at Edenhall, Offerton, Tweedmouth, Doveridge, Donnington and Scorton

St Michael has 7 wells. There is one early example at Minehead (1582), with another at Great Crosby (early sixteenth century), although this seems almost certain to be a hagiologising dedication of an original *micel wella*, 'powerful well'. Later references are found at Addingham, Beetham, Horwood, Olveston and Well in the North Riding.

There are 7 wells dedicated to the Holy Trinity. Two of these are medieval – at Millom (1200s) and Lincoln (1318) – and later references are found at Abbotsham, Bagendon, Clifton, Gloucester and Weare Gifford. Veneration of the Trinity was not authorised until 1162 so the dedications must all be later than this.

St George has 6 wells. There is one medieval record at Wilton in Somerset (1425) and later references are found at Cullompton, Hethe, Holsworthy, Kirkwhelpington and Stamford.

St Oswald, already considered above under the English saints, is next in popularity, with 6 wells (excluding the earlier focus of his cult at Lee St John and the later ones

St Chad's Well at Kings Cross as drawn in about 1830. (From Foord 1910: 74.)

at Elvet and Oswestry). There is one medieval instance at Astbury (1300). Later references are found at Burneside, Grasmere, Hotham, Newton under Roseberry and Winwick.

St Chad has 5 wells, excluding the original focus of his cult at Stowe near Lichfield and the later promotion of it at Lastingham, as discussed among the English saints. The medieval ones are at Abbots Bromley (about 1300) and Wilne. Later references are found at Chadkirk, Chadshunt and St Pancras in London. However, Chadshunt owes its dedication to a hagiologising interpretation of the village name, which is really 'the spring of a man called Cædel'. This is a layman's name not related to the saint's name Ceadda and the two would not have been confused until the fifteenth century.[78]

St Leonard has 5 wells. The medieval ones were at Dunster (1377) and Sheepstor (1570), while later references are found at Belthorpe, Rowney Priory and Winchelsea.

There are 5 wells dedicated to All Saints. Three of these are medieval – at Norwich (1377), Colchester (1387) and Wareham (1545) – and later references are found at Colne and Stamford.

St Patrick, as we have seen, has 5 wells in the north-west; these are Bampton, Bromborough Bridge, Lancaster, Patterdale and Slyne, none of them medieval, although Lancaster may be associated with a fifteenth-century chapel in the parish church.

There are 5 wells dedicated to St Bride. The first reference is at Fawsley (1330), while St Bride's Well in the City of London appears in 1487, when it had given name to an inn of the Bishop of St David's. The Fawsley spring is called *Seyntebridewell*, but the London one simply *Brydewell* and the absence of 'saint' is unusual in a fifteenth-century form. It seems to take its name from a well which remained when all the rest of the royal palace of St Bride was swept away. This palace in turn took its name from the church, which is an unexpected outlier of the Irish cult of St Bride, possibly due to Danish influence. Three later sites are recorded, at Pucklechurch, St Briavels and Ripon. That at Pucklechurch seems to derive from the common spring-name Bridewell and it is possible that the other two have the same origin.[79]

There are 4 wells dedicated to St Agnes, all of them reported in the nineteenth century – Cothelstone, Egham, Tedstone Delamere and Whitestaunton. St Agnes is extremely rare as a medieval dedication, but she appealed to Victorian sensibilities and it seems more likely that these wells were given their name in the modern period. Those at Egham and Cothelstone were near large houses; the Tedston well was improved by a cross and wall, probably put up by a mid-Victorian vicar and that at Whitestaunton is recorded on the authority of Charles Elton, who subsequently rebuilt a Roman shrine nearby and seems to have been of a Romantic frame of mind.

St Botolph, another of the indigenous saints, also has 4: two medieval – at Weybourne (thirteenth century) and Hadstock (1587) – and two later references at Farnborough and Frosterley.

St Hilda has 4 wells, with medieval evidence for Aislaby (1110s), Guisborough (1150s) and Aldfield (1310s) and a presumed fifteenth-century origin for the one at Hinderwell. Her cult is strongly regional, although the actual shrine of Hilda at Whitby, like that of Botolph at Bury St Edmunds, is not not marked by a well.

Dunstan also has 3, at Mayfield, Tottenham and Witham Friary, in addition to the unknown site in Kent which had an actual historical connection with him. Mungo, another of the regional saints, has 3 wells at Brompton, Caldbeck and Copgrove. The other saints with 3 wells each are Anthony, Clement, James, Lawrence and Nicholas. Wells of St Anthony appear at Northowram (1535), Crookes and East Dean; those of St Clement at Westminster (1174), Marfield and Stamford; those of St James – no doubt the Great – at Berkhamsted (1400), Hedgeley Moor and Midhopestones; those of St Lawrence at Norwich (1297), Nantwich (late thirteenth century) and Great Harwood; and those of St Nicholas at Strood (1444), Totnes (1475) and somewhere in Cambridgeshire (1429).

The saints with 2 wells each are St Faith at Hexton and Leven; St German at Faulkbourne (1587) and Rousham; St Giles at Chester (1574) and Knowle St Giles;; St Loy at Tottenham and Weedon Lois; St Martin at Winchester (1564) and Ewyas Harold; St Pancras at Marshfield and Scampton; St Stephen at Belford and Banbury; and St Sunday (i.e. St Dominic) at Newcastle-under-Lyme and Willenhall. There are also two wells dedicated to the Holy Sepulchre, one at Leicester (1458) and one at Sudbury.

Finally come those saints who were honoured with a single well. These are St Augustine of Hippo at Leicester; St Blaise at Bromley; St Clare at Philham; SS Cosmas and Damian at Stretford Court; St Dennis at Naseby; St Erasmus at Ingestre; St Julian (probably the bishop of Le Mans, rather than the mythical Hospitaller) at Wellow; St Juliana at Ludlow; St Lambert at Burneston; St Maurice at Ellingham; St Morel, apparently Maurilius the bishop of Angers, at Hallaton; St Owen, apparently Ouen the bishop of Rouen, at Much Wenlock; St Simon at Coverham; and St Vincent, presumably of Saragossa, at Clifton. St Vincent's well is recorded in 1587 and St Lambert's in about 1200, but otherwise all references are of the seventeenth century or later, though the account of St Faith's Well at Hexton appears to be a genuine description of pre-Reformation practices there.

The growth of saints' cults

We have already suspected from the sequence of dates that dedications to foreign saints began in the early twelfth century and comparison with the series of saints listed above tends to bear this out. The dedications to St Nicholas would postdate the arrival of his relics at Barri in 1087, those to the Holy Sepulchre are likely to follow the First Crusade in 1095, and those to Holy Trinity must have been made after 1162. St Magnus died in 1116, while St Thomas was canonised in 1173, St Dominic in 1234 and St Clare in 1255.

There is very little in the dedications that would reflect cults earlier than these. Only the two wells of St Pancras are unusual, since his cult is typically early. At Scampton there was a chapel of the saint, dating to the twelfth century; that at Marshfield is also named after a building, either the church of a very small parish or another chapel. It seems likely that these were twelfth-century chapels on previously unoccupied land, perhaps dedicated in memory of a pilgrimage to Rome. The well at Scampton is on the edge of a Roman villa, which might have been recognised as such in the antiquarian climate of the time. St Michael is generally taken to be an early dedication, with a focus in the west of Britain, but his wells received their dedications much more recently. One appears to be a sixteenth-century hagiologising dedication, while St Michael's Well at Arthuret seems to have been both built and dedicated when the church was built in 1609.

In fact, if we review the major dedications (5 wells or more), we can make a tentative distinction between the high and late medieval cults by singling out those saints who do not have any wells recorded before the fifteenth century. Michael is among their number; so are Anne, Catherine, George and Margaret. These are all characteristically late cults. None of the five indigenous saints appear in this category and, as one would expect their cults to be early, this gives a certain confidence in the method. On the other hand, John the Baptist is also a latecomer among the recorded dedications and so is St Peter (if we discount the atypical miracle story from Westminster). It seems that there were factors which held up the extension of their long-established cults to holy wells until the fifteenth century or thereabouts.

James Rattue, in his pioneering work, was the first to draw attention to the disparity between the dedications of holy wells and churches.[80] The top ten dedications for wells (excluding the Virgin Mary, as before) are Helen, John the Baptist, Thomas Becket, Anne, Peter, Catherine, Andrew, Margaret, Mary Magdalen and Cuthbert. The corresponding series for churches is All Saints, Peter, Michael, Andrew, John the Baptist, James the Greater, Nicholas, Peter & Paul, Lawrence and Holy Trinity. Seven out of the ten most favoured patrons for wells do not appear in the preferred list for churches; and significantly three of these – Anne, Catherine and Margaret – belong, as we have seen, to the later years of the Middle Ages.

The origin of parish churches is a controversial topic, but most of them seem to have come into being in the tenth and eleventh centuries. The list of favoured church dedications therefore reflects the saints who were most venerated in that period. By the late Middle Ages, patterns of cult had changed, with new saints rising in popularity and the old ones declining. The wells of continental and Biblical saints were dedicated long after churches had received their names and that is why they have a different list of patrons. If we were to take a list of typical late medieval dedications – of lights, altars, chantries – it would be much closer in its choice of saints to the priorities found at holy wells.

Where are the saints' wells found?

The wells dedicated to saints seem, by and large, to be later than the Holywells. But do they simply continue that tradition under a new name, or are they a genuinely new idea of what a holy well should be? Of course there is an overlap and some saints' wells can be found in the idyllic settings typical of the rustic Holywells. At Ashington, St Margaret's Well was 'a sacred fountain… pleasant and soft to the taste… the north side faced with stone, natural, and semicircular, covered with moss, and a thin crust of earth, in which the primrose and meadowsweet have taken root, emitting their pleasant odours round it in their season of flowering' (Wallis 1769: 2.338). But individual examples do not have the weight of statistics and the statistics tell a different picture.

If we look at the location of saints' wells and wells of the Virgin, applying the same threefold analysis used on page 25 for Holywells, the results are shown below.

This is quite different from the earlier tradition, which showed a preference for sites on the outskirts of settlement, with a substantial number of isolated wells and fewer in central locations. The saints' wells are quite the reverse of this, with a strong

Comparison of locations of saints wells and wells of the Virgin with Holywells		
	Saints' wells and wells of the Virgin	*Holywells*
location	**percent**	**percent**
Isolated	28	32
Outskirts	31	48
Central	46	20

preference for sites in villages and towns. Only 4 Holywells (Halifax, Sherborne, Shoreditch and Wolverhampton) are found in towns, as against over 50 wells of saints and the Virgin. This is what you would expect if saints' wells were a later development.

The saints' wells of the twelfth century onwards also differ from their predecessors in the kind of waters which were consecrated. When a well is said to be particularly powerful – St Helen's Well at Rushton Spencer 'supplied an overshot Mill not far distant', as did another well of St Helen at Great Asby and St Anne's Well at Locko House – it usually turns out to be a saint's well.[81] Some of these were later co-opted as municipal water supplies; St Kenelm's Well supplied water for Winchcombe, St Helen's Well for Brigg, St Peter's for Coggeshall, St Thomas's Well at Danbury and St Catherine's at Coventry. Whether this sanctified water did anything for the morals of the inhabitants, or even their health, is not clear, but it must be significant that the water of Holywells was not sought after by Water Boards in this way. This suggests that the name of Holywell was given to what were, by and large, minor springs, supplying only enough water for the needs of travellers or hermits, whereas the names of saints were given later on to the larger and more important springs which served the whole community.[82]

The wells of continental and Biblical saints are more closely linked with other buildings than their predecessors, the wells associated with indigenous cults. If we look for patronal dedications – those shared by a well with the parish church or some other consecrated building – then they are found among 46 percent of the wells dedicated to universal saints, as opposed to 30 percent for the wells of indigenous saints. Holywells cannot be analysed in this way, but it is remarkable how few of them – only 7 percent – are in or near a churchyard or chapelgarth.

The wells of women saints

The choice of patron saints was not always a free one; there were certain limiting factors. All Saints, like Peter & Paul, was clearly felt to be more appropriate as a dedication for churches than for other kinds of sacred place. There are wells of All Saints, it is true, but four out of the five take their dedication from a neighbouring church or chapel. There is no instance at all of a well jointly dedicated to Sts. Peter & Paul – the only claimed example, at Shrewsbury, being based on a suspect reinterpretation of a field-name

Is there a corresponding effect among well dedications, with certain patrons being reserved for them rather than for churches and chapels? In comparing the most favoured dedications for wells with those for churches, one factor stands out. None of the top ten dedications for churches is a woman – remember that we are excluding the Virgin Mary, whose cult is theologically and culturally of a quite different order from other saints – whereas women account for five of the ten saints most commonly associated with wells.[83] Surely this is significant, but what are we to make of it?

The first historian to notice this preference was the Rev Thomas Whitaker, historian of the Craven district, who observed 'that in the Popish superstition, few springs and fountains were dedicated to male saints' and went on to argue that this was 'proof of the affinity of that and the Pagan ritual, in which the Nymphs exclusively enjoyed the same honour… thus St Mary, St Margaret and St Helena were the νυμφαι λειμωνιαδες of Craven' (1805: 371). Later writers have repeated the theme, most of them inheriting Dr Whitaker's dislike for Catholicism if not his taste for quoting Sophocles. And there is no doubt that springs in the ancient world were always placed under the tutelage of female figures. Sulis and Coventina had no male equivalents; a Roman altar found at Chester is dedicated *Nymphis et Fontibus*, as if this was the most obvious combination in the world. Should we not see Sts. Helen, Anne, Catherine, Margaret and Mary Magdalen as the natural successors of these figures?

Not if historical evidence is to count for anything. The passage of seven hundred years between the end of Roman paganism and the spread of these later cults cannot be simply airbrushed out of the picture. There is no reason to suppose that the Anglo-Saxons, even in their heathen days, associated springs of water exclusively with female figures.[84] And if we look at the dedications to local and regional saints, which give a picture of well-cults as they existed between 700 and 1100, we find that there are 59 men and 28 women saints: a proportion of 2:1, the same as existed between men and women in the selection of saints generally, or indeed between high-ranking male and female clergy in common life.

But this is too quantitative an approach; it is a different story if we look at the symbolic value which saints had for their worshippers. The legends of Arild, Juthware, Osyth or Winifred are fantasias on a female theme: the saint is young, beautiful, perfect, vulnerable and desired, one who suffers tragically and overcomes triumphantly. Catherine and Margaret are female martyrs in this mould. Mary Magdalen is the repentant soul personified in a female form. Helen the queen mother and the holy grandmother Anne represent other stages in a woman's life cycle. There is no doubt that their femininity was important in the choice of these figures for veneration. But it did not necessarily link them with the water supply and indeed there is nothing to suggest that female saints were pre-eminently patrons of wells in preference to other things or places. A votary of St Catherine in the late Middle Ages was just as likely to name a pub or a bell or a ship after her as a spring.[85] We are looking at a general movement of society to the idealisation of high-born maidens and not at a particular tradition which survived at or responded to springs of water.

The cult of St Helen

But out of the twelfth-century patrons, was there anyone who came to mind, not just because their cult happened to be popular at the time, but because they were felt in some way to be suitable to wells? The obvious choice here would seem to be St Helen. She heads the ranking for holy well dedications, but comes far down the list for churches – about twentieth in sequence, next to St Thomas Becket. And whereas Becket's cult took off rapidly in the decades following his martyrdom, at a time when most English churches had received their dedication, St Helen's appeal does not seem to have risen or fallen much throughout the Middle Ages.

Her position as the foremost patron of holy wells is, on the face of it, unexpected. And it is an outstanding precedence. It's not just that she has more than twice as many wells as any other patron in the country; that patronage is concentrated into a much smaller area, for Helen is predominantly a saint of northern England. If we analyse the northernmost six regions of the country, she appears with 43 wells, four times as many as the next most popular (John the Baptist) and constituting 40 percent of all the wells dedicated to non-indigenous saints.

There is some doubt, in any case, as to whether St Helen should be numbered among the native or the foreign saints. The real Helen was a partner of Constantius Chlorus, who ruled as emperor in 305–6, several years after they had separated. It is not known where she came from. Later sources suggest Drepanum in Bithynia, but this is not certain; Constantius could have met up with her in many other places on his career path. The Roman empire was large and Helen was not, at first, a very important person. That changed when Constantius died at York and their son Constantine was acclaimed as emperor. He fought his way to supreme power, converted to Christianity and gave his mother a free hand to promote the religion which she, too, had embraced. Her pilgrimage to Jerusalem was accompanied by a lavish founding of churches and according to the ecclesiastical historians (though not those who were strictly contemporary with her) it was then that she discovered and enshrined the True Cross.

This was an excellent thing to do, especially by the standards of the relic-hungry Middle Ages, but it did not necessarily make Helen into a saint. Her tomb in Rome attracted little interest in the years following her death; it was not until 840 that her relics were taken, or supposed to have been taken, to Trier, where Altman wrote a *Life* attesting to her cult and miracles there. This attempt to appropriate the saint did not go uncontested, especially in York, a city which also had a claim to her cult. This was based on the slightly confused reasoning that, as her son Constantine was proclaimed emperor there, she must therefore have come from York herself – presumably as a native princess, for the Anglo-Saxons could not imagine rule by anyone without noble blood. York was in no position to press its claims as a Christian shrine until the conversion of its Danish rulers, but from the time of Wulfstan onwards, the clergy were able to encourage increased veneration of St Helen and the Holy Cross in their city.

But St Helen's legendary life was soon to take a fresh turn. The Welsh, inspired by the idea of her British descent, had found a place for her within their creative genealogies, with Coel Hen as her father. He was a legendary king of the North, but this was unknown to the Anglo-Norman historians, who preferred instead to see him as the eponymous founder of Colchester. By the 1120s, Colchester folk were claiming Helen as their fellow-citizen. This rapidly became part of the narrative of British history, accepted without any apparent dissent at York. By 1200 a northerner, Jocelin of Furness, could write a *Life* in which Helen is presented unambiguously as a native of Colchester (Harbus 2002: 44–51, 64–71, 102).

So St Helen's career as a Yorkshirewoman was a short one, existing only in the eleventh and early twelfth centuries. This is roughly what we would expect from her holy wells, which are amongst the earliest of this kind, with five dedications recorded before 1300. Their distribution, too, corresponds with the cultural boundaries of the time; they are bounded, not by the limits of old Northumbria, but by those of the later Danelaw, with dedications extending southwards into Lincolnshire. This contrasts with the churches of St Helen, which are found further south, though not in such great numbers; some of these seem to have been dedicated much earlier, possibly even in the seventh century, before Helen had acquired her specifically Northern identity.

But why should she have a special role as a patron of holy wells? Researchers have been puzzled by this for many years. One answer has been to explain the connection away as a corruption of words. We have already met with an example at Stainland, where the *Heliwelle* of 1285 had given rise by the late Middle Ages to a chapel of St Helen, the place-name evidently being linked with the saint and not given its true etymology in *hælig*. At Reighton in the East Riding, the modern St Helen's Well appears in the thirteenth century as *Elnewelle*, where the qualifier must be OE *ellern*, 'elder'.[86] But some hagiologising forms are to be expected in the wake of a popular cult. People only confused other words with the name Helen because they were already familiar with wells which belonged to her.

Is it possible that these wells were not dedicated to the historical Helen at all, but to someone else of the same name? Researchers have uncovered a number of candidates, including Helen the wife of Magnus Maximus, Elen Lluyddog (Helen of the Hosts), the mythical founder of roads called Sarn Elen, Elen the water sprite of the Lleyn Peninsula and various damsels called Elaine in the pages of Arthurian romance. But all these figures are derivative; ultimately they take their name, and often their legend, from the original Helen, mother of Constantine. Elen the wife of Maximus – the fairytale bride in the *Mabinogion*'s 'Dream of Macsen Wledig' – is simply a genealogist's repetition of the historical Helen, also the wife or partner of a Caesar, and also distinguished by the epithet *Luitdauc*. The Arthurian romances feature damsels called Elaine because the saint's name was commonly used for twelfth-century girls. And Elen the Celtic goddess, who continues to live a half-life on the fringes of scholarly research, is simply an amalgam of all these later figures projected into the prehistoric past.[87]

In any case, none of these figures had a connection with wells: nor, for that matter, did the historical Helen. What she was famous for was the foundation of churches and the conversion of unbelievers. 'She built many fine churches', says Jocelin, 'in cities and newly strengthened fortresses. She beautified them with fittings of the best quality and had them illuminated by lamps; she endowed them with funds and lands and the service of clergy and monks; she put learned and holy men in authority over the faithful'.[88] This is exactly what Cnut – like Constantine, a converted heathen with ambitions of empire – was doing in the eleventh century and it was the North of England which benefited most from this treatment. It had to be returned to Christianity; but it also stood in need, more than any part of the country, of pastoral care for the new communities who were settling on former wasteland, away from the older parish churches. This was the motive behind the foundation of chapels and many of these were also dedicated to St Helen. If this interpretation is right, we should see her, not so much as a patron of wells, but as the all-purpose saint for new dedications made after 1100 – a category of which wells formed only a part.

Saints' wells and lonely places

Earlier we had noted how saints' wells and wells of the Virgin, when plotted for their distribution on the map, were found in inverse correlation with the population. They are most common in Yorkshire, Cumbria and the North-East; rarest in the South-East and East Anglia. There is a close match here with the history of the parish. All of England derived its pastoral care by the splitting up of original large minster territories into smaller units based around a local sacred building, but this took place earlier in the South than the North. The process was underway in the Lowland Zone by the tenth century and the local buildings there have the status of churches, each typically with a small parish. In the Highland Zone it happened much later, after the crystallisation of parish boundaries under canon law in about 1100, and the local buildings have only the status of chapels. If the holy wells dedicated to the saints of the universal church are most frequent in this region, that would be because they were established after the formation of a rigid parish system. Probably they were intended to act as a kind of surrogate chapels. It is not easy to raise funds or get permission for building in a poor countryside and in the meantime people must have somewhere to meet, to hear preaching and to have the sacraments administered by a travelling cleric. Wells are a natural centre for gatherings of this kind. Later, in the community expanded onto previously uncultivated land, a small chapel might be built next to the venerated spot.[89]

This sheds a new light on the wells dedicated to the forest saints – patrons who were associated with wild and lonely places. St Anthony Abbot, the archetypal hermit, has a well in the isolated Forest of Dean and two others in the former wastes of the West Riding at Crookes and Northowram.[90] St Leonard, often associated with forests, has one at Sheepstor on Dartmoor and another lonely site at Belthorpe. St Giles, the huntsman's saint, often invoked in combination with St Leonard, has one at Knowle St Giles. One might expect St John, the voice crying in the wilderness, to belong to this group, but his wells do not seem to favour isolated places. Here, the association with baptism may have had a greater symbolical importance.

Giles and Leonard are typically French dedications and it is clear from the list of saints that several others were chosen by people familiar with their cults on the Continent. St Lambert of Liège, Loy (Eligius) of Noyon, Julian of Le Mans, German of Auxerre, Faith of Conques, Dennis of Paris, Owen (Ouen) of Rouen and Morel (Maurilius) of Angers are not names which would at first have come readily to an English congregation, although some of their cults were naturalised later on.[91] One of the two dedications to St Loy, that at Weedon in Northamptonshire, may in fact mask an original cult of St Lucien of Beauvais, since the Priory at Weedon was a cell of Beauvais Abbey. These French dedications suggest that the patrons of wells were

St Anthony's Well at East Dean. (From Nicholls 1858: 182.)

sometimes chosen by Norman landowners rather than the local congregation. If this is popular tradition, its popularity evidently comes from a higher rank of society than the English peasantry. The consent and support of a landowner would certainly be needed for the economic support of a new church or chapel nearby and the dedication of a well might have been the first step towards this.

Wells and the later medieval foundations

The patronal associations of wells can also give a clue to the date of their dedication – in some cases, at least. Most patronal wells cannot be dated in this way as they are associated with churches and these would have themselves have been dedicated long before the fashion began for naming wells after continental and Biblical saints. A few churches are known to have changed dedication, however. Hexton was rededicated to St Faith in about 1110, Morwenstow in Cornwall to St John in 1285 and Box in Wiltshire to St Thomas at some time after 1373. The wells, which in each case are dedicated to the new saint, must have been named after these dates. Some wells are to be found in the new towns of the Middle Ages. A great flood swept away most of Winchelsea in 1287 and the present town was built in the early fourteenth century, so its wells of St Catherine and St Lawrence must date after this.

With chapels we are on sounder ground, as these were being founded at all times up to the Reformation. Their first appearance in documents may not be the date of their foundations, although the twelfth-century chapels of St Helen at Colchester and St Thomas at Repton cannot be any earlier than her cult's arrival in Essex in the 1120s and his canonisation in 1173. The wells at these sites, though recorded later, are probably as old as the chapels whose dedication they share. Another well of St Thomas, at Northampton, is associated with a chapel which must have been dedicated in this first wave of enthusiasm for his cult; it appears in documents of about 1210. The chapel of St Catherine in Eckington stood on the scarp of Bredon Hill, part of the fashion for hilltop chapels of this saint in the early thirteenth century, and the associated well would be of the same date. St Swithin's chapel at Stanley is thirteenth-century and so is St Juliana's at Ludlow, although her well is at some distance on one of the roads entering the town.

In the fourteenth century we have chapels of St Helen at Harlepool and Tarleton, and of St Mary Magdalen at Coleham. The chapel of St Margaret at Stowe in Gloucestershire is recorded as *conventum de Stowe* in 1338, but given the early associations of *stow* as a place-name element it is likely to have had a previous history. It is significant that here, as Binsey, a women's retreat had a dedication to St Margaret. The fifteenth century provides the first records of St Nicholas's chapel at Totnes and St Vincent's at Bristol. Given the urban context, it is likely that we would have heard of these if they had existed earlier. The chapels of St Thomas at Windleshaw, St Alphege at Charlcombe, St Patrick at Lancaster, St Anne at Nottingham and St Helen at Almondbury all appear to have been founded in the fifteenth century and so presumably were their wells.

The same devotional impulse which founded chapels led the more wealthy to establish hospitals. These also began in the twelfth century, when that of St Mary Magdalen was set up at Newcastle and that of St Helen at Derby; St Helen's Well is first mentioned about sixty years after the foundation of the hospital, although Magdalen Well does not appear until later. Hospitals flourished in the following century. Among other foundations associated with wells, the hospital of St Giles at Chester was founded in about 1200, that of St John at Lutterworth in 1219 and that of St Mary Magdalen at Bamburgh in 1246. The hospitals of St James at Berkhamsted, St John at High Wycombe, St Lawrence at Nantwich and St Peter at Windsor also appear to be thirteenth-century foundations, so their associated wells cannot be any earlier than this. The hospital of St Michael at Well in the North Riding was a late foundation, being established in 1342. Whether the wells received their names at the same time as the foundations cannot always be established, but this is likely at Derby and certainly seems to have happened at Nantwich, where St Lawrence's well is also recorded in the late thirteenth century.

There are several wells associated with subsidiary altars and chapels within parish churches and with chantry chapels. These are likely to date to the last century or two before the Reformation. The dedications include St Helen, again, at Kirkby Overblow; St Patrick at Lancaster; and St Loy (or Lucien) at Weedon Lois. At Newcastle-upon-Lyme, the chapel of St Sunday had an important guild, established by 1493, which eventually took over the dedication of the church. St Anne's chapel at Fersfield had a fifteenth-century guild; there was also a guild of St Anne at Knowle in Warwickshire, but unfortunately there are no early references to her well there. At Fersfield the memory of processions in honour of St Anne survived until the eighteenth century, but generally these dedications faded from sight after the Reformation. The wells associated with chapels must therefore have been created during their time as centres of active worship, between 1350 and 1550 at a rough estimate.

Holy wells as a water supply

The association of wells with hospitals seems most appropriate; at least, it does if one associates holy wells with healing, which most of us would naturally do. But there is very little in the evidence itself to bear this out. It's true that at St John's Well at Wembdon, an observer found that many people 'distrustful of the cures of the

St Lawrence's Well at Norwich.
(From Willis 1885: pl.15.)

physicians are daily relieved of their sufferings and restored to health' in 1464 (Bekyngton 1934–5: 1.414). Holy Well or St Anne's Well at Buxton was healing with its warm waters from a very early period and there are supposed to have been cures at St Erasmus' Well at Ingestre, though the source for this is late and suspect. But against these 3 examples we must set the 217 wells of continental and Biblical saints which did not work cures – not according to contemporary evidence, at any rate. Medieval records are always imperfect, but even so the rarity of healing at wells of the universal saints stands out in sharp contrast to the accounts from those with indigenous dedications. Here we find that 17 out of a total of 180 are associated with miraculous cures, often described in vivid detail. The difference lies, not so much in the saint's place or origin, as in their perceived presence at the shrine. Cures were only worked at wells which partook of the numinous power of the relics which were enshrined nearby and which had sometimes been exhumed from the very site of the well itself. Simply naming a well after St Helen or St Peter was not going to evoke that frisson of awe.

In fact people seem to have regarded the wells of the universal saints in a very matter-of-fact way. They were protective about them, of course. When an anonymous malefactor threw a dead lapdog down Magdalen Well at Bamburgh, people protested – not because he was abusing the sacred, but because he was contaminating their water supply. Nowhere do we find the water of holy wells tabooed for common use; on the contrary, these were often the common spouts of a village or district within a town.[92] When the manorial court at Hythe objected, in 1400 or thereabouts, that 'John Beyngham and Robert Rykedone have thrown dung upon the Holywelle' (Dale 1931: 88), or Berkhamsted's Portmote Court presented people for washing their clothes at St James's Well (*Victoria CH Herts.* 1908–23: 2.163), they were concerned with hygiene, not sacrilege.

We often find holy wells cited as important sources of domestic water. At Eccleshill the elaborate arrangements made in 1585 so that 'the whole towne of Eccleshill should have libertye to fetch water att the aforesaid well and a sufficient way thereunto' show the importance placed on its domestic use (Preston 1927–32). This shows up more clearly in the later records. St Mary's Well, described in 1883 as 'the only supply of wholesome ordinary water accessible to the inhabitants of this part of Penwortham' (Hewitson 1883: 388–9), was typical of many.

St Lawrence's Well, near the saint's church at Norwich, is one of the first to be recorded as a water supply; there was a 'common way leading to St Lawrence's Well' in 1297. When this alley was enclosed by Robert Gibson in 1576, he laid down sixty feet of pipework with a tap at the end so that water could be drawn off at the main street, providing a florid surround of carved stonework to commemorate the occasion (Sandred & Lindström 1989–2002: 1.132; Knights & Morant 1888). Many holy wells survived as conduit heads in this way. St Kenelm's Well at Winchcombe had its original shrine replaced by a well-house. St Giles' Well at Chester enjoyed a second life in 1622 as a conduit head under the name of Barrel Well, feeding a cistern near the High Cross, and St Rumbold's Well at Buckingham was adapted in this way in 1667.

This was not just a matter of callous secularisation, for a number of holy wells had previously been tapped for drinking water by monastic houses and cathedral chapters. The Gilbertine canons of St Catherine's Priory proposed to construct a conduit to their house in Lincoln from a well in Canwick, in 1306, although the work was never finished, the spring subsequently became known as Holy Well (Mills & Mills 1996). Holywell at Worcester was the conduit head for the Priory there. Similarly St Wilfrid's Well fed Ripon Cathedral, where the fifteenth-century accounts are full of payments for maintaining the well-house. At Otford, masons laid in water pipes to feed the bishop's palace in 1440.

These conduit heads needed to be protected from mud, falling leaves and cattle. From the fifteenth and sixteenth centuries it became usual to cover them with small well-houses, usually square stone buildings with a high-pitched roof and a little door at the front. W.G. Fretton's reference to the well-house over St Catherine's Well at Coventry as 'something between a dog kennel and a mortuary chapel' (1893: 21–2) is unromantic but accurate. Other dog-kennel well-houses can be found at St John's Well next to Mount Grace Priory, Lady Well at Edington, and St Agnes' Well at Cothelstone. Lady Well at Ickles appears to have been of the same pattern, although it had been demolished by the time an archaeological record was made. Lady Well at Kilnwick sounds as if it was similar, as does St Leonard's Well at Dunster. But the queen of the conduit-head wells is Lady Well at Hempsted, a graceful building of the early fourteenth century. It is on land which belonged to the Augustinian canons of Llanthony Priory, in the suburbs of Gloucester, which suggests that it was established as a source of water for them.[93]

Lady Well at Hempsted. (From Maclean 1888–9: 54.)

The dedication of Lady Well is not recorded before 1875, but there is a sculpture over the doorway, thought by some to represent the Virgin, though others have identified is as a family group with St Anne. Clearly the canons of Llanthony Priory had made some effort to give a religious cast to their springhead, but it was not in any sense a consecrated place; it was holy only because it ministered to the needs of holy men in the town below. Exactly the same process was carried out at Waverley in 1216, when Brother Symon excavated a new source of water to feed the abbey's pipework and then called it St Mary's Well. The dedication to the Virgin was apt, as Waverley was a Cistercian house, but it referred to their ownership of the spring, not to any expectation of cult or miracles there.

Wells dedicated in name only

A well could bear a saint's name without being consecrated in any other religious sense. At Ovington the name of St Andrew's Well simply reflects ownership by a nearby cell of St Andrew's monastery at Hexham; at Coley Hall there is a St John's Well taking its name from a grange held by the Order of the Knights Hospitaller, as there is at Ribchester. At Bagendon, Trinity Well is found on land which belonged to the chantry of Holy Trinity in the parish church of Cirencester. For good measure, we can add St George's Well at Cullompton, apparently taking its name from the field where a fair was held on St George's Day. This was established by Buckfast Abbey in 1317.

In the grounds of the bishop's palace at Wells, water from the abundant springs is channelled though a square well-house built by Bishop Beckington in the fourteenth century to feed the town. The area was known as St Andrew's Well at this time, but there are no earlier references to the name; no legend, no chapel, no pilgrimage, no cures. Evidently St Andrew's Well was dedicated in name only and the earlier sources feature it simply as the well or the great spring. This is remarkable because the spring is such a powerful one and must have been influential in determining the site for the eighth-century minster at Wells. But it did so as a landmark, not as a sacred site.

St Andrew's Well at Wells is a classic example of what Rattue calls dedication 'by association' (1995a: 66). We are to understand that the well rises on the land of St Andrew's representative the bishop, that it emerges in the shadow of his cathedral – but nothing more. In the same way townspeople would name a well after the dedication of a nearby church, meaning only give a rough idea as to where it could be found. We hear of All Saints' Well at Colchester just the once, in 1387, and of St Martin's Well at Winchester only in 1567. These references come from towns with exhaustive records of their medieval property and the failure of these wells to be named in any other source suggests that they were not really thought to be dedicated. 'St Martin's Well' was simply a scrivener's way of defining the well by the gate near St Martin's on the Wall. There is at least one town, Stamford in Lincolnshire, where this kind of naming seems to have become general. In Butcher's history of 1646, we meet with wells at almost every church in the town – wells with the names of St Clement, St George, St Mary and St Peter. This means only that they were near the churches of the same name.

Indeed, some wells were not dedicated to individual patrons at all. There was a well of All Saints at Stamford, as there was at Colchester, with others at Norwich, Wareham and Colne. All of these bar the last (which appears only in the suspect form Hullown Well) take their names from churches or chapel. Presumably the Holy Trinity was not directly involved with wells named Trinity, either; that at Bagendon, as we have seen, refers to a landowner, while in Lincoln, as at Gloucester and Weare Giffard, the patronal Trinity Well takes its name from the church. Only Millom stands alone; it is first recorded in about 1200, not long after dedications to the Trinity were officially authorised, and may represent the first step in founding a chapel which never came to be built.

Some dedications could take on a kind of surrogate personality. We sometimes hear of St Pulchre's Well, as if Pulchra were to be numbered among the virgin saints, but on closer examination the name dissolves into a corruption of Sepulchre. At Sudbury a well near the chapel of the Holy Sepulchre had this name. In Leicester the *fons S. Sepulchri* of 1458 is *Pulchre Well* in 1476, again after a nearby chapel. This was demolished at the Reformation, but the nearby chapel of St James survived, so the well becomes 'the spring at St James Chapell' in 1573 and later St James's Well, though it also appears as 'the spring & well in the Southe gate', 'the hermitage well' and 'the Chappell Well' (Cox 1998–2004: 1.229). Clearly it did not have any dedication in its own right and the use of a saint's name to describe it was just a convenience.

This is all a little deflating. We had begun with high hopes for our holy wells, convinced that they would turn out to be ancient, magical places. But when it comes to these wells of the international saints – St John, St Peter and the rest – it is beginning to look as if hundreds of sites have no sacred meaning at all. If the story of Pulchre well is anything to by, these places are mere dedications by association. A site like St Pancras's Well in London turns out to have no more religion to it than the nearby St Pancras Station.

But it is not the wells that are disappointing us; it is the medieval mind. People in the Middle Ages did not think about religion in the way that we have grown to expect. Our notions of the holy are conditioned by an ethos of individual feeling and imaginative response, and sacred places come very short of our expectations if they fail to arouse that profound but ill-defined sense of the numinous. Five hundred or a thousand years ago, the world was a much more matter-of-fact place. God and his saints were the fixed landmarks of life and their presence could be expressed just as much through landownership as through epiphany.

Cult and worship at holy wells

We cannot hope to distinguish wells that were really sacred from those with merely nominal dedications. There is a continuum between these points. At one end, certainly, there are the ordinary conduit cisterns and crossroads wells given saints' names; but at the other, we have a handful of truly venerated sites. At Hexton, the well-house contained an image of St Faith, to complement the one at her altar which was added to the nearby church at some time after the thirteenth century. A causeway was made for pilgrims to pass from the church to the well (Whiteman 1936: 151–3). The 'neat and much frequented walk' leading from Bicester to St Edburgh's Well, and called 'Seynt Edburghes grene way' in 1325, may have served for similar processions (Kennett 1818: 1.191–2). At Bromley the well of St Blaise was linked in some way with his shrine or oratory, a pilgrimage site which had a grant of indulgences in the 1480s (Philipott 1659: 84). The oratory of St Chad at Chadshunt also attracted pilgrims and had an image of the saint; his well must have formed part of their itinerary, even though both shrine and well are based on a misunderstood place-name (Camden 1695: 510). The chapel of St Erasmus at Ingestre, with the saint's well close by, attracted considerable offerings up to the Reformation and may have been built fifty years earlier (Plot 1696: 99). The chapel of St John at Stanford on Teme appears to have attracted pilgrims who subsequently drank of his well (Nash 1781–2: 2.366) .[94]

The evidence for these cults is poor. Nowhere do we have a clear, contemporary account of people visiting, venerating the saint and drinking at the well – it all has to be construed from later evidence. This is very different from the well-cults of indigenous saints, for which there is a wealth of evidence; but then those were the sites where records were kept, since stories of the well's healing power helped prove the holiness of the patron commemorated there. The cults of the universal saints are much later in date, seemingly fifteenth or sixteenth century, and at this time the well was evidently thought much less important than the church or oratory which stood beside it. There are a few suggestions that more isolated wells may also have received some sort of cult. At St Catherine's Well on the outskirts of Barton-upon-Humber stood 'the image of that Saint well cut in white marble standing by it, within the memory of several men now living, but it was all broke to pieces in Cromwell's time'.[95] St Clare's Well, near a farm at Philham, had the battered figure of a saint associated with it in the twentieth century. But this evidence is more suggestive than

*St Anne's Well at Nottingham, as drawn in the 1850s by C.T. Moore.
(From Stapleton 1899: 167.)*

conclusive. Putting statues in niches over well-houses was a common practice among modern landowners and can hardly be taken as evidence for an earlier cult. At Astrop the newly dedicated St Rumbold's well was provided with an image of the saint soon after 1749, although having failed to do their homework, they portrayed him as a knight of romance and not a miraculous babe.[96]

These dedications to Sts. Faith, Blaise, Chad, Erasmus and John are very mixed; evidently there was no expectation that any one of them would be a patron specifically of wells. That role is reserved for St Anne. 'Until late in the fifteenth century, Saint Anne had functioned as a saint among other saint. By the 1470s, however, there are signs that North European Christians were beginning to pay somewhat more attention to her, and attention of a different kind' (Nixon 2004: 21). It is in this context that she appears as the patron of at least four sites with an active tradition of ritual. At Fersfield the congregation would line up after a service and process from St Anne's chapel in the south aisle of the church to her well on the slopes of the hill nearby (Blomefield 1739–75: 1.70). The starting-point at Caversham was a chapel built on the bridge over the Thames and worshippers passed by a great oak, which like the trees in the *Lives* had got somehow incorporated into the sacred story (Margrett 1906). The hot spring at Buxton, originally Holy Well, had become associated with St Anne by 1500 or thereabouts, when the Cottrell family seem to have put about a story that her image had been miraculously found there. The Reformation put stop to this, although after a brief eclipse the enterprising Cottrells found a new role promoting the well as a place for music and dancing (Langham &

Wells 1986: 33–4). A similar development seems likely at Nottingham, where music attended the annual procession of the Corporation to St Anne's Well on Easter Monday. This custom is first recorded in 1557, but as it was then associated with the maintenance of forest rights, it is likely to have been a long-standing practice (Stapleton 1899: 163–92). St Anne's chapel was built in the fifteenth century and appears like its counterpart at Buxton to have gradually taken over old traditions; the well was Robin Hood's well until the 1500s and, when the chapel was pulled down, it reverted to this old description.

Nottingham people kept up their outings to St Anne's Well long after it had lost its religious affiliation and even its name. There was a place selling food and drink, with summerhouses and arbours around it, where large oak planks served as tables and the seats were made from 'banks of earth, fleightered and covered with green sods, like green carsie cushions' (Stapleton 1899: 178). The rural setting must have formed part of the attractions, even before the Reformation, when the purpose of the visit was partly devotional. The sixteenth-century St Anne's Well at Rotherham was also on the outskirts of the town, in a field where people met for recreation. St Anne's chapel at Brislington has much the same relationship to Bristol as the one in Nottingham forest does to the town there, although Brislington's holy well is not recorded until the nineteenth century. None of these pilgrimages were particularly onerous – the well at Fersfield was only sixty yards from the church – and this suggests that a visit to St Anne's Well often formed a pretext for a country stroll.[97] In this, as in other ways, well-cults of the fifteenth and sixteenth centuries were already anticipating the social pleasantries that would be familiar at spas after 1600.

Wells of the Virgin Mary

The late medieval development of the cult of St Anne took place against a background of increasing domestic piety and idealisation of the holy family. Nowhere is this clearer than in the honours paid to St Anne's daughter, the Virgin Mary, from the fourteenth century onwards. These were only the latest upswelling of devotion to Mary, whose cult had been revived or introduced many times over. She is prominent in the earliest dedications in England, she had received new honours in the Benedictine Reform and she aroused a special devotion among the urban elites and new theologians of the early twelfth century. She would feature again in the mid-thirteenth century through the popular and passionate preaching of the mendicant orders. But none of this led to her being chosen as a patron for holy wells. There are some 160 wells dedicated to her, as against 400 dedicated to other saints and 340 Holywells, and they are for the most part late creations.

There is some evidence to suggest that Mary first received the dedication of holy wells in the religious houses. Given that her wells are much less common overall than those of other saints, or the Holywells, it is a surprise to find that they are the most frequent category at monastic foundations. There are 9 wells dedicated to Mary at monasteries, as against 6 of other saints and 2 Holywells. Significantly, most of these houses were established late, so their wells must be late dedications too. Southwell is the only pre-Conquest foundation in the group and that was reformed as a collegiate church. Wells are found at Nunburnholme which, though a Benedictine priory, is first recorded in the 1270s; at the Augustinian priories at Walsingham, Bradley and Haltemprice, founded in 1169, 1230 and 1326; at the Cistercian houses of Roche Abbey, which was founded in 1147, and Waverley, where the well was dedicated, as we have seen, in 1216; and at the friaries of Appleby and Preston. The one example of a hospital with a well of the Virgin is the Maison Dieu at Dover, founded and dedicated to Mary in 1203. Grey monks, hospital brethren, canons and friars seem to have initiated a special interest in springs of the Virgin and they did so in the thirteenth century or later.

The same picture of late dedications emerges from the wells associated with churches and chapels. The Ladywell at Tuesley is associated with a minster that had come down in the world, but that at Hermitage must postdate the change of dedication of the parish church to the Virgin Mary in the fourteenth century. The chapel at Oxford, where a well is first mentioned in the fifteenth century, is likely to have been founded a hundred years earlier. Other wells are found at the chapel at Cheswick, founded in 1360; at one in Bothal, founded in the mid-fifteenth century; and at another in Bradford-on-Avon, of about 1500. The Lady Well at Bradley in Staffordshire may be associated with *Seyntmarieslond*, which belonged to the chantry of the Virgin in 1460, while the chantry itself is probably thirteenth century. The Ladywell at Wokingham derives from a chantry founded in 1443 and St Mary's Well at Brough must have come into being on the eve of the Reformation, as this chantry was only established in 1506. The picture is consistent: wells dedicated to Mary are found at chapels which themselves are late medieval foundations.

We have already seen that well-cults of the other universal saints did not establish themselves until the 1150s, but that of Mary is later even than these. There are no dedications known at all from the twelfth century and it is surprising just how few are recorded at any date in the Middle Ages: just 15, which is 10 percent of the known wells. Of the other saints' wells, on the other hand, 34 percent are known from medieval sources, and 41 percent of Holywells. In the North of England, if we had nothing but medieval records of wells to go on, it would be St Helen who emerged as the most important patron and not the Mother of God.

This cannot be a true reflection of the facts; almost all of the wells dedicated to Mary must go back to a time before the Reformation, even if they were not recorded until much later. But the lack of medieval evidence suggests that the movement to dedicate wells to her must have begun very late, perhaps not gaining any real popularity until the fifteenth century and continuing into the first half of the sixteenth and the suppression of Catholic faith. That would leave very little time for Marian wells to appear in contemporary documents or place-names, and would explain why we are so dependent on later evidence for the existence of her cult.[98]

Sites called Ladywell

There is another factor to be considered when it comes to place-names, since the wells of the Virgin appear here in a double character, for which there is no parallel in any other cult. Some sites are called St Mary's Well in the usual way – *Sancte Marie fons* in Latin, as at Waverley – and *Saintemariwelle* in English, as at

Southampton. But there are many others called Lady Well, or a variation on this name. From the contemporary evidence, limited as it is, it seems clear that the name Lady Well grew in popularity as the Middle Ages progressed. We have wells explicitly dedicated to St Mary at Scotforth (1200s), Waverley (1216), Southampton (1230s), Prestwath (1237), Allerton (1240s), Belford (1399), Walsingham (1400s), Gateshead (1403) and Bristol (1434). By contrast, the earliest Ladywell is recorded at Sacombe as *Lavediwelle* (1294) and another at Kniveton as *Ladiwalle* (1290s). After that there is a gap of over a century before we meet with *Ladewell* (1418) at Austhorpe and *Ladywell* at Hungarton (1470s). In the sixteenth century the new form takes over with *Ladyswell* (1528) at Sockbridge, *Our Ladyes well* (1550s) at Barton near Grantchester and *Lady Well* (1592) at Lewisham.

The spring at Barton rose at Whitwell Farm and is in fact called 'our Ladyes well of Whytewell' (Gray 1894–8: 74). It looks very much as if the original spring-name was in the process of being replaced by a dedication, but the two names co-existed for a while side by side. The renaming of a well is definitely known to have happed at Whelmstone Barton, where the 'cress well' of an Anglo-Saxon charter became Lady Well and had a chapel built beside it. If this happened elsewhere, it would explain why the overwhelming majority of Ladywell names are not recorded until modern times. The 6 which are found in medieval records contrast with over 120 in later sources – the great majority of them on tithe maps and the early Ordnance Survey. The proportion of modern names to early ones is five times higher than in the wells of St Mary and these themselves, as we have seen, show a higher proportion of modern forms than other types of holy well name. An origin in the very late Middle Ages seems the best explanation of this.[99]

St Mary's Well and Lady Well both mean the same thing: it is clear from the language used at Barton that the lady in question is the mother of Christ and not any secular landowner.[100] 'Lady' is often employed in this way – always in the vernacular, never translated into Latin – for things pertaining to the Virgin. This idiom is still used when we speak of Lady Chapels, but it was used much more extensively in the Middle Ages.

ME *Leuedi* is especially common as a qualifier in field-names.[101] It does not appear in these names until the thirteenth century; before that date it seems that places were not being devoted to Mary, whatever other forms her cult may have taken.. But after 1200 Lady- field-names are frequent and remain so without any apparent increase or fall until the end of the Middle Ages. This is quite different from the Ladywells, with their marked increase in numbers towards the sixteenth century. Whatever the cause of the late medieval popularity of Ladywells, it must be sought in a growing cult of the wells themselves and not in the use of a qualifier Lady-, since this was current from a much earlier period.

Furthermore, the Lady- field-names are used in a slightly different sense from the Ladywells; they refer not to places of worship but to cultivated ground. These must be lands devoted to the service of the Virgin – small fields whose rent paid for lights in a chapel, the services of a chantry priest and the like. The plot called *Seyntmarieslond* which we have already met in conjunction with a well at Bradley

Lady Well at Lewisham.
(From Knight 1842: 58–9.)

in Staffordshire seems to have served the the chantry of the Virgin in this way. It was consecrated to Mary's service, but it was not a place for her worship.

On the other hand, we have five examples of Lady Cross, most of them from the thirteenth century. Here the name really does refer to cult rather than ownership and it seems reasonable to interpret Ladywell, like St Mary's Well, in the same way. Indeed at Felkirk in the West Riding the two names pair up, with a *Ladycrosse* recorded in 1476 and Ladywell appearing nearby on the modern map.[102] As with the other saints' wells, there seems to be a spectrum of meaning with places of cult at one extreme and, at the other, dedications that are purely notional. These would include the well at Heversham, named after the abbey at York which owned the manor. Market Harborough similarly had a Lady Well at the point where St Mary's Lane leaves the town and becomes St Mary's Causeway. This leads to St Mary in Arden, the original mother church of the settlement (Nichols 1795–1815: 3 pl.152). The name of the well seems to allude to this and not to any cult that it may have received in its own right.

Pilgrimage to wells of the Virgin

At the other end of the spectrum we have wells like those at Walsingham which, as even Erasmus acknowledged, held 'a wonderfully cold fluid, good for headache and stomach troubles… that stream of water, they declared, suddenly shot up from the ground at the command of the Most Holy Virgin' (1997: 631). It's true that, in his gentle mockery of the cult, he seems to be suggesting that the temperature of the water accounted for more cures than its divine origin. Bishop Erghum had said the same thing about Bisham in 1385 and it was to be a staple of Protestant responses to St Winifred's shrine at Holywell. Like many other traditions at holy wells, scientific rationalism had put down its roots long before the Reformation.[103] But the cult which Erasmus saw at Walsingham was a comparatively recent one. Although the abbey was founded in 1169, and claimed a back-story of Marian devotion stretching a hundred years earlier, its fame as a scene of pilgrimage did not really spread until the fourteenth century. St Mary's Well is first heard of in the 1400s, when a small boy (the future sub-prior) fell in, drowned and was restored to life through the intercession of the Virgin (Dickinson 1956: 12, 136).

The Ladywell at nearby Woolpit would have connected with pilgrimages made to the Virgin there, which included visits by royalty in 1448 (Webb 2000: 99–100). Other cults must have flourished right at the end of the Middle Ages, since we only hear about them in post-Reformation sources. The 'image of Our Lady at Eastwell, yet standing, whereunto was continual oblation in times past' and presumably connected with the Ladywell there, was fondly remembered in 1543 (Webb 2000: 142). At Oakham we are told in 1565 that offerings and pilgrimages were paid to 'the late image of Blessed Mary at the spring' (Jones 2007: 120). Whilst not quite prepared to speak out for the lost religion, people of the town were clearly unhappy about being deprived of the revenue which it had created. It was the same at Newcastle, where folk-memory pointed out a whole street of houses which had been necessary to accommodate pilgrims to the nearby shrine at Jesmond. Certainly in 1428 there were many people resorting 'on account of divers miracles wrought therein through the merits of St Mary, the Virgin' (Brewis 1928; Fraser 1983), but although the chapel had existed in the fourteenth century, and perhaps earlier, there is no pre-Reformation evidence for the dedication of the well. Excavation showed that it had been extensively remodelled in the seventeenth century and it may be that Catholic devotion was transferred to this site, where prayer was less easily observed by suspicious eyes, after the disuse of the chapel. This is also true of Lady Well at Holystone, 'wall'd about with a curious stone resembling porfire' at some time before 1715 and a site of Catholic pilgrimage (Hodgson 1916: 3). It certainly seems to be the case at Fernyhalgh, where a Lady Well near the ruins of a chapel of unknown dedication kept the old religion alive despite the exactions of the penal laws. At these sites a late medieval devotion to Mary continued as the inspiration for post-Tridentine observance, but this doesn't necessarily mean that the actual wells themselves had been receiving cult before the Reformation.

The suppression of Ladywells

There was much about the cult of Mary which appealed to popular devotion. She was the supreme intercessor and in the devotional tradition of the *Miracles de Nostre Dame*, the workings of that mercy are presented almost as a kind of caprice, a reward for devotion and not for virtue. Ordinary people wanted a patron like this – someone who could overturn the grim machinery of law and punishment. And Mary could be present anywhere; because she had been translated bodily to heaven, she was not limited in her sphere of influence to any place on earth.

In the earlier Middle Ages people had wanted the assurance of relics. The most effective saint was always the new saint and, as soon as a cult had begun to flourish, there would be miracles associated with the place that held their bodily remains. But the supply of new saints was gradually strangled by the Church authorities, who saw local cults as little more than a nuisance. After the Council of Constance in 1418, canonisations effectively ceased. Devotion to Mary, on the other hand, had the highest authority; not being bound by corporeal relics, she could manifest at any rock or well or tree. Her universal presence was experienced against the comfortingly local reality of the cult site or image. And anyone, however humble, could be the first recipient of such a grace.

This caused much grief to the bishops. Robert Mascall of Hereford found in 1410 that 'many of our subjects are in large numbers visiting a certain well and stone at Turnastone… with genuflections and offerings' (Durham 1932). The cult was evidently a new one and must have taken off like wildfire, for the spring was unable to supply all the crowds who wanted a touch of its miraculous power; when the water ran out 'they take away with them the mud of the same and treat and keep it as a relic'. He does not specify why they were gathering at the spring, but Turnastone, where the parish church is dedicated to the Virgin, has a Ladywell and this is likely to have been the site that was being venerated. Similarly at Linslade, the cult which Bishop Oliver Sutton suppressed in 1291 is described simply as 'pilgrimage to a well in Linslade open field, under colour of a fancied devotion' (Sutton 1954–69: 6.186–7). But even if this popular devotion was 'fancied', it was still being supported by the vicar, since we find him being disciplined for his part in the proceedings. Forty years earlier, the village had been granted a fair on the week following Lady Day. It was shortly after this festival that Sutton pronounced his condemnation, so the crowd which he describes as 'thronging from all parts' must have been attending the fair, and the cult of the well would have been a natural extension of the veneration for the Virgin which had brought them there in the first place.[104]

The suppression of these cults follows the same course, even using the same rhetoric, as the earlier denunciations of well-worship in the penitential tradition.[105] People had previously been forbidden to venerate obscure or imaginary saints at wells and stones; now they were being told not to presume on unauthorised kindnesses from the Virgin at the same sort of place. But it is only the failed cults which come to our attention like this. There must have been many others which received the blessing of a bishop, or simply got established while his attention was directed elsewhere and then took their place unobtrusively in the religious landscape. At Chulmleigh there was a chapel authorised for divine service in 1378 under the name of *capella Sancte Marie atte Wille* (Brantyngham 1901–6: 1.391). The site is evidently the Lady Well which appears on the modern map. Here a cult of the Virgin seems to have begun around a well, as at Linslade and Turnastone, but it received enough support from authority for a chapel to be built. Now both the building and the cult are lost and only the well remains. There was a 'chapel of St Michael and St Mary by Dertmouth, called Holywyll' and the Bishop of Exeter granted an indulgence of forty days towards its repair in 1452 (Lacy 1963–71: 3.136); here, too, a well chapel seems to have received the sanction of orthodox religion.[106]

A pattern of rapid establishment and decline would explain the frequency with which Ladywell survives, not as a spring-name, but as an adopted name for some other feature of the landscape. 29 percent of Ladywells have given their name to streams, fields, tracks and farms; indeed, 16 percent of them are only known from names of this kind, the location of the original well having been lost. This compares strikingly with the sites called St Mary's Well, which hardly ever give a name to anything else; there is only one exception, St Mary Well Street at Beaminster. The adoption of names from saints' wells for other landscape features is not common; as we saw earlier, it only happens in 8 percent of cases, whereas 65 percent of

Holywells have given rise to other names in this way. Ladywells (but not the wells of St Mary) fall in the middle point between these two categories. What can this mean?

The choice of a spring-name to name other places implies that it was already part of people's mental map. Most field-names are given by farmers or labourers and, if they preferred to name woods or brooks after Holywells and Ladywells, this suggests that these dedications were more important to them than the wells of the saints. They were closer to ordinary people's idea of religion; indeed, in the case of dedications to the Virgin, we can suspect that Ladywell was used in the vernacular as a name for sites of popular cult, as at Turnastone and Chulmleigh, while St Mary's Well would be reserved for sites which had a more formal observance. We have already had reason to believe that Holywell names were given to springs which had attracted popular devotion, but whose cults had no official endorsement. The Ladywells would reflect a similar practice, except that they were being dedicated from 1300 to 1550, roughly speaking, while the Holywells were created earlier, at a range of dates between 750 and 1350. That is why Ladywells have not given rise to so many farm or field-names; there has simply been less time for them to be adopted. In any case they came into being in a world which already had names for these other features.

How did these sites come to be consecrated? Official condemnations always refer to 'the common people' or 'many, weak in the faith'. The sheer speed with which these cults spread evidently took authority off-balance, as did the crush of crowds who descended on sites like Bisham, Linslade, Turnastone, Oxford, Wembdon and North Cerney. Perhaps understandably, the denunciatory bishops deal with people *en masse* and do not look search for any individual who might have started the cult. But we can get a closer view if we compare the English evidence with Catholic shrines on the Continent, where springs of the Virgin continued to attract sudden spontaneous veneration, as they still do today.[107] Before the first crowds and the pilgrim traffic, these cults typically take their origin in the visions or miraculous healing of an individual – often, as is the way of the Virgin, in some special favour which she has shown to the humble and weak. Behind every Lourdes, there is a Bernadette. And it is likely that similar histories underlie many of our medieval English Ladywells.

Ladywells in the landscape

The grotto at Lourdes was a marginal place – scruffy, overgrown and generally thought to be haunted. Until the miracles began, it was just one of those neglected areas that the social geographers call fringeland. Can we identify similar areas in English topography? It is curious how many of the Ladywells are found at abandoned earthworks. The one at Ickles is just east of the Roman fort of Templebrough. At Aconbury, Thornbury and East Brent, Ladywells rise in the fields below hillforts, while that at Brayton is on the isolated Barf Hill. One at Ancaster is associated with a chapel, dedicated to the Virgin, which had been built within a Roman fort near the village. At Belford the spring is found near the chapel of the Virgin on Belford Crags, a chapel which lies just to the south of a hillfort on the highest part of the crag. For good measure we can add the Lady Well at Bampton, which lies within the earthworks of the old Bampton Castle (afterwards Ham Court), although this is not such an ancient earthwork.

Ladywells are not the only sites to be found in locations like this. Holy Well at Ratby is near the hillfort of Bury Camp. The Holy Well at Cholesbury lies near the church within the hillfort which gives the parish its name; the one at Tadmarton is just east of the hillfort and seems to have had a processional route associated with it, for a Victorian antiquary assures us that 'there existed, not many years ago, remains of a paved way made of broad flags, leading to this spring from the camp' (Beesley 1841: 12). We have a St Helen's Well near Castle Ditches at North Stainley, a St Catherine's Well on the outworks of the hillfort at Stretton Grandison, and another at Eckington just below the scarp of Bredon Hill with its multiple hillforts. There is also the enigmatic St Hawthorn's Well on the Wrekin.

Nevertheless, it is the Ladywells which are most often found within earthworks, even though numerically they form a smaller category than Holywells or the wells of other saints. It is the same disproportion that we found with monasteries, where Ladywells occurred more commonly than other types of well. In both cases this must be put down to the special atmosphere of these places. The appearance of holy wells at religious houses is no mystery. We know that from the thirteenth century onwards they hosted individuals with a special devotion to the Virgin and that explains the dedication of their wells. But the abandoned earthworks which lay just outside the village, or on the slopes of the hills overlooking it, seem also to have been centres of a much more unofficial religion. We can perhaps imagine a peasant dreamer spending long days alone in these derelict encampments, hearing and seeing what no-one else could see and hear. The sprites and spectres which other people reported from these places would then be transformed into a religious presence, just as Joan of Arc turned the fairies of Domremy into saints. If other people accepted the visions as true, the local community would begin to venerate a holy well at the site and perhaps found a chapel later on.

Something like this may have happened at the hillfort sites. The preponderance of Ladywells at these sites makes it clear, though, that if this did take place it was at a very late date, probably around the fifteenth century when the well-cults of Mary were at their height. Of course the earthworks themselves were often prehistoric, and much of the traditional lore associated with them may have gone back to the Anglo-Saxon period, but that was another story altogether. Gatherings and supernatural experiences at hillforts certainly have an archaic ring to them, but here as elsewhere we must be vigilant about the distinction between what seems archaic and what is really, historically old. As this example suggests, topographical analysis of holy wells is not, on its own, enough to tell us how old they are, although it may give a clue to the circumstances under which they gained their reputation.

The water of holy wells

Holy wells are created by people. They are found wherever a site would serve the spiritual needs of those who named them – saints, storytellers, vicars, visionaries and many others. Today, when the old worship is forgotten and the chapels all in ruin, it is easy to reverse this process and imagine that the wells came first and people then discovered them, learning to venerate them because of the special qualities they possessed. That may seem to be the natural course of things, but it is not how it happened.[108]

The great Protestant antiquaries of the seventeenth century thought otherwise. Robert Plot supposed that St Edmund's Well at Oxford 'was believed to be so effectual in curing divers distempers, and thereupon held of so great sanctity, that here they made vows, and brought their alms and offerings' (1677: 48) – a complete inversion of the facts as they appear in Bishop Sutton's Register. The well was not made sacred to St Edmund because it cured people. It cured them because of its sanctity, or pretended sanctity, as the bishop saw it; but even he did not claim that it was a naturally medicinal spring, only that it was the scene of religious enthusiasm beyond the bounds of what he was prepared to allow in his diocese.

Plot took a different view because he was writing in the midst of the first spa movement. In his natural histories of Oxfordshire and Staffordshire, he devoted a great deal of space to unusual springs of all kinds, partly from a disinterested scientific curiosity, but also in the faith that these anomalies in the water supply would not have been laid on by a benevolent God unless he intended them to be of use to Englishmen. The nastier a spring tasted, the more evidently it must have have a medicinal value, otherwise what would it have been created for in the first place?

This was not the way that medieval people saw things. Indeed, when the medieval *Lives* describe holy wells, they often make a point of emphasising that their water was of the best possible quality. For Goscelin, the well of a saint was 'pure water', 'a spring of sweet water', 'a spring of bright water', or 'a spring of sweet and clear water'. Other hagiographers took the same line, even when the facts were against them. The anonymous author of the *Life of St Cuthbert* drank from his well on Farne Island and reported that 'the great sweetness of its flavour we have proved and still thankfully prove by tasting it'. It is in fact so polluted with the droppings of Farne's seabirds as to be, by modern standards, absolutely undrinkable (Magnusson 1984: 91–2).

Holy wells and mineral waters

Given this discrepancy between medieval and modern views on healing water, what are we to make of the holy wells that have dissolved mineral content? The Holywells at Catlowdy, Dalston, Staward Peel and Waterhead are all sulphurous, as are St Peter's Well at Barmby-on-the-Marsh and St Erasmus's Well at Ingestre. Wells vaguely described as 'mineral' are reported from Witherslack, Turvey, Windsor and St Pancras. It may be significant that Ingestre, where Plot reports 'sulphurous oleaginous waters' near a chapel of the saint, is the only one of these sites with a medieval cult. The others all appear for the first time in the eighteenth and nineteenth centuries; five of them are from Cumbria or nearby and it may be that in this region Holywell names were applied in modern times to potential spas. This is certainly known to have been done at Humphrey Head.

The situation is quite different with chalybeate wells, for many of these were known as holy wells in the Middle Ages.[109] In the twelfth century there is the spring at the Northumberland village of Holywell and in the thirteenth and fourteenth there are Holywells at Cranfield, Linslade, Rubery and Wolsingham, all described by later observers as being chalybeate. The standard test in the early modern period was to tinge the water with extract of galls, on which it would turn purple if iron was present in significant amounts. Of course we are dependent for this information on amateur chemists, some of them very amateur; Bryant, who describes St Walstan's Well at Bawburgh as a 'strongly chalybeate water', also refers to its daily rise and fall (1900–15: 2.25) and it is only fair to point out that no-one else has made either observation at this much-visited well. But the number of holy wells reported with chalybeate water in the eighteenth and nineteenth centuries is so great that some of the reports must reflect an earlier state of things. Brighton, Farnborough, Longwitton, Shotley Bridge and Siston were all marketed as spas and it is possible that their status as holy wells is a modern invention; but the wells at Banbury, Birtley, Bishops Stortford, Bisley, Gunnarton, Horsted Keynes, Leegomery, Newbrough, Scampton, Wigton and Winton seem likely to be medieval dedications.

The chalybeate springs differ from the sulphurous ones, though, since their water is not particularly unpleasant to the taste. The earliest of them, Holy Well or St Mary's Well at North Shields, seems to have provided drinking water to the village named after it. Chalice Well at Glastonbury, now the most famous of the ritually culted chalybeate springs, was formerly an ordinary water supply to the Abbey. The well at Horsted Keynes was in the hands of the Mid-Sussex Joint Water Board and that at Bishops Stortford was famous for making pea soup.[110] Presumably the iron helped keep the peas green, but at any rate these springs were understood to be acceptable drinking water. The same is true of the petrifying wells recorded at Ditcheat, Eshton, Levisham, Lockton, Rushton and Winterton; they held carbonate of lime in suspension and on any agitation in the stream would deposit this as a stony deposit, but this did not make them any less suitable for drinking than other hard waters. Of course there were many other petrifying springs which were not holy wells, just as there were chalybeate ones. It seems to have been largely a matter of chance that these springs were in places where a holy well happened to be needed. At Leeds there are two wells side by side, one chalybeate and the other not (Thoresby 1715: 110). It is the non-chalybeate one which was dedicated as Lady Well and this suggests that, given the choice, people preferred to venerate waters with the purer taste.

But what of other, less obvious influences? The spa industry has had much to say about the subtle effects of trace minerals in the water from various famous springs. Is it not possible that holy wells might have this too and that some scientifically objective healing power might lie behind the stories of saints and miracles? 'Wells in those ignorant times were believ'd to be tinctur'd with Holiness, instead of Mineral Qualities and Virtues', writes Morton (1712: 283). 'Tis very probably owing to a slight Tincture that they have of one or the other, or of all of the afore-mentioned Minerals'.

St Peter's Well at Rushton.
(From Taylor 1894–5: 61.)

Here we are in the domain of analytical chemistry and need to rely on methods more sophisticated than tincture of galls. Fortunately there is a series of reports on spring waters which will provide information here. They were commissioned between 1899 and 1935 by the Geological Survey, who wanted reliable information on groundwater at a time when much of England was still relying on private wells or local reservoirs. Analyses were published for the Holywells at Eastbourne, Horsted Keynes, Southam and Yatton, together with St Mary's Well at Waverley and St Urian's at Bembridge. Others for St Stephen's Well at Banbury and St Kenelm's at Winchcombe appear in the earlier literature.[111]

None of these holy wells has anything in common with the others, except that they are all sources of reasonably good drinking water, with a slight tincture of minerals that varies according to the different geological strata from which they derive. This may be a disappointment, but should not come as a surprise. From 1928 the Geological Survey had increasingly relied on the work of Linsdall Richardson, who wrote their county surveys for Somerset, Warwickshire, Gloucestershire, Worcestershire, Leicestershire and Herefordshire. As his research progressed, Richardson became fascinated by holy wells and made a point of including information on them amongst the hydrological data. But he never found anything to suggest that they had a common character, either in the formations from which they issued, or in the quality of their water. Richardson remains the only qualified geologist to make a field survey of holy wells and his negative conclusions are fairly damning. 'The blessing of a saint is not usually capable of analysis', as Portishead Urban District Council ruefully admitted after examination of their St Mary's Well, for which they had paid handsomely, could find no miracle element (Wigan 1932: 46).

Cures at holy wells in the Middle Ages

If holy wells are so heterogeneous in their chemistry, how can we explain the long-standing tradition that they had power to cure specific ailments? Peter Binnall was able to classify the wells of Northumberland under five headings, according to whether they were recommended for healing sore eyes, skin diseases, weakness in children, madness, or miscellaneous ailments (Binnall & Dodds 1942–6b: 78). In

Wales, there are springs 'alleged to cure nearly all the ills to which human flesh is heir', according to Jones, who was able to tabulate those with a reputation for handling rheumatism, warts, lameness and sprains (1954: 97–9). Janet Bord in her recent survey lists seventeen ailments for which there are frequent promises of cure at British wells, with a further fourteen evidenced at only one or two sites (Bord 2006: 64–70).

Popular tradition is quite emphatic about the special powers of particular wells. In the eighteenth and nineteenth centuries, they seem to have furnished their devotees with a whole pharmacoepia of patent remedies. So it comes as something of a surprise to find that there is barely a whisper of this in the medieval sources, even though they frequently describe cures. Miracles of healing are reported from Bawburgh, Bellingham, Binsey, Canterbury, Cerne Abbas, Corfe Castle, Clent, East Dereham, Ely, Evesham, Finchale, Oswestry, St Ives, Stockwood, Walsingham and Withersdane. From Wales we can add the *miracula* which are appended to the early twelfth-century *Life of Winifred* and the tributes by poets who went to holy wells for cures, or expressed gratitude for them afterwards; there are several of these from the well-shrine of the Virgin at Penrhys.

These accounts do not spare the medical detail. Alexander from the London parish of St Martin Vintry had suffered for five years from an infirmity in his testicles, which in the end swelled up so much that he could hardly pass water. The doctors suggested that he should slip a straw gently down his prick, as a kind of catheter, and he tried this, being careful to tie a thread onto the end of the straw in case it went astray. But, despite these precautions, both straw and thread disappeared into his orifice and he ended up worse than ever before. It was at this point that a friend recommended the water of Earl Simon's Well at Evesham and in desperation Alexander washed himself with a little of this. Behold! suddenly the tip of the straw could be seen. Gingerly wielding a pocketknife, he worked it loose and out came straw and thread and all, after which he sprinkled himself vigorously with more of the holy water and before long Alexander and his tackle were back in working order, thanks to the miraculous powers of Earl Simon and his well (Halliwell 1840: 102–3).

That's one for the 'miscellaneous' column. But what is particularly revealing about this story, by comparison with later traditions, is Alexander's trust that the water of Earl Simon could cure just about anything. There was no question of going to a particular well with a particular problem; instead, sufferers from any ailment would put their faith in the latest cult. Thus we have particularly vivid accounts of a stroke cured at Bellingham, blindness at Ely, deafness at Binsey and general debility at Bawburgh and Cerne, while the cure of dropsy is reported at East Dereham, Ely, St Ives and Withersdane. There is no suggestion that these wells were good for those particular ailments. The selection of dropsy for frequent treatment is probably just an opportunity for rhetorical exercises by the hagiographers, who liked to expatiate on how wonderful it was that a watery disease should be cured by drinking sacred water.

It seems that the hagiographers themselves were sometimes overwhelmed by the disparate nature of the problems cured at their shrines. The chronicler of St Edwold's

Well at Stockwood reports breathlessly that 'many blind people have seen the use of their eyes restored; cripples have stood upright; the deaf and dumb have regained their faculties; lepers and others troubled by many kinds of illness have been healed' (*Nova Legenda Anglie* 1901: 1.362–4). St Eustace's Well at Withersdane cured the blind, lame and dumb in Biblical style. It is clear from the immense crowds frequenting spontaneous shrines like Wembdon and Turnastone that their waters were thought to be good for all ills.

And the cures at wells form only a fraction of those attributed to the saints whose names they bore. For Bawburgh, Binsey, Canterbury, Ely, Finchale and St Ives our testimony comes from long lists of *miracula* kept by the guardians of the saints' relics in a nearby shrine and in these documents well-cures are very much the exception. At Oxford the deaf woman Brichtiva began her search for healing at St Frideswide's church and it was only after this had been unsuccessful that she followed the advice of a helpful bystander to go to the well at Binsey (*Acta Sanctorum: Octobris* 1853: 8.579). There is nothing in these books of miracles to imply that saints specialised in a particular ailment and it would not have been in the interests of the clergy to suggest it. The powers of their patrons had no limits, at least until the next wonder-working saint came along.

Were there non-Christian healing wells in the Middle Ages?

When medieval evidence presents us with healing wells, they are always found in a religious context and are credited with wide-ranging powers. Of course, much depends on how confident we feel about the representative nature of these twelfth and thirteenth-century shrine-cures. After all, they come from a highly specialised literature, created by and promoting the centres of ambitious cults. People came to these places when they had given up all hope elsewhere. Could it be that there had been a parallel, unwritten tradition of wells that specialised in bad eyes, skin diseases and so on? These sites need not even have been holy wells in the sense that we have been using so far; they could have gone under quite ordinary names, not consecrated but just respected for their natural qualities.

Certainly if we look at the evidence collected by folklorists in the eighteenth and nineteenth centuries, it appears that holy wells had no monopoly on healing. It is not easy to come at statistics, but if we limit ourselves to the springs which which were supposed to cure diseases of the eyes, we find that in the Gloucestershire-Somerset borderlands 67 percent of these were not holy wells at all. In Devon, 66 percent are secular sites; in Richardson's surveys of Herefordshire, Worcestershire and Warwickshire, the figure is 65 percent.[112] In each case, holy wells are in a minority of a third and the same would be found for wells which cure skin diseases, rheumatism and other common complaints. It seems as if natural healing wells were the norm, with only a few being marked out by the Church and consecrated.

That was the way things had been in classical antiquity. Sacred wells were known at shrines, but only a minority of these were invoked for healing, while many profane springs had a medical reputation. Cicero's well cured eye problems; another at Leinus prevented miscarriages. At Sicily there were two fountains side by side, one promoting fertility, the other contraceptive. Pliny and the geographers list curative waters from across the Mediterranean world, some to be drunk and other to be bathed in. Each one of them had a patron who recommended it to friends and correspondents, very much in the manner of eighteenth-century gentry (Dvorjetski 2007: 84–7).

But although the Middle Ages stood between these two eras and, although the classical tradition was known to them, they do not seem to have identified any more wells of this kind.[113] Written sources are not entirely reliable here, since they are biased towards the interests of clerics, but there are other sources of information. If secular healing wells had been part of popular tradition, we would expect them to show up in the place-name record. But they do not. We have more than 120 Holywells recorded before the sixteenth century, but there are no names corresponding to the modern Eye Well or Wart Well.[114] Secular healing wells should appear in some kind of evidence – in medical works, household accounts, family letters, or national and local encomia. The medicinal baths of Bath can be found in writing of all these kinds, which shows that people had no reservations about the idea of non-religious healing waters. Indeed, the *Miracles of St Thomas* feature a monk who is on the verge of setting out for Bath to cure his leprosy when he hears of the martyr at Canterbury and is undecided whether to go to the saint's shrine, or continue with the merely medical objective of taking the waters.[115]

It is not just that healing powers were confined to holy wells; out of that number, it was only a minority – the wells of local saints – which were regularly credited with healing powers. Some of the Holywells must have worked cures too, or they would not have attracted the devotion criticised so strongly in diocesan condemnations; but the only universal saints whose wells performed miracles of healing are St John, in the spontaneous cult at Wembdon in 1464 and the Virgin Mary at Walsingham, where Erasmus in 1524 commented on her well being 'good for headache and stomach troubles'. Here, at least, we have a well which is supposed to be good for a specific ailment, but this may just respect a sceptical attribution of its miracles to the effects of cold water.[116]

It must be relevant, too, that after the Reformation the Scottish Kirk spent a great deal of time in summoning people for superstitiously abusing the waters of their local wells. The answers of the accused are often preserved, but they never defended themselves by saying that the wells were just a source of natural healing water, even when they had used it without any associated ritual and even though the wells from which they took it did not necessarily have the names of saints (Morris & Morris 1982: 187–90). If there had been such things as secular healing wells, it would have been a natural defence to say so. When a Provincial Assembly spoke of 'a well... unto which many of the commons resorts superstitiouselly, pretending the water thereof to have vertew of curing deseases', they took it for granted that this was a survival of the old Catholic worship. And they were probably right.

Holy wells and the origins of the spa movement

If we take the medieval evidence at face value, we must accept that the tradition of secular healing wells had effectively died out in the Middle Ages. When people drank from a curative spring, they did so at one place only – the holy wells which were associated with the cult of a saint venerated nearby. But if that is so, how did popular tradition evolve to the state of things we find in the nineteenth and early twentieth century, where holy wells form only a small proportion of all the curative sites? To answer this, we need to look at the rise of the spa movement.

In the last quarter of the sixteenth century, reports of medicinal springs in England began to be circulated among those who had read or travelled widely. Their points of reference were usually Bath, Buxton and the resort of Spa in Belgium, which gave rise to the word 'spa' itself. At first these springs were uncommon and invalids travelled long distances to them, but by the mid-seventeenth century enthusiasts for natural philosophy had discovered scores of sites. Aubrey was forever sending notes on curious springs to his fellow-gentry, encouraging them to set up a second Epsom or Tunbridge Wells in their grounds. The county histories of the following hundred years contain an immense haul of spas or potential spas, few of which had enjoyed even the briefest flicker of social success.

These spas were almost always new discoveries. It was very rare for them to have had a previous incarnation as holy wells – naturally, since these new sites were usually identified through the undrinkable quality of their waters, while the holy wells had been pure springs. But the hot baths at Buxton had been consecrated about fifty years before the Reformation and it is possible that something similar had happened at Bristol; at all events, the Hotwells near Clifton appear for the first time as St Vincent's in William Harrison's 1587 *Description of England* (1968: 284). William Worcestre, visiting the site a hundred years earlier, had not been told of any name for the springs (2000: 45). He did visit St Vincent's chapel and hermitage on the cliff nearby and it it is possible that these became involved in some common cult with the well before the suppression of Catholic worship, although the name may have just come about because these were the nearest identifiable landmark.

St Richard's Well at Droitwich was later marketed as a spa, although this did not happen until the 1830s; the salt which impregnated its waters, and which had prompted the grateful townspeople to dedicate the well to their local saint, came in handy for brine baths. There is better evidence for continuity at St Mungo's Well in Copgrove, where the dedication appears to be early, although it was not recorded until 1620. At Buxton, the marketers of the spa had been able to overcome Protestant scruples about using a holy well by extolling the medicinal value of its warm waters. Copgrove could make no such claim, so its promoters played the opposite card – it was the forbidding cold of the water which was supposed to be curative. Celia Fiennes, who visited in 1697, observed that 'some of the Papists I saw there had so much Zeale as to continue a quarter of an hour on their knees at their prayers in the Well, but none else could well endure it so long' (1949: 81); evidently the austere reputation of the well acted as a front for continued pilgrimage.[117] At Knaresborough

Holy Well at Great Malvern, drawn about 1830. (From Weaver & Osborne 1992: 95.)

Celia shared lodgings with a relic-hunting Catholic and the availability of a manuscript *Life of St Robert* in the town suggests that there were many others visiting his cave, and perhaps his well, out of devotion rather than curiosity. Harrogate, promoted as the English Spa from 1596 onwards, may have been set up as an unconscious rival to these earlier sites; the original Spa in Belgium had itself been a holy well. At all events, Edmund Deane wrote in 1625 that both St Mungo's and St Robert's Well had been 'in great request in these parts amongst the common sort, much sought unto by many, and great concourse of people have daily gathered and flocked to them' (1922: 72) – but, he adds with a hint of wounded professionalism, chemical analysis has shown that there was nothing remarkable in their waters, so it must all be superstition after all. It was not the last time that scientific know-how would be called upon to put religion in its place.[118]

So there were four or five old holy wells which went on to become spas. It is not a very high figure when one thinks of the abundance of watering-places in seventeenth-century England, even if we add to the list Holy Well at Great Malvern, 'said to heale many Infirmities' from 1654 onwards (Osborne & Weaver 1996: 207–14). The loss of holy wells at the Reformation was not a precondition for the creation of a spa industry; after all, there were plenty of spas on the Continent.[119] There are links between holy wells and spas, but they do not derive from the re-use of particular sites. They show themselves much more clearly in the ambience of healing which was common to the two traditions.

Despite its new claims to scientific objectivity, the early spa literature has many passages which strike a familiar chord. Like the wonder-working saints' wells before them, the spas offered cures not just for one or two ailments, but for everything that human flesh could suffer. The Clifton Hotwells were effective against sterility, blood poisoning, fevers, rheumatic pains, scrofula, cancer, venereal disease, nervous headaches, heartburn, colic, bilious vomiting, painful discharges and urinary problems (Quinn 1999: 131). The last of these is exemplified in the case history of John Gaggs, reported by John Underhill (1703: 18–21). Gaggs, a baker from the nearby city, found himself passing at least three gallons of sweet oily urine each

St Eustace's Well at Withersdane. (From Igglesden 1900–46: 1.20.)

St Eustace's Well

night, something which rapidly reduced him to skin and bones. Casting himself on God's mercy, he begged family and friends to support him as far as the Hotwell and made the journey fainting at almost every step until he had just enough strength to drink the water, on which – to God's glory and the amazement of his friends – his strength all came back and he who had relied on others to carry him to the well, now strode home before them up the slope to Bristol. Everything in this story has its echo in the miracles of healing from medieval wells; St Vincent had evidently not deserted his post.[120]

Significantly, the mere experience of drinking the water was enough to cure Gaggs. He did not need to take it regularly, as one might have expected of a medicine; a single moment's encounter was enough. And that is something which seems to derive from the holy well tradition. The water of saints' wells had no efficacy in itself, but it was charged with the power of the saint and pilgrims would try to get as close to that power as possible by drinking deep, or by washing themselves all over with as much of the water as they could get. Originally, the secular wells of Bath and Buxton had been for bathing only – that was the whole point of going to a hot spring – but under the influence of holy well imagery, their waters began to be drunk too. Elizabeth I wrote skittishly to the Earl of Leicester about being sent to Derbyshire for 'as much of St Anne's sacred water as he lusteth to drink' (Lennard 1931: 9). The idea of drinking medicinal water from springs had disappeared from medical tradition in the Middle Ages. If it returned to favour now, that was due as much to a secularised imitation of religious well-cults as to the rediscovery of classical spa lore.

How spas imitated holy wells

If contact with the water from saints' wells had been desirable, then bathing in them was best of all. At Copgrove this was evidently the goal of pilgrims, who up until the early eighteenth century kept up the practice of walking home with their clothes still wet so that they could prolong the time of contact with the water for as long as possible (Floyer 1702: 230–3, 291). But there is also evidence for bathing as a medieval practice. At Withersdane there was a bathing-place (*natatoria*) at

St Eustace's Well and the well of the Virgin at Walsingham seems to have been provided with a bath in the late Middle Ages. The masonry work here shows two phases of construction, the earlier of which has been identified as medieval (Dickinson 1956: 93). The waters of St Withburgh's Well at East Dereham ran into some kind of deep tank; the county historian Blomefield thought it 'a very ancient baptistery', but it is more likely to have been a fourteenth-century bath and it was as a bath that it was rebuilt in 1752 (Manning 1993: 186). The eighteenth century was the great era for constructing these baths at holy wells. Some were installed for the convenience of landowners, often as a garden feature, but others seem to have been intended to benefit visitors who were already coming to the wells to immerse themselves. The excavators of the cold bath at St Mary's Well in Jesmond found it to be eighteenth-century, but the possibility remains that work of this date may have upgraded something at earlier, especially at sites which are known to have had well-cults such as Doulting, Knaresborough, Newton under Roseberry and North Marston.[121]

When St Catherine's Well at Westhorpe was made into a cold bath in 1720, the proprietor (a Mr Burton of Norwood Park) set up a Latin verse praising St Catherine and extolling waters which were as pure and efficacious as their patron saint (Dickinson 1819: 263). This is an odd bit of rhetoric to come from a good Protestant landowner, but it reflects a widespread tendency amongst the proprietors of baths and spas to place their establishments under the patronage of a saint. The builders of New Cold Bath in Shoreditch, which opened in 1731 under the tutelage of St Agnes, evidently thought they needed all the class they could get, although they had to do some violence to the traditional name of Dame Agnes the Cleere to make her into a saint (Foord 1910: 108–12).

Anne was the saint most favoured by the inventors of tradition; this seems to be a tribute to the original site at Buxton. St Anne's Well at Malvern is not recorded before 1744 and, given the extensive documentation for other medicinal wells in the town, this suggests that the dedication was added as part of the development of its spa facilities.[122] Similarly, St Anne's Well at Inglewhite first appears on a date stone carved in an old-fashioned style in the early eighteenth century (Cookson 1887: 341–2). At Brighton, Dr Richard Russell discovered and perhaps named another St Anne's Well in the 1750s, at a time when the resort was beginning to expand along the coastal strip towards Hove (Musgrave 1970: 54, 57–8). St Anne's Well at Siston may be older than this, but it was certainly marketed as a medicinal well on the basis of its name in 1790, when a plaque was put up by the well (Mardon 1857: 143)). Some said that its patron was not the saint, but Queen Anne, and in 1830 a Queen Anne's Well at Chalvey was dressed up as a spa in much the same way (Walters 1953–60).

St Radegund's Bath in Canterbury was fitted for cold bathing in 1777 and given a name borrowed from the nearby St Radegund's Hospice (Gardiner 1939: 112). At least St Radegund had a local connection; St Vincent's Well, a spa at Cosgrove, seems to have begun as Finches Well (Bridges 1791: 1.285). The spring at Astrop was turned into St Rumbold's Well in 1749, when a new wellhead was built, complete with a statue of the saint in a little niche. The medicinal waters at Stoney

Middleton came under the patronage of St Martin, taken from the dedication of the parish church at some time after the late eighteenth century (Cox 1875–9: 2.246).

In two areas – Somerset and the region around Cumbria and Northumberland – we have seen eighteenth-century spas being called Holywells. The voice of the entrepreneur can be heard at at Eastbourne, where the potential of a spring called Holy Well near a fashionable watering place sent one observer into prophetic rapture. 'Time may be when the now almost neglected springs of Holywell, fostered by the sons and daughters of fashion, shall have raised over them splendid saloons and pillared porticoes, rivalling in elegance and beauty the pump-rooms and spas of Cheltenham' (Horsfield 1835: 1.291). A more successful promotion had taken place earlier in London, where Sadlers Wells was founded in 1684 around 'a certain Spring in the middle of a Garden, belonging to the Musick-house, built by Mr Sadler'. The attractions of his music soon proved much superior to those of the well, which was quietly forgotten. But the original publicity for the venue makes a great feature of it, telling how the spring had just been discovered, but then (without any sense of contradiction) adding that 'the water whereof was, before the Reformation, very much famed for several extraordinary cures performed therby, and was therefore accounted sacred, and called Holy-Well' (Hood 1813: 553–4). Needless to say, there are no records of such a site, which could hardly have gone unnoticed in the centre of London. But the proprietors of Sadlers Wells evidently felt that a spa was incomplete unless it could trace an earlier existence as a holy well.

As we have seen, some 5 holy wells actually had a previous history as spas. But these are greatly outnumbered by those which claimed a spurious past – between 15 and 25, depending on how you reckon the evidence.[123] Landscape forgery of this kind has proved an impediment to the study of the original medieval well-cults, but as with other forgeries, the spurious identifications of holy wells tell us much about the era in which they were created. People seem to have felt that a place of healing waters required some sort of patronage from the saints in whom, officially, they no longer believed. The manifest Protestantism of eighteenth-century England co-existed with a twilight world of joke, make-believe and popular memory in which the old religion was not as dead as it seemed.

Did holy wells owe their powers to superstition?

But boundaries were still placed between legitimate and illegitimate belief, and it did not pay to get on the wrong side of them. In the winter of 1751 Matthew Chancellor fell asleep after a violent fit of asthma, and had a dream. Standing in the roadway at Glastonbury, he saw water running along the track, and in his dream he was told that on seven successive Sundays he should drink of the waters, for they ran 'from holy Ground, where a vast Number of Saints and Martyrs have been buried'. Waking, he followed this mysterious advice, after which he was cured. And so began Glaston Spa (Stout 2007). The fame of the waters bought in people from all around – first 800, then 6,000, then 10,000 or 20,000 strangers camping out around the town awaiting a cure. Upper-class observers were evidently taken aback by the speed with which this reputation grew, just as Thomas Bekyngton had been four hundred years earlier by the 'great concourse of people' hurrying to St John's Well at nearby

Wembdon. And then there were aspects to the initial story which made people uneasy. Was it really acceptable to talk about visionary dreams and the bodies of saints, or to lay down a ritual for drinking the drinking the waters? Chancellor had definitely overstepped the mark.[124] By the summer of 1751 the new spa, despite the presence of a Pump Room and the usual medical testimonies, was being dismissed as 'the Popish invention'.

Significantly, although educated bystanders were sceptical about Chancellor and his dream, they had no doubts that the waters of a well might be able to heal ordinary diseases. That was still taken pretty much for granted and many of the contributors to the *Gentleman's Magazine* would have gone for spa cures themselves. It was the unacceptable beliefs held by common people that were too much for them, just as they had been for the high-ranking clerics confronted by spontaneous well-cults in the Middle Ages. Up to the end of the eighteenth century ordinary people were taken seriously by the gentry when they talked about healing wells. There might be something in it, after all. Polwhele in his *History of Devon* (1793–1806: 1.21) records the popular reputation of healing wells amongst the healing springs analysed by doctors, without making anything mysterious out of their claims.

But as the nineteenth century progressed, this level-headed attitude to popular reports of healing water was transformed into something much more emotive. Holy Well at North Molton, which Polwhele had mentioned in passing as 'famous for its medicinal qualities', was the subject of two lengthy surveys in the 1880s (X 1882; Doe 1884: 123). The benefits of the water have become 'imaginary', 'miraculous'; the annual Ascension Day fair is described as a great curiosity. You feel that the people of the Devon countryside are being watched from a distance, through a telescope.

Holy wells, writes Mabel Peacock, are 'imagined to be extraordinarily successful in preserving or giving back the vision'. Indeed so; but after this level-headed observation, she strays into a discussion of Odin's eye, Mimir's well and the learned lore of Northern paganism, as if that explained everything.[125] The folklorists' concept of ancient survivals had begun as a working hypothesis, but it rapidly become a kind of defensive shield with which upper-class observers could protect themselves from listening too seriously to what common people had to say.

Did holy wells owe their powers to medicine?

The treatment of eye diseases was by far the most common use for medicinal waters; it is reported from 65 holy wells, with skin diseases in second place at 25 and rheumatism trailing with 15. 'The enquiry that I always make on the spot is, "Do you find this water of use for any special purpose?". The reply that comes with as much frequency as certainty is "It's wonderful good for the eyes"' (Horne 1923: 7). As a good Benedictine, Horne preferred to trace the origin of this belief to the symbolism of baptism and not to heathen rites, but that was simply another way of ignoring what people were actually telling him. The situation had been very different at the beginning of the spa era. When the Evelyns were told that a well in Upper Deptford was 'famous for the eyes, and many other medicinal purposes', they did not speculate on Viking myth or sacramental symbolism, but simply rebuilt the well with a chain and drinking dish so that everyone could benefit from it (Aubrey 1847: 21).

The discovery of eye wells was not an ancient tradition. It took place in the seventeenth century, along with the promotion of other spas. Copgrove, Great Malvern, Longwitton and the Flintshire Holywell each had an Eye Well to one side of the main curative spring. Aubrey mentions Holywells with this tradition at Sheepscombe and Great Haseley together with several other undedicated examples. The plethora of examples appearing after 1600 seems to represent a new phenomenon, not just an increasing willingness to record an old one. Of course the miraculous wells of the Middle Ages had cured blindness – they could cure anything – but they had certainly not specialised in this treatment.

Of the holy wells which have been identified as healing springs in modern times, a quarter are dedicated to the saints of the universal church and yet this is exactly the category which did not report cures in the Middle Ages. This suggests that their modern healing traditions developed at some time after 1600. There may be a broader cultural continuity in the idea of healing waters, but the belief in cures has certainly not been handed down from generation to generation at the same place. In fact, of the 15 or so wells which were celebrated for healing in the Middle Ages, at least 10 no longer have any modern reputation at all, while the rest are not celebrated now for any of the ailments that they cured then. St Augustine's Well at Cerne Abbas was famed in recent times for promoting fertility and dealing with infant problems (Harte 1986: 43; March 1899: 479) – virtues which are unlikely to have been in much demand when it was part of a monastic precinct.

The advantages of washing sore eyes are more universal, but it is not so clear why people should have identified certain springs as particularly powerful in this respect. Beeby Thompson, after his detailed fieldwork in Northamptonshire (1915–16: 66–79), thought that chalybeate waters had been singled out as eye wells, but the national evidence does not bear this out; only 5 of the eye wells are chalybeate and two-thirds of the chalybeate holy wells have no specific healing reputation at all. There was in any case no general rule by which individual wells cured individual diseases. Floyer (1702: 17) notes casually that St Chad's Well at Stowe had 'the Reputation of curing Sore Eyes, Scabs, &c. as most Holy Wells in England do'.[126] Barmby-on-the-Marsh, Carnforth, East Dean, Hereford, the Huntingdonshire Holywell, Horwood and Maugersbury were all credited with curing both eyes and skin diseases, an odd combination if their powers had genuinely been derived from minerals in the waters, but typical of the mix-and-match lists of ailments whose cure was credited to the early spas.

The one disease whose cure seems to have depended on objective physical qualities of the medicinal well was rheumatism. Here it was not the mineral content of the water that mattered, but its temperature. Half of the 15 holy wells which rheumatics used were said to be extremely cold; among the 10 coldest wells in the country (judging by contemporary report) only 3 did not have rheumatic sufferers resorting to them. They must have been sufferers in more ways than one – St Anne's Well at Nottingham was said to be so cold that it would kill a toad – and yet total immersion was the preferred method of treatment. At the Holy Well in Kentisbeare 'a respected resident … cured himself of a sharp rheumatic attack by lying all along in his clothes in the healing spring' (Chalk 1910: 279).

Rheumatism lacks much of the mythic resonance of blindness. Perhaps that is why it has not featured in any symbolic interpretations of well lore; but it is a disease like any other and one which seems to have been successfully treated by the cold-water cure. The link with water quality is less obvious with other diseases for which holy wells offered a cure, among them colic (Sheepscombe), fits (Bampton), lameness (Charlcombe), King's Evil (Church Eaton), ague (Wark), consumption (Yatton), rickets (Jarrow), gravel (Belford), headaches (Harpham) and swollen glands (Stanley). This is an impressive list, but it is nothing to what was being claimed for England's spas in the eighteenth century, any one of which would have advertised the cure of all these ailments and many more. If we are to question why holy wells had the reputation of being able to heal disease, we should ask the same of Harrogate, Tunbridge, Astrop, Barnet and Scarborough.

Traditional claims about the healing power of water may have originated at the wells of miracle-working saints, but by the 1700s they formed part of the accepted medical pharmacoepia. Doctors would later lose their faith in wonder-working springs, but ordinary people did not. When they continued to visit sites, or to recommend those which they had found particularly helpful, their medical advice was dismissed by educated observers as nothing more than folk tradition. So it was that these healing springs became added to that strange bricolage of lore from many periods that defines what we think of as the holy well.

Conclusions

At the beginning of this survey, I promised to go into some detail about holy wells and then try to answer a few simple questions. Why did people in England decide that certain springs and wells were sacred? When did this happen and what use did they make of them afterwards? We've seen a little of the detail and now it is time for some conclusions.

Holy wells, as we encounter them in today's guides and gazetteers, are supposed to derive from a single ancient tradition, but they are really much more diverse than that. Here is a very rough attempt at a typology of holy well traditions. It begins with the conversion of England to Christianity, even though that is not the beginning of holy wells. There must have been hundreds up and down the country long before then, with an intricate and complex history, but we know next to nothing about that part of the narrative because it ended before the time of written records. The real story, with known facts and actual people, begins after the conversion with:

1. Wells which were used by the great saints of English history – Cuthbert, Chad and Aldhelm. The springs which they had employed for drinking or bathing in life were venerated afterwards in their memory. This tradition begins in the seventh century and similar sites were still being established in the twelfth.

2. Wells which were associated with local holy men – hermits and country priests whose reputation never spread beyond a few villages. Popular from the eighth century, these were called Holywells up until 1250 after which the tradition declined, though some took saints' names. In the countryside, they were often in waste ground or parks, in which the original hermitage was sometimes transformed later into a farm. In towns, they could be found just outside the walls, where the main road brought travellers in.

3. Wells which served as popular religious gathering places, in the same way as crosses or holy trees. These originated in the eighth and ninth centuries as focal points for religion in a countryside where the only buildings were minsters. Some of them may have belonged to that grey area where orthodox faith met the new superstitions of prophecy and revelation. Later most of these Holywells became superseded by parish churches, which in some cases may have been built next to them.

4. Wells which feature among the landmarks associated with a local saint. The saint may have been real but the events of their *Life* are mythical and the landmarks have been chosen to illustrate the manifestations of their power in

familiar places. These legends, originally as fluid as folktales, were fixed in writing from the twelfth century onwards. Stories of this kind continued to be created up until the fourteenth century.

5. Wells which were venerated to compensate for the absence of a powerful saint after their relics had been taken elsewhere. Some were said to have risen from the grave where the saint was exhumed, others were pointed out as landmarks in the village where the saint was born or died. The need for these wells began in the tenth century when the centralising of relics became common and they continued to be created until the fifteenth century, sometimes relying on imagined biographical claims.

6. Wells associated with miraculous cults and visionary experiences. These sites of spontaneous devotion were already troubling the authorities in the eleventh century and continued to arise until the Reformation. Up until the thirteenth century they were usually Holywells; after that, revelations and promises were more likely to be attributed to the Virgin, and the springs are Ladywells.

7. Wells which rose near to a major shrine where miracles were common. The water of these wells seems to have been accepted as one of the many media through which the healing power of the saint could manifest. These were often created some time after the main cult had been established. They are found from the twelfth century at the shrines of local saints and were being created later at sites of Marian devotion.

8. Wells dedicated in tribute to a powerful regional patron saint. Like the dedications of churches, chapels and other landmarks, these expressed loyalty and affiliation, usually to one of the handful of English saints whose cults had a wider reputation. The practice began in the eleventh century and declined in the late Middle Ages with the rising popularity of the international saints.

9. Wells which were dedicated to the saints of the universal church, usually as a means to identify new devotional sites in the countryside. These either accompanied a chapel, or consecrated a space where one might afterwards be built. They were dedicated from 1150 onwards and continued until the sixteenth century as part of the extension of parochial provision into areas of new settlement.

10. Wells dedicated by association, with saints' names applied to them because they belonged to an ecclesiastical landowner, or stood in the churchyard of a saint, or were at some corner of a town where the name of a nearby church or chapel formed the easiest point of reference to identify the well. This was a common figure of speech from at least 1300 and did not imply that the well itself was sacred.

11. Wells which acted as conduit heads and water sources. These were called Holywell, or given saints' names, because they supplied water to a monastic house. This practice was common from 1200 onwards but the wells themselves were not originally supposed to be holy.

Lady Well at Hempsted. (From Walters 1928: fig 34.)

12. Wells which were linked in their cult with a freestanding chapel or a chantry chapel in a church and which formed the site of rituals typically involving a small pilgrimage from the statue of the saint in the main building to the well. Sometimes the sacred journey took place from the nearby town to the well and chapel together. The recorded examples are late medieval but similar customs may have existed earlier.

13. Wells whose waters were drunk at new spas and which were claimed to have been holy wells by entrepreneurs who wanted to give them some of the cachet of the earlier sites. These were invented in the seventeenth century and new ones were being identified throughout the spa boom of the eighteenth.

14. Wells which were locally identified as holy because they had a healing reputation. This was a vernacular version of the spa cult, which continued in popular tradition after the use of medicinal waters had declined in elite culture. Any unusual well was likely to gather a reputation, although there was a deliberate choice of cold ones to cure rheumatism.

15. Wells venerated by Catholics after the Reformation. Some of these had survived from earlier generations, while others were supposed rediscoveries, but the ritual of pilgrimage and prayer was usually new. They helped followers of an underground religion to make contact with each other. The identification of new Catholic wells continued into the nineteenth century.

16. Wells which were used in preference to any other for baptismal water and which were called holy because of this. The custom was common in the eighteenth century but is not heard of earlier and seems to have been part of a grassroots feeling for sacramentalism in the Church of England.

17. Wells given a dedication and fitted with rustic shrines or well-houses by landowners. These are common as garden features in the eighteenth century. Their imagery often mixes classical and Catholic themes.

18. Wells which were dedicated to reflect a High Anglican or Anglo-Catholic sensibility, usually with settings or well-houses in Gothic style. Some were old and some were invented, often through creative abuse of names. The practice had already begin in the seventeenth century, although the involvement of their creators varied from playful interest to serious devotion.

To which one might add wells which have been created in the twentieth and twenty-first centuries by enthusiastic consumers of holy well literature... But enough. It is sufficient to have shown that new holy wells are being discovered by each generation, as the old ones fade out of popular memory. The sacred spring does not flow to us unchanged from some elemental otherworld. Holy wells belong to history, not nature.

Notes

1. A photo of the well appears in Noble, Hilton & Varney (2006: 20) with its inscription reading *Qui non dat quod habet, daemon infra ridet. Anno 1414.* As the diphthong in *daemon* and the use of Arabic numbers might suggest, this is not a genuine fifteenth-century inscription, but a modern improvement. 'Considerable doubt exists as to the history of this structure', says Taylor (1906: 182) and it was rebuilt more than once. The couplet is first recorded in 1825 and has been quoted many times since (occasionally with the misreading *videt*). It is also attributed to a well in Staffordshire (Hope 1893: 153).

2. See Hodgson (1820–58: 2i.308–9), Jordan (1998: 17) and *Nova Legenda* (1901: 1.88–90).

3. The journal *Source* ran from 1982 to 1988 in its first series and from 1994 to 1998 in its second, with a subsequent online incarnation as *Living Spring*. All back numbers can be accessed at http://people.bath.ac.uk/liskmj/holywell.htm The archives of two discussion lists can be followed at www.jiscmail.ac.uk/lists/WELLS-AND-SPAS.html and http://nwi.skyphos.co.uk. Useful information for site-hounds can be found on www.megalithic.co.uk and www.themodernantiquarian.com/home/.

4. A disproportionate bias to early periods runs through well literature. Terry Faull's colourful survey of Devon wells (2004) begins with a historical introduction which features the Celts, the Romans and the Anglo-Saxons at such length that 11 pages out of 18 have elapsed before we get to the tenth century and the first actual record of a holy well. Faull admittedly writes as an enthusiast rather than an academic, but this relegation of wells to a pagan Celtic dreamtime can be found in more sturdy historians. *Continuity and Colonisation*, Alan Everitt's study of early Kentish settlement, devotes a section to holy wells and names a dozen of them as evidence of continued use from pre-English times (1987: 296–300). As far as the records can tell us, five of his sites are medieval, three are known from the eighteenth century and three from the nineteenth, while one is not found in any publication before his own: a weak basis for an ambitious superstructure. Tom Williamson made similar observations in his *Origins of Norfolk* (1993: 141–2) and the same strictures apply. Late medieval pilgrimages, Victorian medical superstitions and local etymologies (true or false) are not, as these writers seem to suggest, varied aspects of a single phenomenon.

5.   At St Ives (*Chronicon Abbatiae Rameseiensis* 1886: lxxix–x), Canterbury (Stanley 1857), Stoke near Hartland (Doble 1970: 73–4), Evesham (Halliwell 1840: 67–8), Winwick (Phelps 1909: 169–70), Athersley (Jackson & Morehouse 1877–86: 1.281), Stainland (Watson 1775: 279–80), Passenham (Bridges 1791: 1.310), Loversall (Miller 1804: 217), Birmingham (Pearson 1901: 60–2), Lower Swell (Royce 1861: 40) and Somersby (Rawnsley 1900: 38–9), respectively.

6.   Some local writers specialised in this discovery of imaginary dedications. The Rev F.W. Weaver found St Peter in Pedwell, St Barbara in Babwell and, most ambitiously, St Ursula in Herswell (1893: 45). Then again, this is a man who assures us that 'All my eye and Betty Martin' is a corruption of *O mihi beate Martine*. All proposed dedications of this kind, from the plausible to the preposterous, have been given their own section at the end of the survey.

7.   The earliest reference to Lady Well at Fernyhalgh is in 1687 (Gillett 1957: 133) and the main records, including the creation of a medieval foundation legend, come from the ministry of Christopher Tootel some forty years later (G.C. 1816). At Brislington, by contrast, there are abundant pre-Reformation records of St Anne's chapel (Richardson 1898; Winchester 1986: 10–24); the chapel was certainly served by a draw-well, but the first writer to identify this as a holy well is the romantic Morris (1885: 481). A few years earlier, a detailed exploration of the site by Nicholls & Taylor (1881–2: 2.123–5) had said nothing of the well. Its cult seems to have begun when Father Grant cleared it out in 1878. The gradual accumulation of opportunities for creating holy wells, from the spa period through Catholic and Anglo-Catholic cults to today's Celtic romanticism, suggests that very modern references to sites cannot really be trusted to go back before the Reformation. When a well appears for the first time in a recent author such as Theo Brown – and she mentions more than twenty which are not found in any earlier source – we can only wonder how it escaped the attentions of county historians, glebe terriers, tithe maps, three successive editions of the Ordnance Survey and several prominent folklorists. It would be nice to think that the housing estate called Holywell, first recorded in 1998 at Studham in Bedfordshire, has preserved by sheer fluke an Anglo-Saxon spring-name, but the odds are against it. Reluctantly, I have excluded all uncorroborated twentieth-century references to wells from the main survey, though there is still hope that they may turn out to be supported by earlier evidence. Readers with comprehensive tastes can hunt them down in a section following the main survey.

8.   Using 'medieval' in an inclusive sense to cover everything up until 1599. Place-names are conservative and those recorded in the later sixteenth century can still be accepted as pre-Reformation.

9.   In a much-quoted passage Janet Bord (1985: 146) suggested that 'there may once have been at least 2000 holy wells in England'. This is more than the known figure; of course many references have been lost, but the idea of an 'original' total suggests that all holy wells were once in existence at the same

time, which is not the case. Given the shortlived nature of well-cults, it may be that there were never more than fifty or a hundred springs receiving actual veneration at any one time, with the others in existence only as place-names.

10. The national survey was divided into the 15 regions of North-East (Durham and Northumberland), Cumbria (Cumberland and Westmorland), the West Riding, the East and North Ridings, North-West (Cheshire and Lancashire), North of Midlands (Derbyshire, Nottinghamshire and Staffordshire), Lincolnshire, Welsh Borders (Gloucestershire, Herefordshire, Shropshire and Worcestershire), Midlands (Leicestershire, Northamptonshire, Rutland and Warwickshire), East of Midlands (Cambridgeshire, Essex and Huntingdonshire), East Anglia (Norfolk and Suffolk), Home Counties (Bedfordshire, Berkshire, Buckinghamshire, Hertfordshire, London and Middlesex, and Oxfordshire), West Country (Devon and Somerset), Mid-West (Dorset, Hampshire, Isle of Wight and Wiltshire) and South-East (Kent, Surrey and Sussex). The areas of each county were taken from Bartholomew's *Gazetteer.*

11. Statistics like these will appear at intervals throughout this introduction; they are derived from a spreadsheet containing details of all presumed medieval wells. The information is given in a table at the end of the second section of this book.

12. Gomme's study of wells (1892: 78–108) was a landmark in its time. While admittedly his ethnographic conclusions are all wrong, you cannot help admiring the sheer intellectual energy with which he assimilated Hope's newly-published data. And his central observation, that cult changes as you move from South-East to upland North and West, still stands.

13. Other early county surveys are Hall (1880) for Northumberland, much amplified by Binnall & Dodds (1941–2; 1942–6a; 1942–6b) who extended the coverage to include Durham; Shore (1890–3) for Hampshire; the endearing Fretton (1890; 1893) for Warwickshire, also covered by Patchell & Patchell (1987) and Bates (1993); and a perceptive study of Lincolshire by Peacock (1895), afterwards updated by Healey (1995a; 1995b; 1998) and Thompson (1999). Taylor's work has received an thorough updating in six volumes by Noble, Hilton and their colleagues (1999, 2002, 2004, 2005, 2006, 2007). At the beginning of the twentieth century, we have a brief survey for Wiltshire by Wordsworth (1905–7), supplemented by Jordan (1998); a study of Essex by Christy & Thresh (1910); and the monumental work by Foord (1910) on London and Middlesex. One of the most thorough surveys was carried out for Northamptonshire by Thompson (1909–10 and ten subsequent articles), on ground which was covered again by Valentine (1984). In the 1920s, Horne published his work on Somerset (1923), supplemented now by Scherr (1986) and by Quinn's comprehensive and thoughtful work on North Somerset and South Gloucestershire (1999). The first contribution on Yorkshire wells came from Smith (1923), covering the East Riding. This has been followed by Bonser (1979) and Ni Brìde (1994) for the Leeds area, Wilson (1991) for wells near

Sheffield, Shepherd (1994) for those around Bradford and Whelan & Taylor (1989) for the whole county. Hackwood (1924) published a survey of Staffordshire, followed by Cope (1945); Richardson (1927) covered Worcestershire; and Walters (1928) wrote a charming book on the wells of Gloucestershire. Cheshire gets its own section in the folklore study by Hole (1937) and Derbyshire was dealt with by Binnall (1940) and later in more detail by Naylor (1983). A survey of the literature for Cumberland was published by McIntire (1944), followed by Page (1990) who also includes Westmorland and Lancashire North of the Sands in an ambitious but unreliably referenced work. The first of the post-war surveys was undertaken by Brown (1957 and six subsequent articles) for Devon, subsequently updated in a beautifully illustrated work by Faull (2004). A hiatus in well publishing followed until 1960s landscape romanticism began to inspire a new generation of researchers. Then Norfolk and Suffolk were covered by Burgess (1978), with further work on Norfolk done by Manning (1993). Notes on Surrey appeared in Baker (1982) and Kent was treated by Martin (1985), French (1999) and Parish (1997a–c; 1998a). Much of this work appeared in small press publications, especially the holy wells journal *Source*, where Potter (1985) published a list for Leicestershire and Rutland, subsequently updated by Trubshaw (1990). *Source* was also the outlet for Otter's work on Shropshire (1985 and four subsequent articles) and Pennick's on Cambridgeshire (1985; 2006). Morrell wrote a pamphlet on Nottinghamshire wells (1988) and Sant produced a booklet on those of Herefordshire (1994). The list would end with Parish on Hertfordshire (1998b), except for the work of the multi-talented Rattue, who has published successively on Oxfordshire (1990), Dorset (1992), Leicestershire (1993), Buckinghamshire (2003a) Kent (2003b) and Surrey (2008). For good measure, we can include the two surveys of Britain published by Bord & Bord (1985) and by Thompson & Thompson (2004). Any remaining deficiencies can be supplied from Gribben's bibliography of wells and well lore (1992). The latest in a series of gazetteers from Bord (2008) builds on all the previous work, both practical and theoretical, and is extensively illustrated.

14.   This body has been gathering and publishing county volumes on place-names since 1925 and their survey is now almost comprehensive, but there is a catch in this for researchers into wells. The pre-War volumes did not include field-names and it is in these that references to Holywells and Ladywells are most commonly found. This means that the counties with full coverage of field-names by the EPNS are those published post-War – Berkshire, Cheshire, Cumberland, Derbyshire, Gloucestershire, Oxfordshire, Rutland, Westmorland and the West Riding – while surveys for Dorset, Durham, Leicestershire, Staffordshire, Lincolnshire, Norfolk and Shropshire are still in progress to a greater or lesser degree.

15.   The adjective *heilag* is found in every Germanic language, derived from the noun *heil* 'omen, good fortune' which also yielded an adjective *heil* 'whole, healthy'. In its original sense, *heilag* must have had the senses of 'awesome, strong in power, knowing what is to come, fortunate' (Green 1998: 16–20).

The missionaries would have found this a helpful adjective to convey the power, not just of God, but of his saints. It was no great step from the pagan king who stepped invulnerably through conflict, '*heilag* in battle', to a spiritual warrior like Oswald or Guthlac. And pagan toponymy had already used collocations of *heilag* with terms for water features. Heiligenbrunn is common in German place-names, as is Heilbrunn. *Helgi-* is common as a qualifier in Norse names and this certainly goes back to the pagan period; when the hero Helgi was born, 'the holy streams were flowing from the hills of heaven' (*Helgakviða* 2). The well of Urð in Snorri is a *helgi brunnr*, which suggests a link with divination lost in later Christian understandings, but certainly present in folklore

16.   The element *halig* is discussed by Smith (1956: 1.225). The final *g*, originally a consonantal *y*, was silent in historic times. In a compound like *haligwella*, the long *a* at the beginning would be pronounced as a short vowel and then gradually this became modern short *o*. The date of this vowel change varies across the country. In Derbyshire it is found as early as the thirteenth century at Breaston, Hognaston and Snelston; over the next hundred years this pronunciation appears in Nottinghamshire, Staffordshire, Warwickshire and Gloucestershire. At the same time it develops in the south-east, with an unlocated *Holiwelle* of 1270 in Surrey followed by forms from Sussex, Essex and Kent. In the south-west, the long Devon *a*, a slightly different sound, is indifferently written *a* or *o* from the fifteenth century onwards. By the late sixteenth century, *o* had become standard throughout the south, but the North of England dialects retained *a* for much longer. Forms such as Hali Well at Welbury were still current at the time of the Ordnance Survey. Change, when it came, was often only a matter of spelling convention; during his work on place-names in Northumberland, Mawer (1920: 116) found that people would write 'Holy Well' but still say 'Halliwell'.

17.   A *holwella* would be a 'well in a hollow', which most wells are, so there is nothing in the landscape to distinguish it from a holy one. A parasitic vowel sometimes develops between the *l* and *w*; this is usually written *e*, but then the medial *i* of *halig* often develops to *e* as well. So in the Midlands and south-east, a fieldname Holewell or a contracted form Holwell could come from either *halig* or *hol* and only the judgement of an English Place-Name Society editor can tell the two apart. The last letter of a name is often sounded indistinctly, so it is not surprising that after the change from *a* to *o* there is occasional interchange between Holywell and Holloway. Fortunately a spring of water looks quite different from a sunken trackway, so that it is possible to check names against the topography. Thus the Holywell at Hognaston in Derbyshire (often attested in medieval forms as a well) is now to be found in Holloway Flat, a field which is wet and has no hollow way in it. On the other hand, Youlgreave in the same county has an equally well-attested hollow way which appears quite clearly on the map, but was reinterpreted as Holy Well by an enthusiastic twentieth-century vicar. Confusion between the two names can be found at Hale in Cheshire, Radipole in Dorset and Chenies in Buckinghamshire, where the original word was 'well' and at Holywell Lake in

Somerset, where it seems to have been 'way'. *Hall*, the modern 'hall', has been suspected as a qualifier for forms such as *Hallewelle*, where one would not expect *halig* to produce a geminate *ll* (Gover, Mawer & Stenton 1940: 293; Dodgson & Rumble 1970–97: 4.285). *Halh*, a corner of land, has yielded modern Hallow Well in at least one instance (Cameron 1959: 1.117), although here there is more risk of confusion with the dedication 'All Hallows' Well'.

18. This is what happens when *hæl* appears in the name of Elwell, near Upwey in Dorset, which was *Helewill* in 1212 (Mills 1977–89: 1.247). In Devon, the name which was *Hellewelle* in 1238 has become the modern Halwell Farm, but here the vowel change is irregular because it was influenced by the nearby parish of Halwell (Gover, Mawer & Stenton 1931–2: 1.323). Otherwise, *hæl* and *halig* are words which develop separately and are not easily confused.

19. The well at Gloucestershire is *circa* 800 and that at Stoke *circa* 960 but here, as elsewhere in the introduction, I have given the dates as rounded figures. The more accurate date is always given under the entry for the well in the Survey.

20. The frequency of wells on Anglo-Saxon charter boundaries may be misleading – for this period, we know more about borderlands than anywhere else – but there are later records as well. We have boundary Holywells at Barnwell St Andrew, Bingfield, Cam, Clutton, Englishcombe, Harlow Hill, the Northamptonshire Holywell (used for beating the bounds), Seaton, South Dissington, Westerham, Winterton and Yardley Hastings; there are also boundary wells dedicated to Mary at Silverston and Threshfield, Patrick at Lancaster, Dunstan at Witham Friary, and Thomas at Bapchild and Cobham. The Halesowen/ Clent border seems to have been deliberately run through St Kenelm's churchyard, the well being just on the Halesowen side. The most conclusive examples are those wells at three-parish-meets: Clutton, Witham Friary and Yardley Hastings. Beeby Thompson (1917–19: 46) thought that wells were called holy because they were on boundaries. When we add up all the examples, there are only about 30 of these, too few to suggest any regular association of boundaries and holy wells, but enough to show some kind of bias to border locations. It may a side-effect of the dedication of wells in isolated places, or *halig* may have had a boundary sense, as it did in pagan antiquity (Green 1998: 19); Halmpstone in Devon and Holybourne in Hampshire are also on boundaries.

21. Assuming that OE *wella* always means 'well, spring of water', an interpretation which is not as secure as it might seem, since Gelling (2000: 31) allows for a secondary meaning 'stream'. Compounds with *crymbed*, 'crooked *wella*', and *ford*, 'ford of the *wella*', certainly cannot refer to springs. Layamon (*Brut* line 10587) uses the word for a stream but this sense is not found in later ME. In charters, all the references to *halig wella* definitely belong to springheads (at Olney the well is distinguished from the *halig broc*) and generally the sense 'spring' will fit all the Holywell place-names. There does not seem to be any difference in meaning among the regional variants of *wella*. *Wiella* in Devon

yields modern forms in -will and in the West Midlands the modern dialect -wall (rhyming with pal, not pall) derives from OE *wælla* (Smith 1956: 2.250). This is conventionally described as a Mercian form, but Watts (1999–2000: 61) has shown that it belongs to a very specific social-geographical area of woodland with non-nucleated villages.

22. Welsh Holywells can be found in Jones (1954: 153, 176, 184, 195, 200, 210).

23. I am following the views on language assimilation of Townend (2002), though he doesn't mention *kelda*.

24. For *kelda* in place-names, see Smith (1956: 2.3). Its duration as a productive element can be deduced from the Scandinavian and medieval personal names with which it is compounded – Colmán's keld, Skammbeinn's keld, Baldwin's keld and so on (Smith 1961–3: 5.31, 91, 172 and 7.292–303).

25. At Leigh, the *hwit wylle* of a 972 charter appears in the same place as the Holywell of the Ordnance Survey. In Gloucestershire, Wanswell, 'the well of a man called Wægn', is a small estate and Holy Well is virtually the only water source in it; moreover, it feeds the moat of the manor house, which presumably replaces the dwelling of the eponymous Wægn. At Wells in Somerset, there is no doubt that the late medieval St Andrew's Well was originally just 'the great spring of Wells'. Lady Well at Whelmstone Barton occupies the site of a cress well in an eleventh-century charter and 'Our Ladyes well of Whytewell' *circa* 1550 at Barton near Grantchester sounds very much like a renaming. St Anne's Well at Nottingham had previously been Robin Hood's Well, and perhaps Owswell before that. And it may be that St Swithin's Well at Stanley is the site called Wodwelle in 1284. These six or seven instances are the most reliable evidence for the dedication of previously secular wells. I am much less happy with the other examples that have been proposed – St Anne's Well at Welton in the East Riding, St Michael's Well at Well in the West Riding, Holy Well at Welbury in the North Riding, St John's Well at Welham in Nottinghamshire, Holy Well at Welton in Northamptonshire, Holy Well at Brightwell Baldwin in Oxfordshire, St Mary's Well at Willesden in Middlesex, Lady Well at Eastwell in Kent, St George's Well at Wilton in Somerset, Lady Well at Coffinswell and St Nectan's Well at Welcombe in Devon. In each of these cases the settlement is definitely named after a well of some sort but we have no reason to believe that this was the holy one. St Julian's Well at Wellow is not relevant, as this settlement name is not from *wella*. Lady Well at Abbotskerswell is a spurious dedication.

26. *Halig* also differs significant from the usual set of pagan names in its collocations. Whereas the names of the discredited gods – Woden, Thunor, Tiw and Frig – are typically compounded with words for open spaces, *feld* and *leah*, and sometimes with *beorh* and *hlaew*, *halig* is hardly ever found with these generics (though there is one *halig beorh*, Hillborough in Kent: (Smith 1956: 1.225). And theophoric names never appear with *wella* as a generic. The principal word for temple, *hearg*, belongs exclusively with *dun*, 'hill'.

Weoh, which seems to mean a temple of smaller and more local status, follows the same pattern, although there is a single instance of it combined with *wella*, at Wyville, *Uuiuuella* 1106x23, in the Lincolnshire parish of Saltby (Ekwall 1960: 541). Places called *halig*, it seems, may have formed part of heathen thought but they were not associated with the gods. This suggests that our one pagan holy well known to have been converted by an Anglo-Saxon missionary – the well of Fosite in Heligoland which Willibrord used for baptisms – was never actually called *halig wella*. In Iceland, though paganism survived until much later, sacred springs were identified as something distinctively Christian. When Bishop Guðmund Arason toured Iceland in the late twelfth century, he asserted the rights of the Church by performing miracles and consecrating springs. Many took a dim view of these blessings and counterattacked by pissing in springs which the Bishop had just dedicated (Cormack 2007: 233). This would have been self-defeating if they had been converted heathen sacred places.

27.   Flint (1991: 204–216) has suggested that purist preachers often took their stand precisely because they disapproved of the work of their contemporaries in dedicating and consecrating landscape features; one priest's pagan abomination might very well have been his colleague's popular shrine. But conciliatory clerics of this kind are rare in the records, however much we nowadays would prefer them to the more austere sort.

28.   Thus the *Penitential of Pseudo-Theodore*. In *Pseudo-Egbert* the penance is softened up a bit, with one year on bread and water followed by two as a vegetarian, but returning to the bread and water diet on Wednesdays and Fridays. These clauses against the veneration of trees, stones and wells have been cited as evidence of rural paganism ever since Hammond (1689: 658). A more critical examination (Watkins 2007: 76–9) has shown the derivative nature of the texts.

29.   The continued existence of divination at wells is attested by place-names. The name *freht wella* 'well used for omens', is so common as to be almost a compound appellative; it is discussed by Hough (1996–7) and Baines (1997), to which can be added the field-name Fretwell Close in Tadcaster (Smith 1961–3: 4.79) and possibly a Friswell in Bexley (Rattue 2003b: 36). *Hæl*, probably 'omen', appears in the Lincolnshire Holywell, the Dorset Elwell in Dorset and the Devon Halwell, as noted above. Two Hell- names in Rutland and one in Staffordshire are likely to derive from the same element, although early forms are lacking (Cox 1989–92: 51, 123; Oakden 1984: 1.139), and a case could be made for Hellwell Lane in Kentmere (Smith 1967 1.167) and a Hell Well in the Northamptonshire parish of Maidwell (Thompson 1917–19: 45), although in late forms there may be confusion with *elle* 'elder tree'. As we have seen, *hæl* is cognate with *halig*; both adjectives derive from Gmc *heil* and are distinguished by the use of the intensifier *-ig*. The compounding of *hæl* with *wella* as a qualifier distinct from *halig* implies that it had its own semantic field and this seems unlikely to have happened until *halig* began to develop new meanings under the influence of Christianity. One would therefore expect

place-names of the Helwell type to have originated after Christianisation, expressing an idea ('well of the omens') which was no longer legitimate in the dominant religion. Certainly the Dorset and Devon examples lie far outside the area settled in pagan times. If this were the case, there should be a parallel history behind German Heilbrunn names. I doubt whether the place-names in *seofon* (Briggs 2007) or *run* (Gelling & Cole 2000: 330) should be considered in this context. The first uses 'seven wells' in the idiomatic sense of 'many wells', without necessarily implying anything marvellous about them; in the second, *run* might be interpreted as 'counsel, advice', but is just as likely to mean 'low murmuring sound'.

30.   The right to canonise was not reserved to the Pope in canon law until 1234, but the process had been initiated twenty years earlier by Innocent III.

31.   There are, in theory at least, two sorts of wells by roads or paths – those where the road was laid out to go past the well and those where the well happened to lie beside an existing road. The distinction is important from a historical point of view. The wells in the second category are likely to have begun as wayside sources of refreshment for travellers and then been consecrated; those in the first must owe their dedication to some other cause, after which their well-cult attracted enough people to alter the road system. In Derbyshire, for instance, Baslow, Clutton and Kings Newton seem to have been dedicated beside pre-existing tracks, whereas at Hognaston and Repton tracks have been diverted to go past the well. But without a detailed knowledge of local topography it is not possible to take this further.

32.   This grading of locations is inevitably subjective, especially when it has been done from the written record and not from mapwork. The ideal would be for a consistent corpus of mapped wells, such as those on the Ordnance Survey, to be measured in their distance from some agreed benchmark of centrality, such as the named village points on a road atlas. There would need to be weighting factors, because the density of settlement itself is different for different regions. These methods would yield a more accurate figure for the centrality or isolation of wells. The present survey has been very much document-based and it would be interesting to test some of its conclusions against fieldwork.

33.   Athanasius' *Life of St Anthony* (caps 49–50). The discovery of the chosen site and its well long continued to be a topos; it features in the *Life of St Guthlac*, which is closely modelled on that of Anthony, and more realistically in the account of the twelfth-century hermit of Dale. 'He discovered in the valley a spring, beside which he made himself a hut and built an oratory in honour of God and the blessed Mary' (Hope 1883: 20). Thompson and Thompson (2004: 40–5) list some sites where the topography of well and cliff seems intended to replicate examples from the classic *Lives* rather than serving any immediate practical use. Like Robert, the hermit of Dale had to reckon with local magnates telling him to get off their land. Both men were connected to the trading elites of local cities (York and Derby) and this may have helped their negotiations in ways that the hagiographers do not deign to notice.

34. The eremitical life was an austere one, but not quite as demanding as it looks in the pictures. A close reading of Clay (1914) and the less spiritual sections of the *Ancrene Riwle* reveals the presence of hermits' servants, hermits' cows and even a Mrs Hermit (though she had admittedly married him before he took up religion). In Caradoc's *Life of Gildas* the saint is said to have occupied the hermitage with its well on Steep Holm, living off eggs and seawater, but then we are told that he had to flee before pirate raids because his furniture was likely to get damaged and the servants wouldn't stay – a more realistic assessment of the situation. As Blair has noted (2002a: 462), when eremitical saints were enshrined at minsters they were more likely to achieve a lasting reputation; this could be the result of posthumous patronage, but minster dependencies may simply have attracted a better class of hermit in the first place. At one end of the social scale, a recluse like Edith of Lancelin was evidently retreating to a respectable if frugal existence at Binsey; at the other, it is not altogether clear how one could tell a hermit from a pious squatter. Near Trentham Priory in 1246 there was a *heremitorium fontis de Dunstal, cum terra quam Walterus heremita elaboravit* (Parker 1890: 303; *Victoria CH Staffs* 1908–84: 3.136). If hermits were commonly *elaborantes* land from waste in this way, it would explain many of our isolated Holywell Farms.

35. Holy wells at bridges are not uncommon; we have examples at Barking, Caversham, Clodock, Corfe Castle, Draughton, Linslade, Norham, Oxford, Pateley Bridge, Shotley Bridge, Siston, Stockton-on-Tees and Tottenham, with fords at Thorp Arch and Wetheral. Some of these have developed from roadside shrines on the way out of town, as at Colchester; others may be reflecting the magical and liminal status of bridges, if their location is not just coincidence. Other wells close to streams, but not apparently by bridges, include Brancepeth, Burnsall, Caldbeck, Coverham, Doveridge, Durham, Elvet, Lea Town, Leigh (St Catherine's Well), Swanmore and York (Lady Well). Given the logic of the water table, one would expect sometimes to find springs on or near the banks of a river and it is not clear if these were deliberately chosen for some symbolic value as holy wells, or whether they just happened to be near the right place at the right time. At Carnforth, Clifton and Marden the springs continued to flow though even though covered by the river water and that must have seemed miraculous. See Bord (1985: 80–5) for the veneration of other wells with unusual properties.

36. Goscelin writes of the *fons sancti Eadwardi* at Corfe Castle, the *fons beati Yvonis* at St Ives and the *Augustini fons* at Cerne Abbas. The wording is different each time, as if no standard phrase had yet been agreed. Goscelin's contemporary Osbern says of a well somewhere in Kent *Dunstani nomen celebre facit*, 'the name of Dunstan makes it famous', but this is simply elegant variation. Then in the twelfth century the names take on a more regular form – *fons Sancte Hilde* or the like (Aislaby *circa*1110, Farnham and Sawley *circa*1140, Guisborough *circa*1150, Finchingfield *circa*1180, Derby *circa*1190) or *fons beati Nectani* and so on (Stoke near Gartland *circa*1150, East Dereham *circa*1150). It took English a while to catch up with this formula. We have a *Dewyes Well* in 1242 at Dewsall, although this is on the

Herefordshire border and must be influenced by Welsh practice. Austle in Cornwall, from Augustine's Well, is a similar development (Smith 1956: 2.253). But the same cannot be said for St Aidan's Well in Bamburgh and that appears as *Edynwelle* as late as 1383. Generally, however, the new form was standardised in Middle English by the fourteenth century. The *South English Legendary* of circa1310 routinely speaks of *seint Edwardes welle* and *seint Kenelmes welle*. Rollason (1989: 176) discusses the growth of 'saint' as a title in other contexts.

37.   Among the British saints, I have distinguished very local cults from more regional ones, on the simple (and simplistic) rule that any saint with more than two dedications counts as regional. For a comparative exercise, see Rattue (1995a: 62). His 'Biblical' and 'other' are my non-British, his 'local' my local, his 'dispersed' and 'cluster' my regional.

38.   The division between saints and ordinary folk, in theory so very clear-cut, turned out in practice to be something of a sliding scale, since venerated founders and patrons were remembered with a respect which soon shaded into cult. The prevalence of saints in Wales, compared to England, is due partly to a more tolerant inclusion of these minor figures and partly to a landscape much richer in autonomous churches to celebrate their memory. Blair (2005: 374–83) has argued that the distinction made between England and the Celtic West in the establishment of early medieval churches has been overdrawn. In both regions we find natural features, holy wells among them, which form the focus around which first chapels and then parish churches could grow. Stevington and the Huntingdonshire Holywell are his most convincing examples, although a holy well is not really credible as the origin of a local church unless it can be shown to belong to one of the categories which were current before the eleventh century. Nor can the distinction between the nations be put down entirely to a parting of the ways after circa1000, for the well-cults of universal saints, which must be twelfth-century or later, are still three times more common in Wales than in England.

39.   Loomis (1948: 23, 37–9, 70, 76, 104, 124–5) has a formidable catalogue of saints who worked well-miracles.

40.   See Edwards (2004). She could have added that the name Alchhild actually appears in an Old English text (*Widsith* line 97).

41.   Stories of lovely virgins fleeing from lustful pursuit may have appealed for less pious reasons and hagiographical bodice-rippers of this sort became popular in the eleventh and twelfth centuries. However, local legends like these were only a subset of the numerous *Lives* of virgin martyrs, a genre capable of meaning many different things to different audiences (Winstead 1997). Bede is sober in his approach; he uses the motif of the well springing at the place where blood is shed, but only for the two brothers Hewald, who were killed for preaching in Frisia (*Ecclesiastical History* 5 cap 10). But as his treatment of Oswald shows, Bede was sensitive to the difference between being martyred

and merely being killed, while popular tradition made no such distinction. Nectan and Decuman were martyred only in the sense that they were killed by robbers, as Osyth and Alkelda were by Vikings; Kenelm, Ethelbert. Fremund and Edward by political rivals; and Arild, Sidwell, Urith and Juthware by envious relatives. In the earlier understanding of martyrdom, the deaths of the Hewalds were attended by the miraculous witness of a well because they themselves died as witnesses to Christ. In the later legends, holy wells act instead as testimony to a kind of magical personal sanctity, which is fixed at one spot by the act of violent death. See Webb (2000: 155–9) and Hayward (1993) for this fascination with the victims of violence and Gurevich (1988: 41) for its logical conclusion; on hearing that their local holy man was thinking of moving away, villagers decided to kill him there and then, so that they would continue to enjoy his blessings.

42. Rattue (1995a: 56) gives a statistical analysis of holy wells and minsters, arguing for instance that Dorset with ten known minsters has a well associated with each minster. But without tighter control over the typological analysis of wells, these statistics are inconclusive. Cerne and Wareham both count towards his figure of ten, but whereas the well at Cerne was indeed created by a minster priest in the tenth or eleventh centuries, at Wareham the well is named after a sixteenth-century chapel which happens to be in an old minster town.

43. The *Lives* are discussed by Blair (1987). St Frideswide continues to arouse a certain *tendresse* among Oxonians; to the studies by Mayr-Harting and Blair can now be added a reassessment of her miracles by Yarrow (2006: 169–89).

44. An Exeter relic list refers to *Sancta Satiuola... seo wæs unsceððiglice acweald fram hire fæder mædmannum* (Conner 1993: 186–7). If, as seems likely, the text derives from a *schedula* linked to the relics, this would probably have been written in 932 when the cathedral acquired its main relic collection. She appears in the eleventh-century literature on the resting-places of the saints as Sidefulla or Sidefulle, from which the modern Sidwell has been developed. This might be taken as an eccentric use of OE *sideful*, 'modest, honest' used as a personal name, if it were for the Latin form. This cannot be derived phonologically from Sidefulle. Förster (1932–3) suggested that it was an attempted translation on the lines of *satis voluntatis*, 'of sufficient (good) will (for God)', but his only authority for this rather forced pun was Grandisson's fourteenth-century version of her *Life*, where it is introduced as a typical hagiographical play on names. It is more likely that OE Sidefulle and Latin Sativola both derive from an earlier British name, something like the Sitofolla recorded in the *Life* of St Paul Aurelian.

45. See Whiting (1989: 55–61) for the sacred landscapes of Devon and Cornwall in the generation before the Reformation, with stones, hills, trees and relics taking their place alongside the wells. This was an world of very local devotions, where even pilgrimages seldom involved more than a day's walk to a neighbouring shrine.

46. Stones sometimes make an appearance in the sacred narratives of holy wells. St Nectan rested his head on one after decapitation; it was evidently a light-coloured stone, foreign to the local geology, or the marks of the saint's blood would not have been so visible on it. At St Chad's Well in Stowe, the saint on which the saint rested was shown to visitors, a constant landmark through repeated rebuildings. Maen Beuno is still present at Holywell – 'the only object at the well that St Winefride would recognise if she came back today' (Bord 2006: 126). The 'stone 3 foot in length and 2 in breadth called the holy stone' at Lady Well in Holystone (Hodgson 1916: 3) was also said to be the place where a saint knelt, in this case Paulinus, but since his presence at the well derives from a mistranslation, the tradition may have been transferred from St Winifred's Well. At Moxby and Manningham modern lore identified wishing stones near the holy wells.

47. We may not know what the twelfth-century trees were like, but there are plenty of contemporary examples. A web search for Prado Nuevo will show an ash tree, and not a very old one, growing above a well which was revealed at this Spanish shrine a few years ago by the Virgin Mary; no continuity here. It is curious that these are usually ash trees, though the staff of St Benignus was said to have become a yew (Barber 2001: 147), probably influenced by the nearby yew of St Congar. People preferred flourishing young ash trees as the emblems of their saint, because they looked tall and impressive, not twisted and old. Besides, ash is the tree which sprouts up most readily in fenced-off areas, including the enclosures which often mark out a precinct for holy places. Pagan veneration of sacred ash trees, which has its cosmological equivalent in Yggdrasill, may have come about in the same way. This sheds some doubt on assertions (Blair 2005: 477) that because 'the ash was the archetypal sacred tree of northern paganism... these associations were a veneer on a pre-Christian substratum'. Christians and pagans both venerated trees growing in their sanctuaries, but this was a development which had arisen for the same reasons in both traditions, not an influence of one on the other. Ash seedlings are not particular about where they sprout.

48. Not to mention the eel of St Nectan, the only remarkable fish found in an English holy well, although there are several in Celtic tradition (Bord 1985: 119–22). But we should be wary of regarding this imagery solely as a link with nature. The fish stories are primarily about the right forms of hospitality and generosity. They always involve a feast of some kind; the Nectan miracle takes place in a guildhouse.

49. The traditions are found in Royce (1861: 16). St Edward the Confessor can be ruled out, since the settlement already appears as *Eduuardestou* in 1086. The donation of lands by Ethelred is recorded in a charter purportedly of 1016, but this is not a reliable document; it is part of the process by which the original obscure Edward was upgraded to royal status (Jones 1999: 127–9). Even the existence of a local saint Edward is unproven, since the dedication may be a hagiologising form, like Plemstall.

50. But the motif of the pissing oxen did not emerge unprompted from the Norfolk mind; it is found also in the Irish *Life of St Faucee* (Loomis 1948: 37). It is hard to believe that the story was deliberately adopted by a Latinate hagiographer, since the redactor in the *Nova Legenda* is clearly embarrassed by the whole business. There must have been a vernacular underworld of story-telling about saints.

51. There is a well-miracle associated with St Modwen; unable to supply her noble guests with fitting hospitality, she sent her servants to the spring outside the monastery, where they drew beer instead of water (Geoffrey 2002: 179). This comes from one of the Celtic lives, although it is tempting to think that the story appealed to an author based in Burton upon Trent; certainly the miraculous brew had 'a flavour that had never been achieved in those parts by human efforts'. The analogy between the saint-abbess and her real-life counterpart, harassed by having to entertain prestigious visitors from limited funds, is very close to the surface here (cf. Wogan-Browne 1992).

52. But we might suspect direct Celtic influence in two Cumbrian well chapels. Excavation showed that a stream ran south out the door at Holy Well at Gosforth, while sketches of St John's Well at Skelsmergh make it clear that the water ran westwards inside the chapel. Thompson & Thompson (2004: 15–16, 77–9, 195–204) discuss similar arrangements in Wales and Cornwall and suggest that the church at Kirkoswald was aligned on the stream running through it. Page (1990: 4) proposes that all Cumbrian churches were built over springs, but he means the 'underground springs' of dowsing theory, which are not the same as ordinary hydrological water. Calder (2003) argues that Kewstoke also had a well-chapel in Celtic style though nothing survives in tradition. It is not clear if the Continental examples cited by Morris (1989: 87) belong with this group. The chapels or churches at Slepe/ St Ives, Clent, Cerne and (possibly) Marden are a quite different phenomenon; they were built from the eleventh century onwards to incorporate a venerated spring, but the water did not have the ritual significance that it seems to have been given in the Celtic well chapels.

53. See Jankulak (2000) for the cult of St Petroc.

54. The building at Woolston was shown by Dovaston (1886) to be a folly, reusing timbers from West Felton church. It has recently been reidentified as a converted medieval chapel, on the basis of a dendrochronology date of 1485 for the timbers (Bord 2008: 111), but this misses the point; the timbers are old, but they do not come from Woolston.

55. Wells of St Winifred in England are discussed by Gray Hulse (1994). Scully (2007) provides a short history of the original St Winifred's Well. A longer study is in preparation by Tristan Gray Hulse.

56.　Sharpe (2001) discusses the textual evidence for the *Passio*, which exists in three forms of which the shortest (his E) is the original. The claims for a third-century date in Morris (1968) are not valid.

57.　Liveing (1906: 22–3) tells the story. St Modwen, too, 'on winter nights used to chant the whole psalter, staying awake all night in prayer, immersed in water up to her shoulders, while the other sisters slept' (Geoffrey 2002: 179) and the well in which she did this was later the scene of miracles. Other austerity wells are discussed by Clay (1914: 119), Doble (1970: 12) and Bonser (1937). The ascetics professed to imitate St Paul 'in weariness and painfulness, in watchings often, in hunger and thirst, in fastings often, in cold and nakedness' (2 Cor 11: 27).

58.　The account in *Liber Eliensis* (2005: 145–8) is a great story, but it may not be true; the conformity to other accounts is too strong (Rollason 1989: 180; cf. Geary 1978)

59.　The well at East Dereham appears first in Goscelin's *Life of St Withburgh* and slightly later in his *Miracles of St Withburgh* (Goscelin 2004: 66–7, 206). The place where a saint's body had lain was often venerated *faute de mieux*, as Bede illustrates in his account of Oswald's death-place. After the translation of a saint's body, the empty grave continued to be venerated (Blair 2002a: 490–1) and if the grave was dug deep enough to expose water, then so much the better. This seems to lie behind the wells recorded after the translation of Kenelm, Ive, Audrey, Withburgh and Edward. At Meare a well arose miraculously when St Benignus made a hole in a reed bed, which even on the most charitable reading isn't much of a miracle.

60.　Of course all wells acted as substitutes for the saints, wherever their bodily remains might be. Spiritual *potentia* needed to be conveyed from the body itself to the devotee and this meant contact; by the sixth century Rome was exporting pieces of cloth which had been in touch with the holy bodies and absorbed some of their power. Already in Bede, water is accepted as the medium by which the power of sacred relics can be more fully ingested, as happens in the cults of Oswald and Chad (*Ecclesiastical History* 3 cap 11, 13; 4 cap 3). 'The dipping of relics in water or wine remained the commonest method of healing practised in the pilgrimage churches of the eleventh and twelfth centuries' (Sumption 1975: 82), although there were those who gagged at the practicalities; a monk of Mont St Michel announced that he would prefer to die than to drink wine swilled in the head of a corpse and, in the early stages of the cult of St Thomas, the martyr's blood was deliberately diluted with water so as not to cause offence. The holy well, whose connections with the blood of martyrdom were purely metaphorical, might be expected to appeal to such fastidious types. But in practice it does not seem to have competed with other practices, such as water in which the dust from a tomb had been soaked. We find both methods listed in the cures from St Walstan's shrine at Bawburgh. One miracle worked by the well linked with

St Frideswide contrasts with many worked by 'blessed water' at her tomb (Ward 1982: 85).

61. Blair (2005: 217) discusses *stow*; the element was in regular use to characterise places with local cults by the tenth century. Although there is no necessary connection with holy wells, it may be relevant that Stow in Lincolnshire (*Estou* in Domesday) has a St Michael's Well.

62. 'It is striking that the greatest concentration of murdered royal saints arose in the late eighth and early ninth centuries, shortly after the papal legates who visited England in 786 had presided over the promulagation of one of the strongest condemnations of royal murder ever made in England' (Rollason 1983: 17). If the cult of royal saints arose as a response to historical circumstances, we do not need to explain it by vague notions about 'sacral kingship'. Wells served as outward signs of the victim's innocence, which is why they feature in 4 out of Rollason's 10 narratives of murdered kings and princes.

63. Wulfade and Rufinus first appear in the fourteenth-century *Catalogus Sanctorum Pausantium in Anglia*. Their story is modelled on Bede's account of the killing of two princes at a place called Stone, except that these were the heirs to the Isle of Wight and their *Ad Lapidem* was in Hampshire (Rumble 1997). Why an Anglo-Saxon prince should be called Rufinus is not clear, although his well at Tamworth seems to be the first record of the whole business, being mentioned in 1276. St Chad's Well at Stowe was evidently an existing holy well introduced into the *Passio* to add an air of verisimilitude to an otherwise bald and unconvincing narrative.

64. The proposal that Oswald's death and the exhibition of his body took place at two different places is my own. Stancliffe (1995) assumes they are one and the same, as in Reginald, and indeed follows him in identifying Oswestry as the site. But Bede's account of *Maserfelth* makes it clear that there was no physical focus of cult there – that was why people were taking earth away from the death-spot – whereas the head-stake on which Oswald's remains were exhibited rapidly became the centre of veneration and was whittled away to provide curative chippings. It must have been somewhere else. The *Life* refers to Oswald's head and arms, but we only hear of the right arm; Aidan's blessing, 'may this hand never decay or wither', seems designed to accommodate the fact that it was receiving separate cult, an anomaly in Anglo-Saxon England. Presumably the left arm was lost on the battlefield. It is not clear how anyone ever located the body of Oswald which came to be venerated at Bardney; perhaps it was revealed in a dream, like Edwin's. Rollason (1989: 127) thinks that Reginald's story represents the original cult of Oswald, but then has to explain how none of it appears in Bede by assuming that the marvellous raven and tree were too much for the taste of that solid historian. These difficulties all disappear if we assume that the cult actually evolved from respectable simplicity to pagan complexity, as many cults do.

65. The story of the marvellous raven seems to have been in circulation before Reginald's time. A romance, written in the later twelfth century at the Bavarian city of Regensburg, presents Oswald as a fairytale king who falls in love with the daughter of a Saracen potentate, after which the lovers communicate by means of a wonderful speaking raven. This is an unexpected choice of bird for a romantic messenger and it is hard not to suspect influence from the legend at Oswestry; if this was carried to Germany, it is likely to have been when Judith, sister-in-law of Harold II, married Welf IV of Bavaria in 1066x94 (Stancliffe & Cambridge 1995: 212–30).

66. Unlike *stow*, *stoc* does not appear in association with any later saints, which could be taken as corroborating a pre-Conquest origin for these cults and perhaps their wells. But the Dorset form *Bindonestok* for Bindon Abbey, founded in 1172, shows that it remained productive well into the twelfth century.

67. The author of the *Liber Eliensis* thought of Audrey herself as resisting the assault of Ely; another example of the identification of a saint-abbess with the fortunes of her house and perhaps a reason why the well which served her besieged community could have been named after her (Blanton 2007: 157–66).

68. Charlton (1779: 32) used the form Hilderwell, but he was being deliberately archaic.

69. The presence of the historic Plegmund at Plemstall is 'unlikely in the extreme', according to Blair (2002b: 469). Names in -stow are frequently given hagiologising interpretations when their qualifiers really refer to landowners and not saints at all. Thus, while the wells at Plemstall and Maugersbury could record obscure hermits who have been collated with their more famous namesakes, it is equally possible that there never was an original cult and the dedications were made later in the Middle Ages.

70. The story bears a strong resemblance to that of St Benignus, who was invented (and not just in the ecclesiological sense) at Dijon in the sixth century. Here likewise we have the ancient sarcophagus, the doubting cleric, the dream and the miracles. The monks of Ramsey could have read it all in the *Liber in Gloria Martyrum* of Gregory of Tours.

71. The miraculous well at Canterbury is not recorded before the *Polistoire* (Stanley 1857) but water tinged with the saint's blood had been given out to the faithful since the martyrdom; it came in little leaden *ampullae*, which after the 1200s were imitated by other shrines (Ward 1982: 101–3; Webb 2000: 47, 59, 85). The *ampulla* tradition had precedents going back to the sixth century, if not earlier; Bord (2006: 5–7) illustrates a pottery example from the shrine of St Menas, brought home by a Welsh pilgrim some time before this Egyptian shrine was lost to the expansion of Islam. Holy well water, which anyone could have for the asking, gradually took on the magical aura of the holy water

that had been blessed by a priest; this was one of many ways in which laypeople sought to get their hands on the potency of sacramental things. The keeper of St Eustace's Well at Wye, evidently a layman, had no compunctions about using the waters of his well to banish a pair of demonic black shapeshifting toads. At Slepe the woman who made love to a hare turned up for a tryst with her playboy fiend carrying a bottle of water from St Ive's Well and the demon complained that he could not come near because she was surrounded by a wall of raging waters. For other examples of holy water acting more or less automatically as an apotropaic, see Watkins (2007: 110–2, 115).

72.   But in the *Miracles of St Thomas* we hear of one Fretus who ran a hospice for pilgrims at Shooter's Hill and regretted having no water supply for them. St Thomas appeared to him in a dream and told him where to dig a well. After this promising beginning, however, it seems to have become a purely practical source of water and not a holy well.

73.   There are other places that have two holy wells near each other – leaving aside the towns, where you might expect this to happen by chance. The rural locations include Lundy (Helen and John), Barmby-on-the-Marsh (Helen and Peter), Burnsall (Helen and Margaret), Holsworthy (George and James), Kirkwhelpington (Mary and George), Chew Stoke (Mary and Anthony), Tweedmouth (Mary and Cuthbert), Aconbury (Mary and Anne) and Penwortham (Mary and Anne). Saints' wells are near to Holywells at Hatherleigh, Moretonhampstead and Pucklechurch. In some cases one holy well seems to have been superseded by another, as popular devotion changed its object; in others, such as Burnsall, the springs are so near each other that some kind of double dedication seems to have been intended.

74.   Paradoxically, given the illegitimacy of Earl Simon's cult, we know more about the history and development of his holy well than we do for those of the more regular saints. this is not a coincidence; the well had to prove his sanctity in the absence of more conventional relics. Between 1274 and 1279 it worked ten miracles of healing, usually when sick people drank or washed themselves in water which was brought to them. Water was taken to Elmley, Mickleton in Oxfordshire, Thanet, *Lydeham* in Oxfordshire, London and Dunstable, while people came or were carried in carts from *Novereis Burton* in Leicestershire, London and *Sepham Burland* to drink from the well (Halliwell 1840: 68–9, 97, 102–3, 106–7, 108).

75.   The original date of the Clent chapel is not known; its later configuration, on two stories with the well in the undercroft, is similar to the buildings at St Winifred's Well and Ffynnon Fair at Trefnant. Davis (2003) has excellent reconstruction drawings of these in his survey of the architecture of Welsh wells. St Triduana's Well at Restalrig near Edinburgh was also on two levels, with a chapel above and the spring below (Morris & Morris 1982: 96). Bord (2006: 141–3) discusses other examples of well architecture.

76. Thacker (1999: 384) attributes the spread of Augustine's cult outside Canterbury to the Benedictine Reform, in particular to Æthelwold, who was bishop of Winchester until 984, just before the foundation of Cerne. At Ramsey the saint was dignified as *Anglorum praesul* in a metrical calendar compiled in the 990s.

77. St John is the only saint, apart from the Virgin Mary, to appear with any regularity in field-names; it is not clear whether 'St John's Field' means a site for midsummer bonfires, or whether it is a folk-etymology from something like *singeon*, 'burnt place'. It could be that in some cases St John's Well is to be understood as 'the well in St John's Field', but there is no direct evidence of this.

78. At least sixteen spurious dedications to Chad have been proposed by more recent researchers, usually on the basis of a place-name *ceald wella*, 'cold well', and at Chadwell Heath and Chadwell St Mary in Essex these have given a dedication to modern parish churches. It is possible that something of the sort happened earlier in the Middle Ages; this certainly seems to be the case at St Chad's chapel in Tushington with its *Chaddewalle*, later known as Holy Well. Floyer (1702: 202) quotes 'a Learned Divine' who had observed the abundance of Chad-wells and assumed that they were dedicated to the saint. Baring-Gould (1872–7: 3.32) seems to have started the notion that Chad was 'patron saint of medicinal springs'.

79. The spring-name Bridewell is recorded from the tenth century onwards, but nobody is quite sure what it means. At all events, it has nothing to do with St Bridget. Bridewell at Llanvaches in Monmouthshire would have seem to be an instance of this English-language name in Wales and St Bride's Well at Disserth in Flintshire might be a hagiologising form of it. However, there are six non-English dedications to Sant Ffraid in Wales (Jones 1954: 32), so evidently she had a genuine well-cult there.

80. Rattue (1995a: 71). Some of his details are now open to review; the table of well-dedications gives much too high a ranking for Chad, due to the inclusion of spurious modern forms from *ceald wella*, and for James, due to the interpretation of Jacobs Well as a form of St James's Well. It is in fact a modern Protestant spring-name, coined in allusion to John 4: 6–14 the earliest recorded instance being 1674 (Binnall 1940–1: 126). Rattue's distribution maps (1995a: 47, 80) should also be viewed with a cautious eye.

81. Rushton Spencer appears in Plot (1686: 49), Great Asby in Nicolson (1877: 45) and Locko House in Woolley (1981: 83). Although saints' wells provided, on average, more water than Holywells, the two categories of spring do not seem to differ from each other in the reliability of their flow. Whelan (2001: 7–9) provides several examples of holy wells with never-failing waters in her native Yorkshire. A reliable spring is, in hydrogeological terms, one where the potentiometric surface is always higher than the land surface; this depends on

the location of its aquifer (confined or unconfined) and the contours of its recharge area (Price 1985: 88–92). When people dedicated holy wells, they did not always choose springs with a reliable flow; several wells, including Buckingham, Clent, Costessy, Grantchester, Lastingham and Sefton are now dry.

82. It is surprising how little we know from contemporary sources about the appearance of holy wells in the Middle Ages. By the thirteenth century St Kenelm's Well at Winchcombe had been 'wel faire iheled wiþ freo stone' (*South English Legendary* 1956: 290). St Nicholas's Well at Strood was already *antiquus* in 1444 (Duncan & Hussey 1906–7: 1.75). At Evesham in 1448 'there is over the well an hovel of stone, and a crucifix and Mary and John' (Blaauw 1871: 277), which sounds like one of the Breton well-shrines. At Binsey 'was a covering of stone and theron on the front the picture of St Margaret (or perhaps of St Frideswyde), pulled down by Alderman Sayre of Oxon, a little before the late war, anno 1639' (Wood 1889–99: 1.323–9). At Hexton 'over this well, they built a howse, and in this howse they placed the Image or Statue of St Faith' (Whiteman 1936: 151–3), at Oswestry Leland saw a wooden well chapel (Leland 1906–10: 3.75) and St Augustine's at Cerne was 'heretofore covered with a Chappell' (Gerard 1980: 65). St Edith's Well at Bristol was given an elaborate cover in 1484 (Boucher 1939) and St Ethelbert's at Hereford had another, probably fourteenth-century (Dingley 1867–8: 1.clii); both were smaller than but similar to market crosses. St Sidwell's Well at Exeter appears in fourteenth-century stained glass at the cathedral, a raised round cistern of white stone; St Neot's in Cornwall looks much the same in the glass windows of the church there. Of St Pandonia's Well in Eltisley, we know only that it had raised stonework round it which the vicar in 1576 thought superstitious (Palmer 1935). A similar well appears next to St Endelient on a bead added in the seventeenth century to the Langdale rosary (now in the Victoria & Albert Museum). There is something like this in Dingley's illustration (1867–8: 2.248) of a Trinity Well near Cardigan. St Anne's Well at Buxton was housed in a square cistern by 1610 (Speed 1988: 63). The well-house over St Margaret's Well at Hasbury would be remarkable evidence for a healing well if it really did have carvings of the sick and the cured, but it survives only in eighteenth-century memories (Nash 1781–2: 1.528). I am grateful to Tristan Gray Hulse for sharing notes with me in the search for these wells.

83. The first researchers to propose a statistical approach were Binnall & Dodds, who claimed (1941–2: 293) that the ratio of women to men was 2: 1 among Northumbrian wells. The actual figures seem to be 8 men, 6 women, if we exclude the Virgin Mary with 21.

84. Hall (2007: 87) has shown that Anglo-Saxon readers of the classics were confused by the concept of *nymphae* at springs and other natural places. Their nearest equivalent, the *ælf* (our modern elf), was typically an epicene young man, not an alluring female figure. In southern Europe, by contrast, the *fatae* or *fees* with their fondness for springs and pools came from a tradition with its

roots in classical antiquity. Wells, like water in general, are associated with the feminine in modern folklore (see Bord 1985: 115–9, 132–5, 138–43). Water and gender are considered by Strang (2004: 23–4, 83–94), an interesting but historically illiterate discussion; see also Varner (2004: 54–62). Queens, witches, brides, ghosts, mermaids, ladies and fortunetellers are all certainly associated with wells but that does not necessarily mean that their waters are manifestations of some timeless *ewige weibliche*. Much depends on context.

85. St Catherine, like St Helen, was seen as both royal and British (Lewis 2000: 63–79), which may account for the spread of her cult, especially in the patriotic atmosphere of the fifteenth and early sixteenth centuries.

86. Morris (1989: 86) has often been cited in this connection, but his source (Charles 1938: 165) simply cites OE *ellern* as the etymology for Ellenwell Lake in Glamorgan. There is no suggestion that this site, or others in *ellern-*, were linked with St Helen.

87. 'In their kaleidoscopic incoherence, these manifestations look more folkloric than hagiographical' (Blair 2005: 380), but most of the incoherence derives from the folklorists and not from their material. Graham Jones's classic article on the lore of St Helen (1986) has now been superseded by the section in his *Saints in the Landscape* (2007: 126–9), a book which arrived too late to be fully considered in this study, but which will advance our knowledge of many of the saints considered here.

88. Translated from the text in Harbus (2002: 172–3). The guild of St Helen at Beverley had an annual procession in which her discovery of the True Cross was re-enacted (Peacock 1891: 358). Peacock seems to have been the first writer to observe St Helen's popularity in the North and her frequent appearance as a patron of holy wells.

89. This raises questions of historical sequence. Were wells dedicated by themselves in remote districts, with chapels later built next to them, or were chapel and well planned as a single unit? The number of isolated saints' wells without any chapel nearby suggests the former; we have at least 50 like this in remote spots, compared to 25 similar sites with chapel and well. Some buildings could easily have fallen into ruin and never been recorded, but not on this scale. The more plausible sequence is recorded in the eleventh-century *Life of Cadoc*: 'after the Cornishmen had perceived that by divine pity frequent recoveries of health of both sexes were incessantly being effected at the same well, they built a little church of stone by the fountain in honour of St Cadog' (Wade-Evans 1944: 95). At Winchcombe the eleventh-century *Life of St Kenelm* describes only a well, but by the 1280s 'the monkes suþþe of Winchecombe irered habbeþ þer biside/ A uair chapel of sein Kenelm þat men secheþ wyde' (*South East Legendary* 1956: 290); an annex to the building seems to have housed a resident priest. At Cerne, Clent and Slepe/St Ives the cult of the spring came first and the chapel followed later. Blair (2005: 378–9) notes a tendency for these springs to run eastward along the axis of the

churches, and compares Holy Well at Stevington. At Broughton and Thirsk the well also rises east of the church; at Binsey and East Dereham, to the west. Thompson & Thompson (2004: 193) and Rattue (1995a: 76) also discuss orientation relative to the church and the direction in which the well-water flows. It is easy to arrive at premature certainty on the basis of a limited sample. There are some 60 wells rising in and near churchyards and in the nature of things they must flow to the east or west if they don't flow to the north or south; a more comprehensive analysis is needed.

90.   We have already met St Anthony as the archetypal hermit with his well. Later in the *Life* (cap 54) he creates one miraculously: 'the old man seeing they were all in jeopardy… stretched forth his hands and prayed. And immediately the Lord made water to well forth where he had stood praying, and so all drank and were revived'. The story would make him a particularly suitable patron for holy wells, but in fact he has only three to his name. This suggests that dedications were chosen out of general devotion and not for their special appropriateness to wells.

91.   Assuming that the St Owen who has a holy well at Much Wenlock is Ouen of Rouen. The well is only one instance of a regional cult in the West Midlands, with churches of St Owen or Ewan at Bristol, Gloucester and Hereford. A pre-Conquest connection with Chelles has been suggested, since the historical Ouen supported this foundation, where future saint-abbesses including Milburgh of the Hwicce were trained. Despite this pre-Conquest association, it seems more reasonable to include him with the other Norman cults. There are five Welsh wells dedicated to a St Owen, but this is a quite different saint, Hywyn of Aberdaron.

92.   Except that there seems occasionally to have been a prohibition on boiling the water. One of the miracles at Slepe relates to a cauldron of water from St Ive's Well that would not boil; the same story is found at St Nectan's Well at Stoke, although here we are told that the saint's eel had got into the cauldron and that was why the fire was in vain. When St Catherine's Well was consecrated at Skye in the seventeenth century, 'from that time it was accounted unlawful to boil any meat with the water of this well' (Macinlay 1893: 63).

93.   Bond (2001: 93–100) discusses these conduit wells, while Rahtz (1963–4: 159) compares Chalice Well at Glastonbury with other sites of this kind. Chalice Well is now the archetypal holy well, but did not acquire this status until the twentieth century; in the abbey's time it was simply a water source. The conduits of Bath and Bristol, though not formally dedicated, are now attended by annual ceremonies with a religious feel to them (Quinn 1999: 21–3).

94.   It is not clear what these chapels looked like. Comparison with Wales and Cornwall, where the architecture of well shrines has survived much better, suggests that there was a continuum stretching from simple vernacular well-

houses to independent chapels. In Cornwall, Dupath Well at Callington survives from the early sixteenth century; St Cleer was thirteenth-century, but its present form, suggestively resembling a raised shrine with access arches, is the work of nineteenth-century restoration.

95. This was reported to Abraham de la Pryme when he visited in 1697 (De la Pryme 1870: 142). The shrine may be linked to the 'growing general popularity of Katherine's cult amongst the laity in Lincolnshire during the twelfth century' (Walsh 2007: 134); if so, it would stand out from Catherine dedications elsewhere, which seem to be late medieval.

96. The well-head was set up at a new site, half a mile away from the original spa (Osborne & Weaver 1996: 93–101). As this suggests, claims by local historians that their holy well was a scene of pilgrimage should be received with great caution. Even when the site really was a holy well, the pilgrim story usually turns out to be based on some Victorian topographer or one of the classic county histories, which routinely claim that pilgrims came from far and wide to be healed by the waters of some holy well – Collinson's *Somerset* (1791) is full of this sort of thing. For the most part this was just antiquarian guesswork. Finding that the spring had a dedication, they assumed that it must fit their idea of what a holy well should be.

97. 'Woods and water alike provided a frequent setting for the veneration of St Anne' (Webb 2000: 106). Scherr (1986) notes that chapels dedicated to St Anne include St Anne's-in-the-Grove or St Anne's-in-the-Briars at Southowram near Halifax and St Anne-in-the-Willows at Aldersgate in London, as if there were some feeling that wilderness was an appropriate location for St Anne's cult. Macduff (1857) had previously made this point about her wells. The late medieval cult of St Anne, first studied by Ronan (1927), has been reconsidered in Ashley & Sheingorn (1990) as well as by Nixon (2004). Morris considered (1989: 90) that the wells of St Anne originated in the church of St Anne built by the pool of Bethesda by the Crusaders in 1140. This is not plausible; none of the St Anne's wells are recorded before the sixteenth century.

98. The evidence outside England is not so comprehensive but points to a similar history for Marian well-cults. In Wales, the three most famous wells of the Virgin – at Trefnant, Pilleth and Penrhys – all seem to be late medieval. Here, wells of the Virgin represent the same proportion of the whole as they do in England, 15 percent as against 16 percent; but whereas in England they are about as numerous as those of the other Bibical and foreign saints, in Wales they are three times more common than them (Jones 1954: 33). Madeleine Gray's forthcoming study of Penrhys will be particularly illuminating. The earliest Scottish shrine is at Whitekirk, where a popular cult at Our Lady's Well led Melrose Abbey to build a shrine in 1309, and 15,653 pilgrims were recorded in 1413; remarkable evidence for the levels of devotion at these cults, if true. They offered 1,422 merks in total, a spend per head of between

1 and 2 shillings English money. Our Lady of Loretto Well at Musselburgh had, as its name suggests, a sixteenth-century cult, as did the Well of the Virgin at Chapel of Seggat (Morris & Mossis 1982: 27, 142, 146).

99.   In Scotland, Ladywell is the more common name, as it is in England; the index to Morris & Morris (1982) list 38 examples, as against 24 wells of St Mary. Wales has a few examples of the name in the counties bordering England. In Ireland, there are Ladywells not only in Co. Dublin, but in Cork, Clare and Kerry, suggesting that the name had become established after the early sixteenth century when English began to be spoken there, and before the Reformation.

100.   Still less the goddess Freya, as suggested by William Smith (1923: 154–5). The meaning 'Virgin Mary' is almost as old as the word 'lady' itself, going back to the ninth century (sense 3 in the OED, with adjectival compounds listed under sense 16). But even without involving pagan goddesses, there are reasons to be cautious about interpreting every Lady- name as a reference to Mary. The EPNS volumes record a Lady's and Lord's Meadowe in Oxfordshire at Wardington, a Lady's and Lord's Wood in Gloucestershire at Painswick, a Lady's and Lord's Meadow in Shropshire at Preston Gubbals, a Lady's and Lord's Piece also in Shropshire at Northwood, and a Lady's and Lord's Bridge in Sheffield. All these names obviously have a secular interpretation. So does Ladies Bridge in Wiltshire at Wilcot, 'named after Lady and Miss Wroughton of Wilcot Manor' (Gover & Stenton 1939: 326) and Ladies Wash in Cambridgeshire at Sawston where 'tradition has it that this pool was used by the squire's ladies as a bathing-pool' (Reaney 1943: 362).

101.   A quick survey of three counties (Gloucestershire, Derbyshire and the West Riding) finds over fifty medieval names which use ME *Leuedi* as a qualifier. See Smith (1964–5: 1.126, 1.201, 1.234, 2.78, 2.108, 2.138, 3.123, 3.171, 3.235–6, 2.261); Cameron (1959: 1.10, 1.38, 1.43, 1.65, 1.74, 1.84, 1.127, 1.178, 1.184, 2.196, 2.261, 2.265, 2.296, 2.322, 2.333, 2.349, 2.384, 2.411, 2.419, 2.424, 2.427, 2.487, 2.498, 3.525, 3.600, 3.621, 3.633, 3.644, 3.648, 3.661); and Smith (1961–3: 1.34, 1.98, 1.105, 1.220, 1.297, 1.331, 1.333, 2.29, 2.47, 2.114, 3.96 & 113, 3.205, 3.249, 3.252, 4.90, 4.134, 4.167, 4.260; 5.22, 5.23, 5.25, 5.59, 5.73, 5.177, 6.65, 6.95, 6.100, 6.137, 6.164, 6.190). In this sample there are 13 names reported from the thirteenth century, 10 from the fourteenth, 14 from the fifteenth and 15 from the sixteenth. *Croft* is the most common generic, with 7 examples, followed by 5 cases of *holm* 'island' and 3 of *acre*, *flat* 'land in open field' and *ridding* 'cleared land'.

102.   Lady Well appears on the 1854 OS in Felton, while *Ladycrosse* was recorded in the adjoining parish of Great Houghton (Smith 1961–3: 1.98, 269). Other standing crosses are recorded at or near to holy wells at Aislaby, Barnwell St Andrew, Beetham, Coleham, Great Crosby, Sticklepath and Tottenham, with the earliest at Seaton where it is recorded as *Halywelcros*, *circa*1275. A brief survey of local well studies and county place-name surveys finds a dozen instances of the name Crosswell (including a *Cruchewelle* 1232 at Laxton in

Northamptonshire and a *Crossekelde* 1120x47 in Bolton Abbey). It seems to have been a deliberate policy to site crosses over wells, as in the much-photographed example at Condicote in Gloucestershire. A traveller on a hot dusty day could stop, drink and wash, then say a short prayer before moving on; the wells were not exactly consecrated, but they were not without some religious sense either. In literature, the universal image of well and tree was sometimes developed into that of well and cross, as in the *De Pascha* attributed to Cyprian (Greenhill 1964: 338–40).

103. Miracles, after all, are associated with power; from the time of the conversion onwards they had been used as standard knock-down arguments for the superiority of Christianity over rival systems. Where there was a power vacuum, as in Late Antiquity (Brown 1981), miracles helped to fill it and this may explain why miraculous wells were more common in the Celtic West than they were in Anglo-Saxon England, with its comparatively stable government. It would also explain the decline in the number of officially promoted well-cults as the Middle Ages progessed; by the fourteenth century the power of state and Church no longer needed supernatural buttressing, which meant that miracles started to look subversive rather than supportive (cf. Finucane 1977: 52–3).

104. Webb (2000: 25, 144, 216) discusses the relationship between shrines, fairs and markets at Linslade and St Ives.

105. Mascall commences by reminding his readers that 'it is provided in the divine laws and sacred canons that all who shall adore a stone, spring or other creature of God, incur the charge of idolatry' (Durham 1932), an example of the practice noted earlier by which 'paganism' was retained from the penitential tradition as a label for anything that the authorities didn't like the look of. Bishop Quinel of Exeter had given his condemnations a contemporary edge in 1287 by blaming the revived worship of trees and springs on heretics (Watkins 2007: 79).

106. The Lady Well beside 'a place called The Chapel' at Orton near Tebay (Nicolson & Burn 1777: 1.482) looks very much like a similar development. In Scotland, we find another Lady Well at Kirkton of Menmuir, where John Smith was appointed 'hermit of the hermitage of the chapel of the Blessed Mary in the forest of Kilgery' in 1445 (Morris & Morris 1982: 50).

107. Pyrenean examples are given in Harris (1999: 32–44). Earlier instances of popular Marian cult are discussed in Sumption (1975: 275–80) and Webb (2000: 99–105); Marian apparitions are considered by Zimdars-Swartz (1991). For more recent examples connected with wells, see Varner (2002: 179–82).

108. Cf. Letcher (2006: 26): 'whenever anything is deemed "natural" and "obvious" it almost always turns out, on closer inspection, to be culturally specific, localised and historically contingent – in other words, not at all natural or obvious'.

109. Curiously, none of the springs supposed to rise from the blood of a virgin martyr are chalybeate, although Quinn (1999: 223) does note that the water of St Arild's Well at Kington 'leaves a slight stickiness on the skin and the palate when drunk, very much as blood would do'. Recently, the chalybeate waters of St Botolph's Well at Farnborough have been said to have been coloured red by rust from the nails of the Cross (Bates 1993: 51), apparently a local variation on the belief that Chalice Well was tinged red by Christ's blood. These are modern beliefs, but they show how the appearance of a holy well can be linked with its legends.

110. The water of holy wells at Catwick, Dover, Warminster and Chadwell near Sheriffhales was (we are told) unrivalled for making tea. Presumably these were soft-water springs in a hard-water area. Holy well water was found pure enough to supply breweries at Conisbrough, Ipswich, Kirkby Stephen and Worcester. Murphys is still made from the water of Lady Well at Cork, unwittingly following the advice of Whitaker (1812: 430) that 'it is perhaps, as innocent at such hours of relaxation to drink water, even from a consecrated spring, as to swallow the poison of British distilleries at a public-house'. Cheers!

111. Analysis of the holy well waters of Eastbourne can be found in Whitaker (1899: 108) and Edmunds (1928: 251); of Horsted Keynes in Edmunds (1928: 231); of Southam in Richardson (1928b: 62); of Yatton in Richardson (1928a: 252–3); of Waverley in Whitaker (1912: 286–7); of Bembridge in Whitaker (1910: 184); of Banbury in Beesley (1841: 97); and of Winchcombe in Dent (1877: 54). Rattue (1990) refers to an analysis of Holy Well at Tadmarton, which I have not seen. There is also the handful of holy wells which subsequently became spas; Osborne & Weaver (1996: 159, 225, 111) give analyses of St Mungo's Well at Copgrove, St Vincent's Well at Clifton and St Anne's Well at Buxton.

112. The evidence for Devon comes from Brown (1957 and subsequent papers); that for Gloucestershire and Somerset from Quinn, who reckons 36 eye wells (1999: 37), of which 12 can be identified as holy wells; and that for the other counties from Richardson (1928b: 44, 89; 1930: 33, 39, 45, 70, 110, 119, 149, 212; 1935: 30, 43 (twice),110, 111, 114, 115).

113. Details of Cicero's well and other healing springs were passed down by Isidore of Seville in his *Etymologiae* (13 cap 13), along with a great deal of curious but non-medicinal well lore. In the twelfth century, marvellous wells appear in Gervase of Tilbury and Giraldus Cambrensis, as part of their attempts to develop a scheme of natural philosophy. Geoffrey of Monmouth versifies Isidore's passage in the *Vita Merlini* (lines 1179–1242) after he has introduced a spring which has the power to bring the distracted to their wits. For Geoffrey, if the context is anything to go by, these classical wells belonged to the realm of romance and fantasy. Sir John Mandeville, it is true, drank from a non-sacred well which had the power to cure all diseases (Courtney 1916: 41). But the Well of Youth was a fiction and so of course was he.

114. Names beginning in *hæl* have been identified as medicinal wells, but the element seems to have the sense of 'omen' rather than 'healing'. *Bot*, 'help', is found as a qualifier in the name Botwell, found at in Hayes in Middlesex, Leighfield in Rutland and Hamfallow in Gloucestershire. It is true that *bot* is sometimes found associated with holy wells – St Edward's Well at Corfe was 'of gret botnynge' (*South English* 1956: 1.114) in *circa*1310 – but it is found compounded with other generics as well. The compound Botley, with *leah*, appears four times as a settlement name and this suggests a sense of 'for your needs' rather than 'for healing' (Smith 1956: 1.43). The same goes for *geoc*, also meaning 'help', which has been suspected at Ickwell in Bedfordshire; a Sussex *geocburnan* was helpful because it turned a mill, not because it cured people. ModE 'sound', found in Soundwells at Kingswood in Gloucestershire and Admington in Warwickshire, could refer to drumming sounds rather than sound health. Speedwell appears in fieldnames, but this is a phrasal name – 'speed well' meaning 'may you succeed' – and has nothing to do with wells. The sheer range of qualifiers suggested for the sense 'healing' is itself impressive. People are convinced that there must be evidence for secular healing wells in early England, but each class of evidence which they put forward in its favour turns out to be less than conclusive.

115. Webb (2000: 48). For an Italian example of a sufferer hesitating between a trip to the thermal waters and the invocation of a saint, see Bolton (2005: 168).

116. It may be significant that both of these references are late in date. However, there is evidence for an earlier Welsh tradition in which saints' wells specialised in particular ailments. That of St Brynach was good for the healing of wounds, while St Winifred's specialised in epilepsy, although (as the hagiographer is quick to point out) she could be relied on to cure many other problems – dumbness, blindness, dropsy, the stone, piles, coughs, death etc. An invalid drinking from that of St Cadog 'will receive soundness of belly and bowels, and he will throw up in his vomit all slimy worms out of himself' (Wade-Evans 1944: 7, 95, 301–7). We have an extreme case of worm-vomiting at St Ives, where the unfortunate woman threw up a three-foot snake, but violent purging often followed the ingestion of holy water of any sort. 'The whole thing must have been unpleasant for nearby pilgrims' (Finucane 1977: 90).

117. Osborne & Weaver (1996) have followed in the footsteps of Celia Fiennes. Of the 25 spas she visited, 5 (Buxton, Copgrove, Holywell, Malvern and Bristol) had been holy wells, not including Astrop, which would later claim to have been St Rumbold's. St Peter's Well at Leeds, not visited by Celia, was another early cold bath.

118. The competing languages of science and religion are nicely delineated by Walsham (1999: 249–53); see also Walsham (2005) for the debated status of Holywell as shrine or spa. More wells will appear in her forthcoming *The Reformation of the Landscape: Religion, Memory and Legend in Early Modern England.*

119. Addison (1951: 137–43) states that 'most of the spas had been holy wells', a claim for which he provides surprisingly little evidence, while Finucane (1977: 215–6) more plausibly attributes the rise of the spa tradition at the Reformation to the fact that 'after the shrines were destroyed, English society developed means to compensate for some of the loss'.

120. The décor of a successful spa soon began to look like a holy well, with grateful patients leaving the usual litter of crutches behind. Even scepticism about their healing power was traditional. We hear in the twelfth century of a lad who was ill and cried out for Canterbury water, but none was available, so his friends gave him a cupful from the nearest wellhead and he got better anyway (Sumption 1975: 86–7). Exactly the same story is told of one of the Essex spas (Christy & Thresh 1910).

121. The baths at Brindle, East Dean, Holywell at Oxford, Leeds, Loversall, Moxby, Naseby, Newbrough, Nottingham, Peterchurch, Somersby, Stanley and Windleshaw would also repay attention. Of the twin baths at Brindle, destroyed in 1968, one at least seems to have been in existence in the seventeenth century, at a time when the well was an active Catholic centre. The large number of bathing-places at Welsh wells, many of them cut into the rock and therefore more likely to survive than English ones, suggests that here, too, the tradition may go back to an early date. The *Life of St Winefred* records the miraculous publishment of a woman who used the sacred spring as an ordinary bathing-place (Wade-Evans 1944: 301).

122. I owe this observation to Bruce Osborne, who has written extensively on the wells at Malvern.

123. Dedications seem definitely to have been invented in order to market spas to visitors at Ashill, Astrop, Berwick-upon-Tweed, Brighton, Cornhill, Cosgrove, Edington in Somerset, Great Malvern, Humphrey Head, Inglewhite, Kensington (St Agnes), Kings Cross, Papworth St Agnes, Sadlers Wells, Shapwick, Shoreditch (St Agnes) and Stoney Middleton. I'd reserve judgement on Catlowdy, Dalston, Durham (St Cuthbert), Farnborough, Longwitton, Siston, Staward Peel, Waterhead and Witherslack.

124. Chancellor's story had its roots in longstanding traditions at holy wells. The seven successive Sundays on which he drank are paralleled by the wells at East Dean and Naseby, which were to be visited on nine successive occasions (Nicholls 1858: 180–2; Mastin 1792: 33). At Copgrove, children were immersed in St Mungo's Well five, seven, or nine times – always an odd number. A sevenfold treatment was authorised by the cure of Naaman in 2 Kings 5, often cited by exegetes of well-miracles such as Goscelin. As for dreams, St Augustine had appeared to the monk of Cerne in the tenth century and at St Ive's Well another monk with dropsy was admonished in his sleep to find a cure in the 1120s (William 2002: 216), while fifty years later a woman was similarly told to seek out St Godric's Well at Finchale (Reginald 1847:

389). These stories are only one aspect of the dreams and visions that told people which saint they should approach to seek relief (Finucane 1977: 83–5). In 1640 a sufferer was cured after being told in a dream to drink from Madron Well; his story was witnessed by Joseph Hall, the Bishop of Exeter, whose name carried rather more authority than that of the unknown Matthew Chancellor. Another story of a mysterious stranger and a miracle cure was told in connection with St Thomas's Well at Stamford, but it is noticeable that its author is very circumspect about introducing it (Peck 1727: app.1.15).

125. Thus Peacock (1895: 369–70). Charlotte Burne (Burne & Jackson 1883: 422) had made the same point and it features in the exhaustive list of eye symbolisms proposed by Binnall (1945).

126. Floyer (1702: 17). Space, alas, precludes further discussion of Sir John Floyer, a fascinating character who created his own rationalist mythology out of the holy well tradition. Cold water was his universal panacea and he was convinced that the real business of baptism, preferably by total immersion, was to harden up infants for their life ahead. His theories may have fed back into popular trradition; certainly we find children being dipped in the cold springs of holy wells at Cerne and Copgrove, as they were at Coldkell Well near Egton (Gutch 1901: 27), Craikell Spring (Peacock 1895: 372) and a well at Glanton (Binnall & Dodds 1942–6a: 31). Floyer had no sense of the mysterious, even in the sacraments. The popular customs, by contrast, put his theories into practice by transforming them into lay ceremonies of baptismal rebirth. Courtney (1916: 102–3) discusses these customs in Cornwall and Bord (2006: 75) notes examples elsewhere, while Walsham (1999: 243–4) notes the symbolic replication of Catholic ritual. Within a few generations we have moved from the medical materialism of the spa theorist to this account of 1715 from Lee Hall at Bellingham: 'If the lady of the Hall dip aney children that have the rickets or any other over groone distemper, it is either a speedy cure or death. The maner and form is as followeth: The days of dipping are on Whitsunday Even, on Midsummer Even, on Saint Peeter's Even. They must be dipt in the well before the sun rise and in the River Tine after the sun bee sett: then the shift taken from the child and thrown into the river and if it swim the child liveth, but if it sink dyeth' (Binnall & Dodds 1942–6a: 20). Compare this with Floyer to see how the archaic can arise from the rationalist, as easily as the rational from the archaic.

Bibliography

Acta Sanctorum: Octobris, 1853, Alphonse Greuse, Brussels.

Addison, William, 1951, *English Spas,* Batsford, London.

Ælfric, 1881–1900, *Ælfric's Lives of Saints,* ed Walter Skeat, Early English Texts Society 1st ser 76, 82, 94 & 114.

Amery, P.F.S., 1894, 'Twelfth report of the committee on Devonshire folk-lore', *Tr. of the Devonshire Assoc.* 26: 79–85.

Andrews, J.H.B., 1962, 'Chittlehampton', *Tr. of the Devonshire Assoc.* 94: 233–338.

Arnold, Thomas, 1890–6, *Memorials of St Edmund's Abbey,* Rolls Series 96.

Ashley, Kathleen M., and Pamela Sheingorn, eds, 1990, *Interpreting Cultural Symbols: Saint Anne in Late Medieval Socity,* University of Georgia Press.

Aston, Mick A., and Michael D. Costen, eds, 1990, *The Shapwick Project: A Topographical and Historical Study – The Third Report,* University of Bristol.

Atkinson, J.C., 1874, *History of Cleveland: Ancient and Modern,* J. Richardson, Barrow-in-Furness.

Aubrey, John, 1847, *The Natural History of Wiltshire,* ed John Britton, Wiltshire Topographical Society.

Baines, Arnold H.J., 1997, 'The furlong-names of Chicheley', *Records of Buckinghamshire* 39: 1–17.

Baker, Rowland G.M., 1982, 'Holy wells and magical waters of Surrey', *Surrey History* 2iv: 186–192.

Barber, Richard, 2001, 'Was Mordred buried at Glastonbury?: Arthurian tradition at Glastonbury in the Middle Ages', pp145–59 in Carley, ed, *Glastonbury Abbey and the Arthurian Tradition.*

Baring-Gould, Sabine, 1872–7, *The Lives of the Saints,* John Hodges, London.

Barker, W.G.M. Jones, 1856, *Historical and Topographical Account of Wensleydale and the Valley of the Yore in the North Riding of Yorkshire,* John Russell Smith, London

Bates, A.W, 1993, 'Healing waters: holy wells and spas in Warwickshire', *Warwickshire History* 9ii: 47–61.

Beesley, Alfred, 1841, *The History of Banbury,* Nichols & Son, London.

Bekyngton, Thomas, 1934–5, *The Register of Thomas Bekynton, Bishop of Bath and Wells 1443–1465,* ed H.C. Maxwell-Lyte and M.C.B. Dawes, Somerset Record Society 49–50.

Bestall, J.M., *et al.,* 1974–80, *History of Chesterfield,* Borough of Chesterfield.

Bethell, Denis, 1970, 'The lives of St Osyth of Essex and St Osyth of Aylesbury' *Analecta Bollandiana* 88: 75–127.

Billington, Richard Newman, and John Brownbill, 1910, *St Peter's, Lancaster: A History*, Sands & Co., London.

Binnall, Peter B.G., 1940, 'Holy wells in Derbyshire', *J. of the Derbyshire Arch. and Nat. Hist. Soc.* 61: 56–65.

Binnall, Peter B.G., 1940-1, 'Holy wells in Devonshire', *Devon and Cornwall Notes & Queries* 21: 121–6.

Binnall, Peter B.G., 1945, 'Some theories regarding eye-wells', *Folk-Lore* 56: 361–4.

Binnall, Peter B.G., and M. Hope Dodds, 1941-2, 'Holy wells in Northumberland and Durham: I', *Proc. of the Soc. of Antiq. of Newcastle-upon-Tyne* 4th ser 9: 291–302.

Binnall, Peter B.G., and M. Hope Dodds, 1942-6a, 'Holy wells in Northumberland and Durham: II', *Proc. of the Soc. of Antiq. of Newcastle-upon-Tyne* 4th ser 10: 19–35.

Binnall, Peter B.G., and M. Hope Dodds, 1942-6b, 'Holy wells in Northumberland and Durham: III', *Proc. of the Soc. of Antiq. of Newcastle-upon-Tyne* 4th ser 10: 64–86.

Blaauw, William Henry, 1871, *The Barons' War*, Bell & Daldy, London.

Blair, John, 1987, 'Saint Frideswide reconsidered', *Oxoniensia* 52: 71–127.

Blair, John, 2002a, 'A saint for every minster?', pp455–94 of Thacker & Sharpe, eds, *Local Saints and Local Churches*.

Blair, John, 2002b, 'A handlist of Anglo-Saxon saints', pp495–565 of Thacker & Sharpe, eds, *Local Saints and Local Churches*.

Blair, John, 2005, *The Church in Anglo-Saxon Society*, Oxford University Press.

Blanton, Virginia, 2007, *Signs of Devotion: The Cult of St Æthelthryth in Medieval England, 695–1615*, Pennsylvania State University Press.

Blomefield, Francis, 1739–75, *A Topographical History of the County of Norfolk*, W. Whittingham, Lynn.

Bolton, Brenda, 2005, 'Signs, wonders, miracles: supporting the faith in medieval Rome', pp157–78 in Cooper & Gregory, eds, *Signs, Wonders, Miracles: Representations of Divine Power in the Life of the Church*.

Bond, James, 2001, 'Monastic water management in Great Britain: a review', pp88–136 in Keevill, Aston & Hall, eds, *Monastic Archaeology: Papers on the Study of Medieval Monasteries*.

Bonser, Gerald, David W. Rollason and Clare Stancliffe, eds, 1989, *St Cuthbert, his Cult and his Community to 1200*, Boydell, Woodbridge.

Bonser, K.J., 1979, 'Spas, wells and springs of Leeds', *Tr. of the Thoresby Soc.* 54: 29–50.

Bonser, Wilfrid, 1937, 'Praying in water', *Folk-Lore* 48: 385–8.

Bord, Janet, 2006, *Cures and Curses: Ritual and Cult at Holy Wells*, Heart of Albion, Wymeswold.

Bord, Janet, 2008, *Holy Wells in Britain: A Guide*, Heart of Albion, Wymeswold.

Bord, Janet and Colin, 1985, *Sacred Waters: Holy Wells and Water Lore in Britain and Ireland*, Granada, London.

Boucher, Charles E., 1939, 'St Edith's Well and St Peter's Cross, Bristol', *Tr. of the Bristol & Gloucestershire Arch. Soc.* 61: 95–106.

Brantyngham, Thomas de, 1901–6, *The Register of Thomas de Brantyngham, Bishop of Exeter (AD 1370–1394)*, ed F.C. Hingston-Randolph, George Bell, London.

Brewis, Parker, 1928, 'St Mary's Chapel, and the site of St Mary's Well, Jesmond', *Archaeologia Aeliana* 4th ser 5: 102–11.

Bridges, John, 1791, *The History and Antiquities of Northamptonshire*, ed Peter Whalley, D. Price & J. Cooke, Oxford.

Briggs, Keith, 2007, 'Seven Wells', *J. of the English Place-Names Soc.* 39: 7–44.

Brooks, Nicholas, and Catherine Cubitt, eds, 1996, *St Oswald of Worcester: Life and Influence*, Leicester University Press.

Brown, Mary Gifford, 1990, *An Illuminated Chronicle: Some Light on the Dark Ages of Saint Milburga's Lifetime*, Bath University Press.

Brown, Peter, 1981, *The Cult of the Saints: Its Rise and Function in Latin Christianity*, University of Chicago Press.

Brown, Theo, 1957, 'Holy and notable wells of Devon: I', *Tr. of the Devonshire Assoc.* 89: 205–15.

Bryant, T. Hugh, 1900–15, *Norfolk Churches*, Norwich Mercury Office, Norwich.

Buckley, W.E., 1875, 'St Govor's Well', *Notes & Queries* 5th ser 4: 523.

Burgess, Michael W., 1978, *Holy Wells and Ancient Crosses of Norfolk and Suffolk*, East Suffolk & Norfolk Antiquarians Occasional Paper 2.

Burne, Charlotte, and Georgina Jackson, 1883, *Shropshire Folk-Lore: A Sheaf of Gleanings*, Trübner, London.

Calder, Michael, 2003, 'Early ecclesiastical sites in Somerset: three case studies', *Proc. of the Somerset Arch. & Nat. Hist. Soc.* 147: 1–28.

Camden, William, 1695, *Britannia*, ed Edmund Gibson, Edmund Gibson, London.

Cameron, Kenneth, 1959, *The Place-Names of Derbyshire*, English Place-Name Society 27–9.

Campana, A., 1996, 'Santa Ositha', *Archivio Italiano per la Storia della Pietà* 9: 95–121.

Carley, James P., ed, 2001, *Glastonbury Abbey and the Arthurian Tradition*, D.S. Brewer, Woodbridge.

Cartularium Abbathiae de Whiteby, 1879–81, ed J.C. Atkinson, Surtees Society 69 & 72.

Cartulary of Darley Abbey, The, 1945, ed Reginald R. Darlington, Titus Wilson, Kendal.

Chalk, Edwin S., 1910, 'The town, village, manors and church of Kentisbeare', *Tr. of the Devonshire Assoc.* 42: 278–93.

Charles, B.G., 1938, *Non-Celtic Place-Names in Wales*, University College London.

Charlton, Lionel, 1779, *The History of Whitby and of Whitby Abbey*, A. Ward, York.

Christy, Miller, and May Thresh, 1910, *The Mineral Waters and Medicinal Springs of Essex*, Essex Field Club.

Chronicon Abbatiae de Evesham, ad Annum 1418, 1863, ed William Dunn Macray, Rolls Series 29.

Chronicon Abbatiae Rameseiensis, 1886, ed William Dunn Macray, Rolls Series 83.

Clay, Rotha Mary, 1914, *The Hermits and Anchorites of England*, Methuen, London.

Colgrave, Bertram, 1940, *Two Lives of Saint Cuthbert: A Life by an Anonymous Monk of Lindisfarne and Bede's Prose Life*, Cambridge University Press.

Collinson, John, 1791, *The History and Antiquities of the County of Somerset*, R. Cruttwell, Bath.

Conner, Patrick W., 1993, *Anglo-Saxon Exeter: A Tenth-Century Cultural History*, Boydell Press, Woodbridge.

Cookson, Richard, 1887, *Goosnargh: Past and Present*, H. Oakey.

Cooper, Kate, and Jeremy Gregory, eds, 2005, *Signs, Wonders, Miracles: Representations of Divine Power in the Life of the Church*, Ecclesiastical History Society.

Cope, F. J., 1945, 'The holy wells of Staffordshire' *Tr. of the.Old Stafford Soc.* 1945: 9–13.

Cormack, Margaret Jean, ed, 2007, *Saints and their Cults in the Atlantic World*, University of South Carolina Press.

Cormack, Margaret Jean, 2007, 'Holy wells and national identity in Iceland', pp229–45 in Cormack, ed, *Saints and their Cults in the Atlantic World*.

Coster, Will, and Andrew Spicer, eds, 2005, *Sacred Space in Early Modern Europe*, Cambridge University Press.

Councils and Synods, with Other Documents Relating to the English Church, 1964–81, ed F.M. Powicke *et al.*, Clarendon, Oxford.

Courtney, R.A., 1916, *The Holy Well and the Water of Life*, Beare & Son, Penzance.

Cox, Barrie, 1989–92, *The Place-Names of Rutland*, English Place-Name Society 67–9.

Cox, Barrie, 1998–2004, *The Place-Names of Leicestershire*, English Place-Name Society 75, 78 & 81.

Cox, Edward W., 1895, 'Leaves from an antiquary's notebook', *Tr. of the Historic Soc. of Lancashire & Cheshire* 47: 235–52.

Cox, John Charles, 1875–9, *Notes on the Churches of Derbyshire*, Bemrose & Sons, Derby/ W. Edmunds, Chesterfield.

Crabtree, John, 1836, *A Concise History of the Parish and Vicarage of Halifax, in the County of York*, Hartley & Walker, Halifax.

Cubitt, Catherine, 2002, 'Universal and local saints in Anglo-Saxon England', pp423–53 in Thacker & Sharpe, eds, *Local Saints and Local Churches in the Early Medieval West*.

Curwen, John F., 1925, 'Heversham Church', *Tr. of the Cumberland & Westmorland Antiq. & Arch. Soc.* 2nd ser 25: 28–79.

Dale, Herbert D., 1931, *St Leonard's Church, Hythe, With Some Account of the Life and Customs of the Town*, John Murray, London.

Davis, Paul, 2003, *Sacred Springs: In Search of the Holy Wells and Spas of Wales*, Blorenge, Abergavenny.

Day, W.I. Leeson, 1934, *Holsworthy*, Devonshire Assocation.

De la Pryme, Abraham, 1870, *The Diary of Abraham de la Pryme*, ed Charles Jackson, Surtees Society 54.

Deane, Edmund, 1922, *Spadacrene Anglica: Or, the English Spa Fountain*, ed James Rutherford and Alex Butler, John Wright, Bristol.

Dent, Emma, 1877, *Annals of Winchcombe and Sudeley*, John Murray, London.

Dickinson, J.C., 1956, *The Shrine of Our Lady of Walsingham*, Cambridge University Press.

Dickinson, William, 1816, *The History and Antiquities of the Town of Newark*, M. Hage, Newark.

Dingley, Thomas, 1867–8, *History from Marble*, ed John Gough Nichols, Camden Society 94 & 97.

Doble, Gilbert H., 1962, *The Saints of Cornwall II: Saints of the Lizard District*, Dean & Chapter of Truro.

Doble, Gilbert H., 1970, *The Saints of Cornwall V: Saints of Mid-Cornwall*, Dean & Chapter of Truro.

Dodgson, John McNeal, and Alexander Rumble, 1970–97, *The Place-Names of Cheshire*, English Place-Name Society 44–8, 54 & 74.

Doe, G., 1884, 'Seventh report of the committee on Devonshire folk-lore', *Tr. of the Devonshire Assoc.* 16: 122–3.

Dovaston, Adolphus, 1886, 'Woolston Well, Shropshire', *Tr. of the Shropshire Arch. & Nat. Hist. Soc.* 1st ser 9: 238–43.

Dugdale, William, 1817–30, *Monasticon Anglicanum: A History of the Abbies and Other Monasteries in England and Wales*, ed John Caley, Henry Ellis & Bulkeley Bandinel, Longman, London.

Duncan, Leland L., and Arthur Hussey, 1906–7, *Testamenta Cantiana*, Kent Archaeological Society.

Duncumb, John, *et al.*, 1804–1915, *Collections Towards the History and Antiquities of the County of Hereford*, E.G. Wright, Hereford.

Durham, Mary Edith, 1932, 'Extracts from Hereford Cathedral Registers', *Folk-Lore* 43: 431.

Dvorjetski, Estée, 2007, *Leisure, Pleasure and Healing: Spa Culture and Medicine in Ancient Eastern Mediterranean*, Brill, Leiden.

Edmunds, Francis Hereward, 1928, *The Wells and Springs of Sussex*, Memoirs of the Geological Survey.

Edwards, Heather, 2004, 'The saint of Middleham and Giggleswick', *Yorkshire Arch. J.* 76: 135–44.

Ekwall, Eilert, 1960, *The Concise Oxford Dictionary of English Place-Names* 4th edition, Clarendon, Oxford.

Erasmus, Desiderius, 1997, *Collected Works of Erasmus 40: Colloquies*, tr Craig R. Thompson, University of Toronto Press.

Everitt, Alan, 1987, *Continuity and Colonization: The Evolution of Kentish Settlement*, Leicester University Press.

Eyton, R.W., 1854–60, *Antiquities of Shropshire*, John Russell Smith, London.

Farbrother, John E., 1859, *Shepton Mallet: Notes on its History*, Albert Byrt, Shepton Mallet.

Faull, Terry, 2004, *Secrets of the Hidden Source: In Search of Devon's Ancient and Holy Wells*, Halsgrove, Tiverton.

Fell, Christine, 1971, *Edward King and Martyr*, University of Leeds School of English.

Fiennes, Celia, 1949, *The Journeys of Celia Fiennes*, ed Christopher Morris, Cresset Press, London.

Finucane, Ronald, 1977, *Miracles and Pilgrims: Popular Beliefs in Medieval England*, J.M. Dent, London.

Flete, John, 1909, *The History of Westminster Abbey*, ed Joseph Armitage Robinson, Cambridge University Press.

Flint, Valerie, 1991, *The Rise of Magic in Early Medieval Europe*, Clarendon, Oxford.

Floyer, John, 1702, *The Ancient Ψυχρολονσια Revived: Or, An Essay to Prove Cold Bathing Both Safe and Useful*, Samuel Smith & Benjamin Walford, London.

Foord, Alfred Stanley, 1910, *Springs, Streams, and Spas of London,* T. Fisher Unwin, London.

Förster, Max, 1932–3, 'The etymology of "Sidwell"', *Devon & Cornwall Notes & Queries* 17: 243–5.

Fox, Cyril, 1959, *The Personality of Britain: Its Influence on Inhabitant and Invader in Prehistoric and Early Historic Times*, National Museum of Wales.

Fradenburg, Louise Olga, ed, 1992, *Women and Sovereignty*, Edinburgh University Press.

Fraser, R., 1983, 'St Mary's Well, Jesmond, Newcastle upon Tyne', *Archaeologia Aeliana* 5th ser 11: 289–300.

French, Helen, 1999, *Ancient Sites in Kent,* Privately.

Fretton, W.G., 1890, 'The Warwickshire Feldon: a sketch of its hills and valleys, waters, famous trees, and other physical features', *Proc. of Warwickshire Naturalists' & Archaeologists' Field Club*, 35: 23–45.

Fretton, W.G., 1893, 'The waters of the Arden: a sketch of its springs, wells, rivers, lakes, pools, and marshes, within the basin of the Avon', *Proc. of. Warwickshire Naturalists' & Archaeologists' Field Club* 38: 19–36

G.C., 1816, 'The Catholic antiquary: III', *Catholicon: Or, the Christian Philosopher* 3: 128–33.

Gameson, Richard, 1999, *St Augustine and the Conversion of England*, Sutton, Stroud.

Gardiner, Dorothy, 1939, 'Notes on an ancient house in Church Lane, Canterbury', *Archaeologia Cantiana* 51: 108–12.

Geary, Patrick, 1978, *Furta Sacra: Thefts of Relics in the Central Middle Ages*, Princeton University Press.

Gelling, Margaret, 1990–2006 (and ongoing), *The Place-Names of Shropshire*, English Place-Name Society 62/3, 70, 76, 80 & 82.

Gelling, Margaret, and Ann Cole, 2000, *The Landscape of Place-Names*, Shaun Tyas, Stamford.

Geoffrey of Burton, 2002, *Life and Miracles of St Modwenna*, ed, tr Robert Bartlett, Clarendon, Oxford.

Gerard, John (as John Coker), 1980, *Coker's Survey of Dorsetshire*, Dorset Publishing, Sherborne.

Gillett, H.M., 1957, *Shrines of Our Lady in England and Wales*, Samuel Walker, London.

Gomme, George Laurence, 1892, *Ethnology in Folklore*, Kegan Paul, London.

Goscelin of Saint-Bertin, 2004, *The Hagiography of the Female Saints of Ely*, ed, tr Rosalind C. Love, Clarendon, Oxford.

Gover, John, Allen Mawer and Frank Stenton, 1931–2, *The Place-Names of Devon*, English Place-Name Society 8–9.

Gover, John, Allen Mawer and Frank Stenton, 1939, *The Place-Names of Wiltshire*, English Place-Name Society 16.

Gover, John, Allen Mawer and Frank Stenton, 1940, *The Place-Names of Nottinghamshire*, English Place-Name Society 17.

Grainge, William, 1871, *The History and Topography of Harrogate, and the Forset of Knaresborough*, John Russell Smith, London.

Gray, Arthur, 1894–8, 'On the watercourse called Cambridge in relation to the river Cam and Cambridge castle', *Proc. of the Cambridge Antiq. Soc.* 9: 61–77.

Gray Hulse, Tristan, 1994, 'The other St Winifred's Wells', *Source* 2nd ser 1: 18–20.

Gray Hulse, Tristran, 1995, 'What makes a Holy Well "holy"?', *Source* 2nd ser 3: 33.

Green, D.H., 1998, *Language and History in the Early Germanic World*, Cambridge University Press.

Greenhill, Eleanor Simmons, 1964, 'The child in the tree: a study of the cosmological tree in Christian tradition', *Traditio* 10: 323–71.

Gribben, Arthur, 1992, *Holy Wells and Sacred Water Sources in Britain and Ireland*, Garland, New York.

Grosjean, Paul, 1953, 'Vie de S. Rumon; Vie, invention et miracles de S. Nectan', *Analecta Bollandiana* 71: 359–414.

Gurevich, Aron, 1988, *Medieval Popular Culture: Problems of Belief and Perception*, Cambridge University Press.

Gutch, Eliza, 1901, *Examples of Printed Folk-Lore Concerning the North Riding of Yorkshire, York and the Ainsty*, Folklore Society.

Hackwood, Frederick M., 1924, *Staffordshire Customs, Superstitions and Folklore*, Mercury Press, Lichfield

Hagerty, R.P., 1988, 'The Buckinghamshire saints reconsidered III: St Rumwold (Rumbold) of Buckingham', *Records of Buckinghamshire* 30: 103–10.

Hall, Alaric, 2007, *Elves in Anglo-Saxon England: Matters of Belief, Health, Gender and Identity*, Boydell, Woodbridge.

Hall, G. Rome, 1880, 'Notes on modern survivals of ancient well-worship in North Tynedale', *Archaeologia Aeliana* 2nd ser 8: 60–87.

Halliwell, James Orchard, ed, 1840, *The Chronicle of William de Rishanger of the Barons' Wars and the Miracles of Simon de Montfort*, Camden Society 1st ser 15.

Hammond, Henry, 1689, *A Paraphrase and Annotation upon All Books of the New Testament*, Margaret Royston, London.

Hamper, William, 1821, 'Observations on the site of the Priory of Halywell in Warwickshire, a cell to Roucester Abbey in the County of Stafford', *Archaeologia* 19: 75–8.

Harbus, Antonina, 2002, *Helena of Britain in Medieval Legend*, D.S. Brewer, Cambridge.

Harris, Ruth, 1999, *Lourdes: Body and Spirit in the Secular Age,* Penguin, Harmondsworth.

Harrison, William, 1968, *The Description of England*, ed George Edelen, Folger
Shakespeare Library.

Harte, Jeremy, 1986, *Cuckoo Pounds and Singing Barrows*, Dorset Natural History
& Archaeological Society.

Hasted, Edward, 1778–99, *The History and Topographical Survey of the County of
Kent*, Privately.

Hayward, P.A., 1993, 'The idea of innocent martyrdom in late tenth- and eleventh-
century English hagiography', pp81–92 in Wood, ed, *Martyrs and
Martyrologies.*

Healey, Hilary, 1995a, 'Lincolnshire holy wells: I', *Lincolnshire Past & Present* 19:
3–6.

Healey, Hilary, 1995b 'Lincolnshire holy wells: II', *Lincolnshire Past & Present* 20:
3–5.

Healey, Hilary, 1998, 'Holy wells in Lincolnshire: some further comments',
Lincolnshire Past & Present 31: 22.

Hearne, Thomas, 1885–1918, *Remarks and Collections of Thomas Hearne*, ed H.E.
Salter *et al.*, Oxford Historical Society 2, 7, 13, 34, 42, 43, 48, 50, 65, 67
& 72.

Henig, Martin, and Phillip Lindley, eds, 2001, *Alban and St Albans: Roman and
Medieval Architecture, Art and Archaeology*, British Archaeological
Association Conference Transactions 24.

Hewitson, Anthony, 1883, *History of Preston*, Preston Chronicle, Preston.

Historia et Cartularium Monasterii Sancti Petri Gloucestriae, 1863–7, ed William
Henry Hart, Rolls Series 33.

Hodgson, J.C., 1916, 'Notices of ruined towers, chapels etc. in Northumberland
circa 1715', *Archaeologia Aeliana* 3rd ser 13: 1–16.

Hodgson, John, 1820–58, *History of Northumberland*, Thomas and James Pigg,
Newcastle.

Hole, Christina, 1937, *Traditions and Customs of Cheshire*, Williams & Norgate,
London.

Hood, E., 1813, 'Of the London theatres: V', *Gentleman's Magazine* 1st ser 83ii:
553–63.

Hope, Robert Charles, 1893, *The Legendary Lore of the Holy Wells of England*,
Elliot Stock, London.

Hope, W.H. St John, 1883, 'Chronicle of the Abbey of St Mary de Parco Stanley, or
Dale, Derbyshire', *J. of the Derbyshire Arch. and Nat. Hist. Soc.* 5: 1–29.

Horne, Ethelbert, 1923, *Somerset Holy Wells*, Somerset Folk Press 12.

Horsfield, Thomas Walker, 1835, *The History, Antiquities and Topography of the
County of Sussex*, Sussex Press, Lewes.

Hough, Carol, 1996–7, 'The place-name Fritwell', *J. of the English Place-Name Soc.*
29: 65–9.

Hoveden, Roger de, 1868–71, *Chronica*, ed William Stubbs, Rolls Series 51.

Igglesden, Charles, 1900–46, *A Saunter Through Kent with Pen and Pencil*, Kentish
Express, Ashford.

Jackson, Charles, and H.J. Morehouse, eds, 1877–86, *Yorkshire Diaries and
Autobiographies in the Seventeenth and Eighteenth Centuries*, Surtees
Society 65 & 77.

Jankulak, Karen, 2000, *The Medieval Cult of St Petroc*, Boydell & Brewer. Woodbridge.

Jones, Francis, 1954, *The Holy Wells of Wales*, University of Wales Press.

Jones, Graham, 1986, 'Holy wells and the cult of St Helen', *Landscape History* 8: 59–75.

Jones, Graham, 1999, 'Authority, challenge and identity in three Gloucestershire saints' cults', pp117–37 in Mowbray, Purdie & Wei, eds, *Authority and Community in the Middle Ages.*

Jones, Graham, 2007, *Saints in the Landscape*, Tempus, Stroud.

Jordan, Katy, 1998, 'Seven Wiltshire wells and their folklore', *Source* 2nd ser 6: 17–20.

Keevill, Graham, Mick Aston, and Teresa Hall, eds, 2001, *Monastic Archaeology: Papers on the Study of Medieval Monasteries*, Oxbow, Oxford.

Kennett, White, 1818, *Parochial Antiquities Attempted in the History of Ambrosden, Burcester, and Other Adjacent Parts*, Clarendon, Oxford.

Knight, Charles, 1842, *The Journey-Book of England: Kent*, Charles Knight, London.

Knights, M., and A.W. Morant, 1888, 'St Lawrence's Well, Norwich, and Gibson's Conduit', *Tr. of the Norfolk & Norwich Arch. Soc.* 10: 185–91.

Lacy, Edmund, 1963–71, *The Register of Edmund Lacy, Bishop of Exeter, 1420–1455*, ed G.R. Dunstan, Canterbury & York Society 60–3.

Langham, Mike, and Colin Wells, 1986, *Buxton Waters: A History of Buxton the Spa*, J.H. Hall, Derby.

Leland, John, 1906–10, *The Itinerary of John Leland In or About the Years 1535–1543*, ed Lucy Toulmin Smith, George Bell, London.

Lennard, Reginald, ed, 1931, *Englishmen at Rest and Play: Some Phases of English Culture 1558–1714*, Clarendon, Oxford.

Letcher, Andy, 2006, *Shroom: A Cultural History of the Magic Mushroom*, Faber & Faber, London.

Lewis, Katherine J., *The Cult of St Katherine of Alexandria in Late Medieval England*, Boydell, Woodbridge.

Liber Eliensis: A History of the Isle of Ely from the Seventh Century to the Twelfth, 2005, tr Janet Fairweather, Boydell, Woodbridge.

Liveing, Henry G.D., 1906, *Records of Romsey Abbey: An Account of the Benedictine House of Nuns, with Notes on the Parish Church and Town (AD 907–1558)*, Warren & Son, Winchester.

Loomis, C. Grant, 1948, *White Magic: An Introduction to the Folklore of Christian Legend*, Mediaeval Academy of America.

Love, Rosalind C., 1996, *Three Eleventh-Century Anglo-Latin Saints' Lives: Vita S. Birini, Vita et Miracula S. Kenelmi, and Vita S. Rumwoldi*, Clarendon, Oxford.

Macduff, Sholto, 1857, 'St Ann's Wells', *Notes & Queries* 2nd ser 4: 318.

Macinlay, James M., 1893, *Folklore of Scottish Lochs and Springs*, William Hodge, Glasgow.

Maclean, John, 1888–9, 'Proceedings at the summer meeting held at Gloucester', *Tr. of the Bristol & Gloucestershire Arch. Soc.* 13: 41–71.

Magna Vita S. Hugonis Episcopi Lincolniensis, 1864, ed James F. Dimock, Rolls Series 37.

Magnusson, Magnus, 1984, *Lindisfarne: The Cradle Island*, Oriel, Stocksfield.

Manning, Mary, 1993, 'Taking the waters in Norfolk', *J. of the Norfolk Industrial Archaeology Soc.* 5: 134–92.

March, Henry Colley, 1899, 'Dorset folk-lore collected in 1897', *Folk-Lore* 10: 478–89.

Mardon, E., 1857, 'Rambles around Bristol', *Bristol Magazine and West of England Monthly Review* 1: 141–7.

Margrett, Edward, 1906, 'St Anne's Well and Chapel, Caversham', *Berkshire Buckinghamshire & Oxfordshire Arch. J.* 12: 25–7.

Martin, Valerie, 1985, 'Some holy wells in Kent', *Source* 1st ser 2: 27–8.

Mastin, John, 1792, *The History and Antiquities of Naseby, in the County of Northamton*, Francis Hodson, Cambridge.

Mawer, Allen, 1920, *The Place Names of Northumberland and Durham*, Cambridge University Press.

Mawer, Allen, and Frank Stenton, 1927, *The Place-Names of Worcestershire*, English Place-Name Society 4.

McIntire, Walter T., 1944, 'Holy wells of Cumberland', *Tr. of the Cumberland & Westmorland Antiq. & Arch. Soc.* 2nd ser 44: 1–15.

Metrical Life of St Robert of Knaresborough, The, 1953, ed Joyce Bazire, Early English Texts Society 1st ser 228.

Meyrick, J., 1982, *A Pilgrim's Guide to the Holy Wells of Cornwall*, Privately.

Migne, J.P., 1844–80, *Patrologiae Cursus Completus: Series Secunda... Ecclesiae Latinae*, J.P. Migne, Paris.

Miller, Edward, 1804, *The History and Antiquities of Doncaster and its Vicinity*, W. Sheardown, Doncaster.

Mills, A.D., 1977–89, *The Place-Names of Dorset*, English Place-Name Society 52–3 & 59/60.

Mills, Joan, and Dennis Richard Mills, 1996 'The holy well and conduit, Canwick', *Lincolnshire Past & Present* 23: 3–5

Morrell, Robert W., 1988, *Nottinghamshire Holy Wells and Springs*, Anomalous Phenomenon Research Association.

Morris, John, 1968, 'The death of Saint Alban', *Hertfordshire Archaeology* 1: 1–8.

Morris, Richard, 1989, *Churches in the Landscape*, J.M. Dent, London.

Morris, Ruth, and Frank Morris, 1982, *Scottish Healing Wells: Healing, Holy, Wishing and Fairy Wells of the Mainland of Scotland*, Alethea Press, Sandy.

Morris, William, 1885, *Swindon Fifty Years Ago (More or Less): Reminiscences, Notes and Relics of Ye Olde Wiltshire Towne*, Swindon Advertiser, Swindon.

Morton, John, 1712, *The Natural History of Northampton-shire*, R. Knaplock, London.

Mowbray, Donald, Rhiannon Purdie & Ian P. Wei, eds, 1999, *Authority and Community in the Middle Ages*, Sutton, Stroud.

Muir, Richard, 2007, *Be Your Own Landscape Detective*, Sutton, Stroud.

Musgrave, Clifford, 1970, *Life in Brighton, From the Earliest Times to the Present*, Faber & Faber, London.

Nash, Treadway R., 1781–2, *Collections for the History of Worcestershire*, John White, London

Naylor, Peter J., 1983, *Ancient Wells and Springs of Derbyshire*, Scarthin Books, Cromford.

Ni Brìde, Feòrag, 1994, *The Wells and Springs of Leeds*, Pagan Prattle, Preston.

Nichols, John, 1795–1815, *The History and Antiquities of the County of Leicester*, John Nichols, London.

Nicholls, H.G., 1858, *The Forest of Dean: An Historical and Descriptive Account*, John Murray, London.

Nicholls, J.F., and John Taylor, 1881–2, *Bristol Past and Present*, J.W. Arrowsmith, Bristol.

Nicolson, Joseph, and Richard Burn, 1777, *The History and Antiquities of Westmorland and Cumberland*, W. Strahan, London.

Nicolson, William, 1877, *Miscellany Accounts of the Diocese of Carlisle*, ed R.S. Ferguson, Cumberland & Westmorland Antiquarian & Archaeological Society.

Nixon, Virginia, 2004, *Mary's Mother: Saint Anne in Late Medieval Europe*, Pennsylvania State University Press.

Noble, A.J., and J.A. Hilton, 1999, *Henry Taylor,* The Ancient Crosses and Holy Wells of Lancashire – A Revised Version I: Lonsdale Hundred*, North West Catholic History Society.

Noble, A.J., and J.A. Hilton, 2002, *Henry Taylor,* The Ancient Crosses and Holy Wells of Lancashire – A Revised Version II: Amounderness Hundred*, North West Catholic History Society.

Noble, A.J., and J.A. Hilton, 2004, *Henry Taylor,* The Ancient Crosses and Holy Wells of Lancashire – A Revised Version III: Blackburn Hundred*, North West Catholic History Society.

Noble, A.J., and J.A. Hilton, 2005, *Henry Taylor,* The Ancient Crosses and Holy Wells of Lancashire – A Revised Version IV: Salford Hundred*, North West Catholic History Society.

Noble, A.J., J.A. Hilton, and W.A. Varney, 2006, *Henry Taylor,* The Ancient Crosses and Holy Wells of Lancashire – A Revised Version V: West Derby Hundred*, North West Catholic History Society.

Noble, A.J., J.A. Hilton, M. Panikkarr and W.A. Varney, 2007, *Henry Taylor,* The Ancient Crosses and Holy Wells of Lancashire – A Revised Version VI: Leyland Hundred*, North West Catholic History Society.

Northumberland County History Committee, 1893–1935, *A History of Northumberland*, Andrew Reid, Newcastle-upon-Tyne.

Nova Legenda Anglie, As Collected by John of Tynemouth, John Capgrave, and Others, 1901, ed Carl Horstmann, Clarendon, Oxford.

Oakden, J.P., 1984, *The Place-Names of Staffordshire*, English Place-Name Society 55.

Osborne, Bruce, and Cora Weaver, 1996, *Aquae Britannia: Seventeenth-Century Springs and Spas*, Privately.

Otter, Laurens, 1985, 'Notes towards a survey of Shropshire holy wells: I', *Source* 1st ser 3: 8–15.

Page, Jim Taylor, 1990, *Cumbrian Holy Wells,* North West Catholic History Society.

Palmer, W.M., 1935, *John Layer (1586–1640) of Shepreth, Cambridgeshire: A Seventeenth-Century Local Historian,* Cambridge Antiquarian Society 8☐ ser 53.

Parish, Ross, 1997a, 'Kent's other spas: a discussion of other mineral spas that hoped to capitalise on Tunbridge Wells', *Bygone Kent* 18: 15–22.

Parish, Ross, 1997b, 'The curious water-lore of Kent I: river lore and the Devil', *Bygone Kent* 18: 345–8.

Parish, Ross, 1997c, 'The curious water-lore of Kent II: ghosts, fertility and living traditions', *Bygone Kent* 18: 427–32.

Parish, Ross, 1998a, 'The Lady Wells of Kent', *Bygone Kent* 19: 45–8.

Parish, Ross, 1998b, 'Holy wells and folklore waters: a gazetteer of Hertfordshire hydrolatry', *Hertfordshire's Past* 43/4: 11–15.

Parker, F., 1890, 'Chartulary of the Austin Priory of Trentham', *Staffordshire Hist. Collections* 11: 295–336.

Parkes, D., 1797, 'Description of St Kenelm's Chapel', *Gentleman's Magazine* 1st ser 67: 738–9.

Patchell, P.M., and E.M. Patchell, 1987, 'The wells of old Warwickshire', *Source* 1st ser 6: 10–15.

Peach, R.E., 1883, *Historical Houses in Bath and Their Associations,* Simpkin Marshall, London.

Peacock, Edward, 1891, 'Saint Helen', *Arch. J.* 48: 354–60.

Peacock, Mabel, 1895, 'Lincolnshire water-lore', *Antiquary* 31: 366–74

Pearson, Howard S., 1901, 'Birmingham springs and wells', *Tr. of the Birmingham & Midland Institute* 28: 55–62.

Peck, Francis, 1727, *Academia Tertia Anglicana: Or, The Antiquarian Annals of Stamford,* James Bettenham, London.

Pennick, Nigel, 1985, 'Holy and notable wells: the Cambridge district', *Source* 1st ser 1: 9–10.

Pennick, Nigel, 2006, *Folk-Lore of East Anglia and Adjoining Counties,* Spiritual Arts & Crafts, Cambridge.

Phelps, Joseph J., 1909, 'Visit to Newton-le-Willows for Newton Old Hall and Winwick', *Tr. of the Lancashire & Cheshire Antiq. Soc.* 27: 160–70.

Philipott, Thomas, 1659, *Villare Cantianum: Or, Kent Surveyed and Illustrated,* William Godbid, London.

Plot, Robert, 1677, *The Natural History of Oxford-Shire,* At the Theater, Oxford.

Plot, Robert, 1686, *The Natural History of Stafford-Shire,* At the Theater, Oxford.

Polwhele, Richard, 1793–1806, *The History of Devonshire,* Cadell Johnson & Dilly, London.

Potter, Clive, 1985, 'The holy wells of Leicestershire and Rutland', *Source* 1st ser 1: 15–17.

Potter, T.R., 1842, *The History and Antiquities of Charnwood Forest,* Hamilton Adams & Co, London.

Preston, W.E., 1927–32, 'Some local holy wells', *Bradford Antiquary* 7: 241–8.

Price, Michael, 1985, *Introducing Groundwater,* Chapman & Hall, London.

Purvis, J.S., 1927–9, 'Seventeenth-century copies of early Yorkshire charters', *Yorkshire Arch. J.* 29: 390–3.

Quinn, Phil, 1999, *The Holy Wells of Bath and Bristol Region*, Logaston, Herefordshire.

Radford, C.A. Raleigh, 1976, 'The church of St Alkmund, Derby', *Derbyshire Arch. J.* 96: 26–61.

Rahtz, Philip, 1963–4, 'Excavations at Chalice Well, Glastonbury', *Proc. of the Somerset Arch. & Nat. Hist. Soc.* 108: 145–67.

Rattue, James, 1990, 'An inventory of ancient and holy wells in Oxfordshire', *Oxoniensia* 55: 172–6.

Rattue, James, 1992, 'An inventory of ancient, holy and healing wells of Dorset', *Proc. of the Dorset Nat. Hist. & Arch. Soc.* 114: 265–268.

Rattue, James, 1993, 'An inventory of ancient, holy and healing wells in Leicestershire', *Tr. of the Leicestershire Arch. & Hist. Soc.* 67: 59–69.

Rattue, James, 1995a, *The Living Stream: Holy Wells in Historical Context*, Boydell, Woodbridge.

Rattue, James, 1995b, 'The wells of St Swithun', *Source* 2nd ser 4: 6.

Rattue, James, 2003a, *The Holy Wells of Buckinghamshire*, Privately.

Rattue, James, 2003b, *The Holy Wells of Kent*, Privately.

Rattue, James, 2008, *The Holy Wells of Surrey*, Privately.

Rawnsley, H.D., 1900, *Memories of the Tennysons*, James MacLehose, Glasgow.

Reaney, Percy, 1943, *The Place-Names of Cambridgeshire*, English Place-Name Society 19.

Reginald of Durham, 1835, *Libellus de Admirandis Beati Cuthberti Virtutibus*, ed James Raine, Surtees Society 1.

Reginald of Durham, 1847, *Libellus de Vita et Miraculis Sancti Godrici, Heremitae de Finchale*, ed Joseph Stevenson, Surtees Society 20.

Richardson, A., 1898, 'St Anne's Chapel, Brislington', *Proc. of the Somerset Arch. & Nat. Hist. Soc.* 44ii: 188–97.

Richardson, Linsdall R., 1927, 'Some notable Worcestershire wells', *Tr. of the Worcestershire Nat. Hist. Club* 8: 138–53.

Richardson, Linsdall R., 1928a, *Wells and Springs of Somerset*, Memoirs of the Geological Survey.

Richardson, Linsdall R., 1928b, *Wells and Springs of Warwickshire*, Memoirs of the Geological Survey.

Richardson, Linsdall R., 1930, *Wells and Springs of Worcestershire*, Memoirs of the Geological Survey.

Richardson, Linsdall R., 1935, *Wells and Springs of Herefordshire*, Memoirs of the Geological Survey.

Risdon, Tristram, 1811, *The Chorographical Description or Survey of the County of Devon*, Rees & Curtis, Plymouth.

Roberts, Askew, 1879, 'Where did King Oswald die?', *Tr. of the Shropshire Arch. & Nat. Hist. Soc.* 2: 97–140.

Rollason, David, 1983, 'The cults of murdered royal saints in Anglo-Saxon England', *Anglo-Saxon England* 11: 1–22.

Rollason, David, 1989, *Saints and Relics in Anglo-Saxon England*, Basil Blackwell, Oxford.

Ronan, M.V., 1927, *St Anne, her Cult and Shrines*, Sands, London.

Roscarrock, Nicholas, 1992, *Nicholas Roscarrock's Lives of the Saints*, ed Orme, Devon & Cornwall Record Society 2nd ser 35.

Rotulorum Originalium in Cura Scaccarii Abbrevatio, 1805–10, ed H. Playford and John Caley, Record Commission.

Royce, David, 1861, *The History and Antiquities of Stow*, T. Clift, Stow-on-the-Wold.

Rumble, A.R., 1997, 'Ad Lapidem in Bede and a Mercian martyrdom', pp307–19 in Rumble & Mills, eds, *Names, Places and People*.

Rumble, A.R., and A.D. Mills, eds, 1997, *Names, Places, and People*, Paul Watkins, Stamford.

Sandred, Karl Inge, and Bengt Lindström, 1989–2002, *The Place-Names of Norfolk*, English Place-Name Society 61, 72 & 79.

Sant, Jonathan, 1994, *The Healing Wells of Herefordshire*, Moondial, Bodenham.

Scherr, Jennifer, 1986, 'Names of wells and springs in Somerset', *Nomina* 10: 79–91.

Scully, Robert E., 2007, 'St Winefride's Well: the significance and survival of a Welsh Catholic shrine from the early Middle Ages to the present day', pp202–28 in Cormack, ed, *Saints and their Cults in the Atlantic World*.

Sharpe, Richard, 2001, 'The late antique Passion of St Alban', pp30–7 in Henig and Lindley, eds, *Alban and St Albans: Roman and Medieval Architecture, Art and Archaeology*.

Shepherd, Val, 1994, *Historic Wells In and Around Bradford*, Heart of Albion, Wymeswold.

Shore, T.W., 1890–3, 'Springs and streams of Hampshire' *Proc. of the Hampshire Field Club* 2: 33–58.

Short, Thomas, 1740, *A Natural, Experimental, and Medicinal History of the Principal Mineral Waters of Cumberland etc.*, John Garnet, Sheffield.

Simeon of Durham, 1882, *Opera Omnia*, ed Thomas Arnold, Rolls Series 75.

Smith, Albert Hugh, 1956, *English Place-Name Elements*, English Place-Name Society 25–6.

Smith, Albert Hugh, 1961–3, *The Place-Names of the West Riding of Yorkshire*, English Place-Name Society 30–37.

Smith, Albert Hugh, 1964–5, *The Place-Names of Gloucestershire*, English Place-Name Society 38–41

Smith, Albert Hugh, 1967, *The Place-Names of Westmorland*, English Place-Name Society 42–3.

Smith, William, 1923, *Ancient Springs and Streams of the East Riding of Yorkshire*, A. Brown, London.

South English Legendary, The, 1887, ed Carl Hortsmann, Early English Texts Society 87.

Speake, Robert, and F.R. Witty, 1953, *A History of Droylsden*, Cloister Press, Stockport.

Speed, John, 1988, *The Counties of Britain: A Tudor Atlas*, ed Nigel Nicolson and Alasdair Hawkyard, Pavilion, London.

Stancliffe, Clare, 1995, 'Where was Oswald killed?', pp84–96 in Stancliffe and Cambridge, eds, *Oswald: Northumbrian King to European Saint*.

Stancliffe, Clare, and Eric Cambridge, eds, 1995, *Oswald: Northumbrian King to European Saint*, Paul Watkins, Stamford.

Stanley, Arthur Penrhyn, 1857, *Historical Memorials of Canterbury*, John Murray, London.

Stapleton, 1899, *Some Account of the Religious Institutions of Old Nottingham*, Thomas Forman, Nottingham.

Stockdale, James, 1872, *Annales Carmoelenses: Or, Annals of Cartmel*, William Kitchin, Ulverston.

Stout, Adam, 2007, *The Thorn and the Waters*, Library of Avalon, Glastonbury.

Stow, John, 1912, *The Survey of London*, ed Henry B. Wheatley, Dent.

Strang, Veronica, 2004, *The Meaning of Water*, Berg, Oxford.

Stubbs, William, ed, 1874, *Memorials of St Dunstan*, Rolls Series 63.

Sumption, Jonathan, 1975, *Pilgrimage: An Image of Mediaeval Religion*, Faber & Faber, London.

Sutton, Oliver, 1948–86, *The Rolls and Register of Bishop Oliver Sutton 1280–1299*, ed Rosalind M.T. Hill, Lincoln Record Society 39, 43, 48, 52, 60, 64, 69 & 76.

Swanton, M.J., 1986, *St Sidwell: An Exeter Legend*, Devon Books, Exeter.

Taylor, Henry, 1906, *The Ancient Crosses and Holy Wells of Lancashire*, Sherratt & Hughes, Manchester.

Taylor, Isaac, 1898, *Names and their Histories: A Handbook of Historical Geography and Topographical Nomenclature*, Rivingtons, London.

Taylor, John, 1894–5, 'Rushton and its owners: II', *Northamptonshre Notes & Queries* 6: 49–72.

Thacker, Alan, 1996, 'Saint-making and relic collecting by Oswald and his communities', pp244–68 in Brooks & Cubitt, eds, *St Oswald of Worcester: Life and Influence*.

Thacker, Alan, 1999, 'In Gregory's shadow? The pre-Conquest cult of St Augustine', pp374–409 in Gameson, ed, *St Augustine and the Conversion of England*.

Thacker, Alan, and Richard Sharpe, eds, 2002, *Local Saints and Local Churches in the Early Medieval West*, Oxford University Press.

Thompson, Beeby, 1909–10, 'A history of the water supply of Northampton: I', *J. of the Northamptonshire Nat. Hist. Soc.* 15: 123–31.

Thompson, Beeby, 1913–14, 'Peculiarities of waters and wells: V', *J. of the Northamptonshire Nat. Hist. Soc.* 17: 101–118.

Thompson, Beeby, 1913–14b, 'Peculiarities of waters and wells: VII', *J. of the Northamptonshire Nat. Hist. Soc.* 17: 190–7.

Thompson, Beeby, 1915–16, 'Peculiarities of waters and wells: X', *J. of the Northamptonshire Nat. Hist. Soc.* 18: 66–79.

Thompson, Beeby, 1917–19, 'The river system of Northamptonshire – springs: II', *J. of the Northamptonshire Nat. Hist. Soc.* 19: 39–48.

Thompson, Ian, 1999, *Lincolnshire Springs and Wells: A Descriptive Catalogue*, Bluestone, Scunthorpe.

Thompson, Ian and Frances, 2004, *The Water of Life: Springs and Wells of Mainland Britain*, Llanerch, Cardiganshire.

Thoresby, Ralph, 1715, *Ducatus Leodiensis: Or, the Topography of the Ancient and Populous Town and Parish of Leeds*, Maurice Atkins, London

Thorpe, Benjamin, ed, 1840, *Ancient Laws and Institutes of England,* Record Commission.

Todd, John M., 1980, 'St Bega: cult, fact and legend', *Tr. of the Cumberland & Westmorland Antiq. & Arch. Soc.* 2nd ser 80: 25–35.

Townend, Matthew, 2002, *Language and History in Viking Age England: Linguistic Relations Between Speakers of Old Norse and Old English,* Brepols, Turnhout.

Trubshaw, Bob, 1990, *Holy Wells and Springs of Leicestershire and Rutland,* Heart of Albion, Wymeswold.

Twinch, Carol, 1995, *In Search of St Walstan: East Anglia's Enduring Legend,* Media Associates, Bawburgh.

Underhill, John, 1703, *Johannis Subtermontani Thermologia Bristoliensis; Or, Underhill's Short Account of the Bristol Hot-Well-Water,* W. Bonny, Bristol.

Valentine, Mark, 1984, *The Holy Wells of Northamptonshire,* Privately.

Varner, Gary R., 2002, *Sacred Wells: A Study in the History, Meaning, and Mythology of Holy Wells and Waters,* Publish America, Baltimore.

Varner, Gary R., 2004, *Water of Life, Water of Death: The Folklore and Mythology of Sacred Waters,* Publish America, Baltimore.

Victoria County History of Buckinghamshire, The, 1905–28, ed William Page *et al.,* Institute of Historical Research.

Victoria County History of Hertfordshire, The, 1908–23, ed William Page *et al.,* Institute of Historical Research.

Victoria County History of Essex, The, 1903–2001, ed H. Arthur Doubleday *et al.,* Institute of Historical Research.

Victoria County History of Shropshire, The, 1908–1985, ed William Page *et al.,* Institute of Historical Research.

Victoria County History of Staffordshire, The, 1908–1984 and continuing, ed William Page *et al.,* Institute of Historical Research.

Wade-Evans, A.W., 1944, *Vitae Sanctorum Britanniae et Genealogiae,* University of Wales Press.

Walker, J., 1934, *Wakefield: Its History and People,* West Yorkshire Printing Co., Wakefield.

Wallis, John, 1769, *The Natural History and Antiquities of Northumberland,* W. & W. Strahan, London.

Walsh, Christine, 2007, *The Cult of St Katherine of Alexandria in Early Medieval Europe,* Ashgate, Aldershot.

Walsham, Alexandra, 1999, 'Reforming the waters: holy wells and healing springs in Protestant England', pp227–55 of Wood, ed, *Life and Thought in the Northern Church c.1100–c.1700.*

Walsham, Alexandra, 2005, 'Holywell: contesting sacred space in post-Reformation Wales', pp211–36 of Coster & Spicer, eds, *Sacred Space in Early Modern Europe.*

Walters, R.C. Skyring, 1928, *The Ancient Wells, Springs and Holy Wells of Gloucestershire: Their Legends, History and Topography,* St Stephen's Press, Bristol.

Walters, R.C. Skyring, 1953–60, 'Notes on Buckinghamshire wells', *Records of Buckinghamshire* 16: 47–8.

Ward, Benedicta, 1982, *Miracles and the Medieval Mind*, Scolar Press, London.

Watkin, Hugh R., 1923–4, 'The manor of Tormohun', *Tr. of the Torquay Nat. Hist. Soc.* 4: 134–48.

Watkins, Carl S., 2007, *History and the Supernatural in Medieval England*, Cambridge University Press.

Watson, John, 1775, *The History and Antiquities of the Parish of Halifax*, T. Lowndes, London.

Watts, Victor, 1999–2000, 'Some place-name distributions', *J. of the English Place-Name Soc.* 32: 53–72.

Weaver, F.W., 1893, 'On a painting of St Barbara in the church of St Lawrence, Cucklington, Somerset', *Proc. of the Somerset Arch. & Nat. Hist. Soc.* 39ii: 42–54.

Webb, Diana, 2000, *Pilgrimage in Medieval England*, Hambledon & London, London.

Welford, Richard, 1885–7, *History of Newcastle and Gateshead*, Walter Scott, London

Whelan, Edna, 2001, *The Magic and Mystery of Holy Wells*, Capall Bann, Chievely.

Whelan, Edna, and Ian Taylor, 1989, *Yorkshire Holy Wells and Sacred Springs*, Northern Lights, Pocklington.

Whitaker, Thomas Dunham, 1805, *The History and Antiquities of the Deanery of Craven*, Nichols & Son, London.

Whitaker, Thomas Dunham, 1812, *The History and Antiquities of the Deanery of Craven* (2nd edition), J. Nichols, London.

Whitaker, William, 1899, *The Water Supply of Sussex*, Memoirs of the Geological Survey.

Whitaker, William, 1910, *The Water Supply of Hampshire and the Isle of Wight*, Memoirs of the Geological Survey.

Whitaker, William, 1912, *The Water Supply of Surrey*, Memoirs of the Geological Survey.

Whitehead, David, 1978, 'In search of St Ethelbert's Well, Hereford', *Herefordshire Archaeological News* 35: 11–13.

Whiteman, Ralph J., 1936, *Hexton: A Parish Survey*, Privately.

Whiting, Robert, 1989, *The Blind Devotion of the People: Popular Religion and the English Reformation*, Cambridge University Press.

Wigan, Eve, 1932, *Portishead History*, Barnicott & Pearce, Taunton.

William of Malmesbury, 2002a, *The Deeds of the Bishops of England*, tr David Preest, Boydell, Woodbridge

William of Malmesbury, 2002b, *Saints' Lives: Lives of SS. Wulfstan, Dunstan, Patrick, Benignus and Indract*, ed, tr M. Winterbottom and R.M. Thomson, Clarendon, Oxford.

Williams, Hugh, ed, 1901, *Gildas*, Cymmrodorion Record Series 3.

Williams, John, 1860, 'St Govor's Well', *Notes & Queries* 2nd ser 9: 388–9.

Williamson, Tom, 1993, *The Origins of Norfolk*, Manchester University Press.

Willis, Edward Preston, 1885, *Quaint Old Norwich*, Privately

Wilson, Rob, 1991, *Holy Wells and Spas of South Yorkshire*, Privately.

Winchester, Evelyn, 1986, *St Anne's, Bristol: A History*, White Tree Books, Bristol.

Winstead, Karen A., 1997, *Virgin Martyrs: Legends of Sainthood in Late Medieval England*, Cornell University Press.

Wogan-Browne, Jocelyn, 1992, 'Queens, virgins and mothers: hagiographic representations of the abbess and her powers in twelfth and thirteenth-century Britain', pp14–35 in Fradenburg, ed, *Women and Sovereignty*.

Wood, Anthony, 1889–99, *Survey of the Antiquities of the City of Oxford*, ed Andrew Clark, Oxford Historical Society 15, 17 & 37.

Wood, Diana, ed, 1993, *Martyrs and Martyrologies*, Studies in Church History 30.

Wood, Diana, ed, 1999, *Life and Thought in the Northern Church c.1100–c.1700: Essays in Honour of Claire Cross*, Ecclesiastical History Society.

Woolley, William, 1981, *William Woolley's History of Derbyshire*, ed Catherine Glover and Philip Riden, Derbyshire Record Society 6.

Worcestre, William, 2000, *The Topography of Medieval Bristol*, ed Frances Neale, Bristol Record Society 51.

Wordsworth, Christopher, 1905–7, 'Some Wiltshire springs and holy wells', *Wiltshire Notes & Queries* 5: 308–9.

Wulfstan, 1957, *The Homilies of Wulfstan*, ed Dorothy Bethurum, Clarendon, Oxford.

X, 1882, 'Holy well revel', *Folk-Lore Record* 5: 160.

Yarrow, Simon, 2006, *Saints and Their Communities: Miracle Stories in Twelfth Century England*, Clarendon, Oxford.

Zimdars-Swartz, Sandra L., 1991, *Encountering Mary: From La Salette to Medjugorje*, Princeton University Press.

Index

Cures and curses

Ritual and cult at holy wells

Janet Bord

Why are some wells said to be miraculously created by saints? Why are the rituals associated with them sometimes about divination or cursing? What evidence is there for the water curing illnesses? Do the wells have guardians? If so, are they humans, fairies, or even dragons? Is there treasure hidden there? What should be left there – rags, pins, coins, pebbles or even votive offerings?

Until recently the answers had been almost entirely forgotten. However a revival of interest in holy wells started in 1985 with the publication of Janet and Colin Bord's book *Sacred Waters* and in recent years research has gathered pace. In this entirely new book Janet brings together the latest understanding of such lore as 75 topic-by-topic descriptions, including their links to pre-Christian practices. There is also a list of 25 recommended wells to visit. The 135 illustrations include historic photographs of wells and rituals.

Cures and Curses provides an enticing overview for those looking for an introduction to holy wells and a source of reliable but little- known information for those already seduced by the allure of sacred springs.

Janet Bord lives in North Wales, where she and her husband Colin run the Fortean Picture Library. They have written more than 20 books on folklore and mysteries since their first successful joint venture, *Mysterious Britain* (1972).

> 'The book contains not only a plethora of illustrations, but also a very full bibliography, referring to many unusual items. But Janet Bord's style is blessedly unacademic. All in all, like the author's other books, this is a synthesis of imagination, poetry and scholarship, a must-have-read for all interested in the ancient traditions of these islands.' **Peter Costello** *Irish Catholic*

ISBN 978-1-872883-953. 2006. 245 x 175 mm, 191+ viii, 100 b&w photographs, 35 line drawings, paperback. **£14.95**

Holy Wells in Britain

A guide

Janet Bord

Holy wells were once widespread throughout Britain. They were often dedicated to local saints and were important features in the medieval sacred landscape. Over many centuries, pilgrims sought the healing powers of their waters, and many left votive offerings in the form of bent pins, coins and rags.

Interest in this aspect of our sacred heritage has been growing since the publication of Janet Bord's first book on holy wells over twenty years ago. Many holy wells have now been restored, and the modern visitor may still experience a quiet communion with the spirit of the place, and come away spiritually uplifted.

For this book Janet Bord has sought out three hundred of the surviving holy wells of England, Wales and Scotland that are most rewarding to visit, and she recounts their histories and traditions in the light of current historical research.

Holy Wells in Britain is the first guidebook to British holy wells to draw upon the extensive research of recent decades. Up-to-date practical information for visitors is also provided to inspire readers to seek out these evocative sacred sites for themselves.

> 'This is a splendidly presented and illustrated book... and is a very worthwhile

ISBN 978-1-905646-09-8 April 2008
245 x 175 mm, 226 + xii pages, 179 b&w photos, 5 line drawings, paperback.
£14.95

Also by Jeremy Harte from Heart of Albion Press

*Winner of the Folklore Society
Katharine Briggs Award 2005*

Explore Fairy Traditions

Jeremy Harte

We are not alone. In the shadows of our countryside there lives a fairy race, older than humans, and not necessarily friendly to them. For hundreds of years, men and women have told stories about the strange people, beautiful as starlight, fierce as wolves, and heartless as ice. These are not tales for children. They reveal the fairies as a passionate, proud, brutal people.

Explore Fairy Traditions draws on legends, ballads and testimony from throughout Britain and Ireland to reveal what the fairies were really like. It looks at changelings, brownies, demon lovers, the fairy host, and abduction into the Otherworld. Stories and motifs are followed down the centuries to reveal the changing nature of fairy lore, as it was told to famous figures like W.B. Yeats and Sir Walter Scott. All the research is based on primary sources and many errors about fairy tradition are laid to rest.

Jeremy Harte combines folklore scholarship with a lively style to show what the presence of fairies meant to people's lives. Like their human counterparts, the secret people could kill as well as heal. They knew marriage, seduction, rape and divorce; they adored some children and rejected others. If we are frightened of the fairies, it may be because their world offers an uncomfortable mirror of our own.

> '... this is the best and most insightful book on fairies generally available... ' John Billingsley *Northern Earth*

> '*Explore Fairy Traditions* is an excellent introduction to the folklore of fairies, and I would highly recommend it.' Paul Mason *Silver Wheel*

ISBN 1 872883 61 3. 2004. Demy 8vo (215 x 138 mm), 171 + vi pages, 6 line drawings, paperback. **£9.95**

Heart of Albion

The UK's leading publisher of
folklore, mythology and cultural studies.

Further details of all Heart of Albion titles online at
www.hoap.co.uk

All titles available direct from Heart of Albion Press.

Please add 80p p&p (UK only; email
albion@indigogroup.co.uk for overseas postage).

To order books or request our current catalogue
please contact

Heart of Albion Press

2 Cross Hill Close, Wymeswold
Loughborough, LE12 6UJ

Phone: 01509 880725
Fax: 01509 881715
email: albion@indigogroup.co.uk
Web site: www.hoap.co.uk